For Graham

Contents

List of figures

Preface to the first edition

My interest in language and languages began at an early age. Being brought up in Wales and having Welsh lessons as a compulsory part of the school curriculum gave me an excellent start in developing an appreciation for the subtleties of language differences and the rich lessons of language and culture to be learned. It also gave me an understanding of differences in status ascribed to languages; of the importance of language in shaping identity; and the prevalence of prejudices and stereotypes around language use and language users.

This early experience led to a later concentration on languages as a major feature of my secondary education and a place on a degree programme in French and linguistics. Ironically perhaps, my studies of the social aspects of language and language use and of French social thought led me away from this course to a broad-based social science degree. However, I never lost my interest in language and indeed widened it to incorporate issues of communication more broadly as I learned more and more about social processes and institutions and their effects on individuals, their families and communities.

From that interest in the social world and its implications for people within it I was drawn into the world of social work and social problems, devoting many years of my life to dealing with people and their problems. These days my career profile as a trainer, consultant and author involves building on all my studies and all my professional experiences in helping people learn about the complexities of 'people problems', the intricate dynamics between individuals, groups, communities, organizations, cultures, genders, classes and so on and the pain, grief, suffering, conflict, tension and pressure that they can, and do, so easily bring. However, one theme that underpins all this is the significance of communication. It is through communication that we live our lives, with language being a major feature of that communication. Writing this book therefore brings me an excellent opportunity to draw on my many years' experience of learning and professional practice with a view to presenting the basic building blocks of communication and language theory in an accessible way and drawing out the implications for practitioners and managers in a variety of settings where effective communication can make all the difference between success and failure, collaboration and conflict, progress and inertia.

Preparing the book has given me immense pleasure and satisfaction, reminding me of how much interest, stimulation and fascination I have found over the years in not only studying the subtleties of communication and language, but also in putting so much of my learning into practice in helping others tackle their problems in a variety of settings and contexts. I recognize that I cannot expect readers to share my enthusiasm to the same full extent, but I can at least hope to provide a platform from which a greater understanding can grow and develop.

Preface to the second edition

In the eight years since the first edition of this book was published there has been an even greater recognition of the significance of communication as a feature of working life in general and the 'people professions' in particular. For example, communication issues regularly feature in the training courses I am asked to run and I frequently encounter a growing awareness of the crucial role of communication in the problem-solving consultancy work I undertake with organizations. So, the need for a book like this would seem to have grown rather than diminished.

I have been delighted with the positive feedback I have received on the first edition. Two aspects that seem to have been particularly well received are (i) the emphasis on the relationship between language use and discrimination and the way in which my approach to these issues has enabled people to move beyond the simplistic limitations of a 'political correctness' approach; and (ii) the successful blending of theory and practice. Both these strengths remain in this edition and are supplemented by a number of new features. First, the theoretical underpinnings of effective communication in Part I of the book have been updated and extended. In particular, there is a stronger focus on the significance of communication in the context of helping and supporting people – for example, through engaging in problem-solving processes (Thompson, 2006a). In this way, effective communication can be seen as an essential part of promoting empowerment.

Second, three new chapters have been added to Part II in order to help draw out more of the practical implications of a sound knowledge of communication. The first of these covers communicating with children and young people, both verbally and nonverbally – for example, through play. The second addresses the challenges involved in working with groups. It includes discussion of the art of making presentations, something that many people find quite stressful if not actually terrifying. The third covers the complications we encounter at times in our efforts to communicate. This includes when we are interacting with people whose communications are affected by a physical or learning disability and the difficulties that can arise in intercultural communication, as well as the issues relating to hearing impairment.

One other change is the title of the book. Originally published as *Communication and Language,* it has now been renamed as *Effective Communication* to emphasize the point that our task is not just to communicate – we are doing that all the time, effectively or otherwise. Rather, it is to make sure that our communications are as fruitful and productive as possible – that they are *effective.*

These new elements add new dimensions to the book in ways that help it to provide a sound foundation for developing your knowledge and skills in communication. Communication is, after all, at the heart of everything we do in the people professions – the complexities of it are a key part of what makes us human, and so maximizing our communicative abilities can be seen as a very worthwhile investment of time, effort and energy. I hope you will find this book a helpful foundation to guide you in investing wisely.

NEIL THOMPSON

Acknowledgements

This book, in both its editions, is the product of many years of study and practice, and so the people I am indebted to for the learning that has gone into it are far too numerous to mention individually. However, I would like to say a general thank you to them all.

At a more practical level, I am grateful to Maggie Holloway for the excellent job she did as an audio-typist. Catherine Gray at the publishers has continued to be a pleasure to work with and I am grateful to her for that and for the excellent support and insights she has provided. Once again I am greatly indebted to Penny Simmons for her excellent copyediting work and the friendly and supportive manner in which she carries it out.

As always, I must acknowledge my enormous gratitude to Susan Thompson, as she makes such a positive difference to me in so many ways.

About the author

Neil Thompson PhD, DLitt is a Director of Avenue Consulting Ltd (www.avenueconsulting.co.uk), a company based in Wales offering training and consultancy services in relation to social and occupational well-being. He has held full or honorary professorships at four UK universities and has over 150 publications to his name, including best-selling textbooks, papers in learned journals and training and open learning materials.

Neil has over thirty-three years' experience as a practitioner, manager, educator, consultant and expert witness in the helping professions. He is very well respected for his ability to communicate complex ideas in an accessible way without oversimplifying them. He has also been involved in developing education and training DVDs and other learning resources (see www.avenuemediasolutions.com).

He has been a speaker at seminars and conferences in the United Kingdom, Ireland, Greece, the Netherlands, Norway, the Czech Republic, Spain, Italy, Hong Kong, India, Canada, the United States and Australia and has qualifications in social work, management (MBA), training and development, mediation and dispute resolution, as well as a first-class honours degree in Social Sciences, a doctorate (PhD) and a higher doctorate (DLitt).

Neil is a Fellow of the Chartered Institute of Personnel and Development and the Royal Society of Arts (elected to the latter on the basis of his contribution to workplace learning). He is also a Fellow of the Higher Education Academy and a Life Fellow of the Institute of Welsh Affairs. In addition, he is a member of the International Work Group on Death, Dying and Bereavement.

Neil has served as the editor of the international journal, *Illness, Crisis & Loss* (published by Baywood) and is currently the editor-in-chief of two online resources, *Well-being Zone* (www.well-beingzone.com) and *Social Work Focus* (www.socialworkfocus.com). He is a sought-after conference speaker, consultant and workshop facilitator. His personal website is at www.neilthompson.info.

Introduction

How far would we be able to get in going about our day-to-day business if we were not able to rely on communication? Clearly, not very far at all is the simple answer. Communication is a basic feature of social life. Good (2001) emphasizes this important point by beginning his discussion of communication and language with the following argument:

> Human language and the ways in which we use it lie at the very heart of our social lives. It is through communication with one another that personal relationships, communities and societies are made and maintained, and it is through these social networks and relationships that we become who we are. (p. 76)

However, this is not a book about the social significance of communication in general. There are already many texts available which cover that ground (see the *Guide to further learning* section at the end of the book). Rather, my focus is more specifically on how an improved understanding of the complexities and subtleties of communication can be of assistance in working with people and their problems across a variety of settings and disciplines. So, while the book includes a considerable amount of material relating to the theoretical underpinnings of communication, this is not presented simply as a set of ideas in their own right, but rather as a basis for informed and sensitive practice in a variety of settings.

And, of course, while we can readily see that communication is an important component of social life in general, it is important to note that it is particularly important in a wide variety of work contexts, especially those that I would characterize as the 'people professions'. This includes not only the helping professions (the traditional 'caring professions' of social work and social care; nursing and professions allied to medicine; counselling, advocacy, advice work and pastoral care; plus criminal and community justice services; teaching in schools as well as higher and further education; and other public services), but also supervisors, managers, leaders and human resource professionals. All of these have communication as a basic building block of practice.

The attempt to appeal to a broad readership is deliberate as part of my attempt to address concerns that I have had for some time about the tendency towards 'silo thinking' – that is, for members of particular disciplines or professional groups to focus too narrowly on communication from their own point of view (communication skills for nurses ...; for social workers ...; for managers ...; and so on) without taking adequate account of the multidisciplinary nature of people work and therefore the need to develop *a holistic, multidisciplinary understanding of communication*, rather than a narrow, single disciplinary one. The goal of working effectively in partnership is not likely to be well served by members of different disciplines focusing narrowly on their own disciplinary niche, rather than appreciating the complexities of the broad field of professional and interprofessional communication. There is a considerable irony in this, of course, in so far as communication – which is about connecting people, bringing them together in meaningful and productive ways – should be tackled by so many people from a narrow, single disciplinary perspective.

The same argument applies to a certain extent to the theory base. For example, it would be a mistake to focus narrowly on psychological aspects of communication, or to concentrate on social factors without considering the organizational factors involved, or to emphasize the organizational factors without taking account of the personal, psychological issues that apply to that organizational context; and so on. In this way, just as a holistic approach in terms of professional contexts is to be seen as a helpful step forward, so too can a holistic approach relating to the range of theoretical perspectives we can draw upon. In order to develop a broad-based understanding of the theory base it is therefore necessary for us to focus on a wide range of theoretical traditions, mainly the following:

- *Communication theory*   This in itself is a broad-based area of study concerned with communication at various levels.
- *Cultural and media studies*   Closely related to communication theory in many ways is the rapidly developing field of cultural and media studies. As the name implies, this area of study concerns itself with the role of culture in society and the part that the mass media play in constructing and disseminating that culture.
- *Linguistics*   Language is a very complex subject, and linguistics is the study of those complexities, covering various aspects of the biological, psychological, social and technical basis of language production and use.
- *Social psychology*   Interactions between and across individuals and groups are part of the bread and butter of social psychology, and so it is not surprising that, as an academic discipline, it has much to say about communication.
- *Sociology*   While overlapping with social psychology to a certain extent, sociology is distinctive, in so far as it offers an analysis of social

factors from a wider structural or 'macro' point of view and pays particular attention to factors such as power which, as we shall see, are very important in relation to communication.

However, I shall not necessarily be presenting these theoretical traditions as separate domains. That is, much of the theoretical material presented will be a blend of these different traditions, drawing on, and combining, diverse aspects of the knowledge base.

As will become apparent in Part I of the book, the theory base is very important in helping us to get to grips with the complexities of communication in general and language in particular. Indeed, this field is so complex as to make a reliance on 'common sense' or general life experience a very risky strategy indeed. However, while the theory base has much to offer us in terms of understanding, this is not the whole story. This is because having an understanding of the theory will not automatically make us into better communicators in our professional lives, as the relationship between theory and practice is a complex one (Thompson and Thompson, 2008). It will therefore be necessary to draw out the main implications for practitioners and managers, and this will be the main focus of Part II of the book. Of course, Part II will only be a guide to drawing out these implications – actually drawing them out in detail is potentially a life's work. That is, simply reading about the practice implications of the theory base is not enough on its own. The real challenges when it comes to effective communication are:

1. To develop at least a basic understanding of the theory base that underpins effective communication (Part I is designed to go a significant way towards achieving this).
2. To draw out, in a spirit of critically reflective practice, the practice implications of the theory base (Part II lays the foundations for this).
3. To continue to develop and extend our knowledge of the theory base over time (the *Guide to further learning* is intended to provide a helpful step in this direction, and it is also to be hoped that the book as a whole will help to give you an appetite, and enthusiasm, for continuing to develop your knowledge and understanding of these fascinating and extremely important issues).
4. To continue to develop our skills by using our growing knowledge base to make sense of the practice situations we encounter – in effect, to *theorize* our practice (Thompson, 2010).
5. To contribute to our professional knowledge base by drawing out the lessons to be learned from our theory-informed practice.

In my work over the years I have come across many people who are, in effect, practising beyond their level of knowledge. Practitioners are often involved in complex and demanding situations which require a high level of communicative skill and sensitivity, and yet a high proportion of them appear to practise on the basis of a relatively simple, undeveloped knowledge of the complexities of communication and interaction, relying mainly on the everyday communication skills they have developed as part of their upbringing. This text therefore offers a basis for developing a much more sophisticated understanding of communication to act as a foundation for the more advanced-level skills that are called for in so many of the situations which, as members of the 'people' professions, we encounter in our work. Without this more sophisticated level of understanding practitioners – and indeed managers – will be relatively ill-equipped to rise to the many challenges involved.

The book is divided into 11 chapters, organized into two parts, one focusing primarily on theory, the other concentrating mainly on practice. Part I provides an introduction to the range of theories that have been developed to account for communication and language. This literature represents both traditional and contemporary approaches, including an analysis of the significance of post-structuralist and postmodernist approaches. Chapter 1 focuses on communication in its broadest sense, while Chapter 2 narrows this down to the more specific topic of human language. This includes a discussion of the mistakes that have been made in the name of 'political correctness' and the relationship between language and inequality. Chapters 1 and 2 introduce a number of concepts and themes that are revisited in more depth in later chapters. In this respect, the first two chapters can be seen as 'scene-setting' chapters. Chapters 3 to 5 narrow down further the broad field of communication and language by concentrating on the use of: writing (3); spoken and nonverbal communication (4); and the range of broader contextual factors which have a bearing on communication and language (5).

Part II explores the practice implications of the theoretical work presented in Part I. It is divided into six chapters. The first provides a general overview of the knowledge and skills involved in maximizing our effectiveness in interpersonal encounters by considering how spoken language, paralanguage (tone, pitch, speed and so on) and body language can be used to best effect. This sets the scene for the more specific aspects of interpersonal encounters to be explored in the following three chapters.

Chapter 7 focuses on communicating with children and concentrates on the additional factors that need to be taken into consideration when attempting to communicate effectively with children and young people. While this chapter focuses explicitly on communicating with children and young people, it should not be assumed that the other chapters do not apply to them. The insights in Chapter 7 should be seen as in addition to what else the book has to say, rather than an alternative to it. Chapter 8 is concerned with communicating with groups which also involves considering an additional set of factors.

The group dimension of communication can be a considerable source of anxiety, and so dealing with anxiety forms part of this chapter.

Chapter 9 explores the issues that need to be considered when communicating difficulties arise, for example, as a result of disability issues or the challenges of intercultural communication. Chapter 10 examines what is involved in writing effectively, with a major focus on clarity. The approach in this chapter is a very pragmatic one, but avoids the dogmatically prescriptive tendencies of much of the literature on effective writing skills.

Finally, Chapter 11 focuses on managing communication, covering systems of communication and related matters. It is argued in this chapter that highly developed communication skills are of little use if systems of communication are ineffectual or non-existent. It also includes a discussion of the use of email and the implications of the 'digital revolution' more broadly.

Each chapter contains a number of 'practice focus' illustrations, short cameos to help present a picture of the issues being discussed. This is a method of illustration I have used in a number of my other books and very many people have told me that such short examples help to bring the ideas to life. However, I am also aware that not everyone finds these helpful. My advice is therefore quite simple. If you find these cameos useful, then please draw upon them as much as you like. However, if they are not to your liking, then feel free simply to skip them as you choose. They are not intended as case studies, although some tutors or trainers may wish to use them as the basis for education and training exercises. Each chapter also contains 'voice of experience' comments. Many of these are direct quotes from conversations I have had with practitioners (for example, as part of a training course), while others are typical of comments I encounter on a fairly regular basis. It is important to emphasize that these relate to the voice of *practitioner or manager* experience. I would love to be able to include direct quotes that reflect the experience of clients, service users, patients and so on, but my work no longer brings me into direct contact with them (whereas I am in full and detailed contact with practitioners and managers on a very regular basis). I do not feel it would be appropriate or ethical for me to speak on behalf of the people we serve or to report their views third hand. I would therefore urge you to supplement the examples I have given here with a consideration of the literature that reports the 'voice' of citizen perspectives and to ask for the views of the people you are seeking to help (see the *Guide to further learning* at the end of the book). In this way we can develop a broader perspective on communication in general and, in particular, on what constitutes *effective* communication.

The fact that theoretical issues come first (in Part I) is not meant to imply that the theory underpinning practice is in any way more important than, or superior to, practice issues. Rather, it is a reflection of the complexity of the theory base that it needs careful consideration before beginning to look at the practice implications. Indeed, even the materials in Part I are merely a 'taster' of the wide knowledge base available relating to communication and language – a very basic introduction and overview to encourage and facilitate further study and learning rather than a sufficient font of knowledge in its own right.

A second reason for the theoretical issues being addressed first (or being tackled at all – some people might argue that you do not need the theory, just the practice 'know how') is that I wish to avoid the book being seen as the sort of 'cook book' which offers prescriptions for practice. Instead, I want it to be seen as what it is intended to be – namely an introduction to the theory base of communication in the context of working with people and their problems, with accompanying discussion which seeks to draw out some of the main implications for practice in a wide variety of settings. My aim is not to provide 'instructions' on how to communicate effectively, but rather to offer the basis for critically reflective practice – to help promote forms of practice that are well informed and well thought through, and which do not rely simply on habit and routine, unquestioned assumptions and (uneducated) guesswork (Thompson and Thompson, 2008).

Given the amount and complexity of theoretical material in Part I, my advice is to read Part I, followed by Part II and then to reread Part I. I believe that this will allow for a fuller understanding of not only the theoretical materials, but also the relationship between the theory base and the practice realities it seeks to cast light on.

An important emphasis in the book is the need to relate communication issues to the demands of working in a context of difference, diversity and discrimination. While, as we shall see, there is a good specialist literature base in this area, it is a matter of some concern to me that so much of the general literature on communication neglects these crucial issues. Promoting equality and valuing diversity owe so much to effective communication and poor or inappropriate communication is often a contributor to discrimination and oppression, and so it is both surprising and concerning that the links between effective communication and emancipatory forms of practice are often not made or only very sketchily drawn. The need to appreciate the connection between these two key areas (equality and diversity on the one hand and communication on the other) can be seen as a vitally important one, and so it is to be hoped that this book can help to fill some of the gaps in the traditional knowledge base.

Given that the book covers such a broad and complex subject matter, quite an extensive guide to further learning is needed to point readers in the direction of relevant texts relating to the various issues that it deals with. Indeed, it is to be hoped that this book can and will act as a gateway to the broader and more in-depth literature in which so much fascinating and thought-provoking material is to be found.

In view of the heavy pressures facing staff and managers in the people professions it is not surprising that people are often faced with situations where their knowledge is not as extensive as they would like, where – in effect, as I mentioned earlier – they find themselves having to practise beyond the limits of their knowledge. Communication is such a central and vital set of skills, and yet my experience tells me that a significant proportion of practitioners practise on the basis of a relatively simple, underdeveloped knowledge of the complexities of communication and interaction. This book will, I very much hope, play a part in rectifying that situation by helping its readers to develop a much more sophisticated and useful understanding of effective communication.

Theory

Introduction to Part I

Developing basic communications skills is part of our upbringing, something that we tend to take for granted. However, in a professional context, we need to have advanced-level communication skills, ones that enable us to go beyond everyday abilities. Consider the following examples:

- A social worker regularly has to deal with conflict, discuss sensitive issues and form empowering relationships that avoid dependency creation (Thompson, 2009a). He or she will need to be able to remain professional and yet engage with people in ways that make them feel comfortable and from which trust and effective working relationships can develop. These all involve a high level of communication skills.
- A nurse could be called upon to care for someone whose communication is severely impaired by their illness or disability, to calm anxious relatives and put them at their ease, to explain complex health conditions to people who may have little understanding of such matters, and to share information with a wide range of professionals from other disciplines. Again, these all involve a high level of communication skills.
- A manager needs to be able to win the trust of his or her team, to boost the confidence of team members where appropriate, help people learn, develop collaborative relationships outside the team, make presentations within and outside the organization, respond to complaints and grievances and handle disciplinary matters. And, of course, all of these also involve an advanced level of communication skills.

To develop such an advanced level of skill *can* come through years of experience without explicitly studying communication theory. However, this is doing it the hard way. By developing our knowledge of how communication works, by building up a more sophisticated understanding of the intricacies of how people interact, we can reach a more advanced level of skill and practice sooner and without making so many mistakes in the process. Of course, having the theoretical understanding will not of itself make us into better communicators. There is, none the less, much to be gained from the combination of (i) a better understanding of the theory base that casts light on communication; (ii) some guidance on how to draw on such theory in practice; and (iii) actual practice experience. Part I of the book is geared towards providing an overview of (i) and a foundation for extending and deepening that knowledge. Part II goes some way to providing (ii), the guidance needed for using the knowledge base and, in so doing, lays the foundations for (iii), actual practice – especially critically reflective practice.

Our focus in Part I, then, is on the range of theoretical concepts and frameworks that can help us develop a better understanding of communication. But this is not theory for theory's sake. It is presented to help develop critically reflective practice (Thompson and Thompson, 2008) – that is, forms of practice that are based on an informed approach to our practice challenges, one that draws on a critical use of an underpinning knowledge base. Part I provides a summary of, and gateway into, that knowledge base.

CHAPTER 1

Understanding communication

Introduction

In this first chapter my aim is to explore and explain some of the complexities of communication. I begin by examining what is meant by the term 'communication' and look at how it operates at a variety of levels. I then move on to look at different models of communication, different ways in which a range of theorists have tried to explain the complexities of communicative patterns, processes and interactions. Following on from this, the role of culture is our topic of analysis. This leads into a discussion of the significance of identity and its role in shaping the way communication takes place. Before ending the chapter, I also concentrate on some of the subtleties that occur as a result of intercultural communication – that is, the various dynamics that can occur as a result of communication taking place between people who have different cultural backgrounds, and therefore make different assumptions about the content of communication, the nature of that communication and, in some cases, its purpose.

What is communication?

Moss (2008) makes the important point that:

> To be human is to communicate. Whether we realise it or not, all of us all of the time are sending out messages to other people, directly or indirectly, about ourselves and others. From the way we choose to dress, to the gestures we make; from the style and choice of language we use, to the company we keep, we are all the time giving out messages to each other. Sometimes we are heard clearly; often we are misunderstood; occasionally we get it completely wrong. The complexity and fascination of communication is part of the joy of being human. (p. 1)

This is a very rich passage and we shall be returning to some of its insights at various points below.

Communication is such a well-integrated part of our day-to-day existence that we tend to take it for granted, rarely pausing to consider what it involves or just how important it is to us. In this regard, Fiske (1994) makes apt comment when he states that: 'Communication is too often taken for granted when it should be taken to pieces' (p. viii). Perhaps the first point that we need to recognize is that communication is a very broad term indeed. For example, when I first began my undergraduate social science studies, one of the modules I undertook was entitled 'Communication'. I was therefore very surprised to begin reading about transport networks, food distribution systems and so on. This was certainly not my idea of communication. However, I quickly realized that communication is used in a number of senses and at a number of levels to indicate the transmission of information or even, as in the transport networks example, the transmission of goods and people. As this topic is such a broad-ranging one, it will be necessary for me to narrow down the discussions, not only in this chapter, but also throughout the book, to those aspects of communication that relate to the personal or interpersonal levels, although reference will be made from time to time to wider factors – for example, the role of the mass media.

Marsen (2006) offers not one definition, but five, each of which can help us to develop our grasp of this important concept:

1. 'social interaction through messages' (Fiske, 1990: 2)
2. 'a process in which participants create and share information with one another in order to reach a mutual understanding' (Rogers, 1995: 35);
3. 'an activity in which symbolic content is not merely transmitted from one source to another, but exchanged between human agents, who interact within a shared situational and/or discursive context' (Price, 1997: 5);
4. 'a process whereby people in groups, using the tools provided by their culture, create collective representations of reality' (Trenholm, 1999: 31);
5. 'a process in which there is some predictable relation between the message transmitted and the message received' (Graber, 2003: 2).
   (p. 3)

These definitions help to paint a picture of what is involved in communication and the remainder of this chapter should help to fill in some of the details in that picture.

Personally, I particularly like Fiske's definition for its simplicity and clarity. It is no coincidence that this definition begins with the word 'social'. Indeed, the social aspect of communication is something that I shall be paying a lot of attention to. We can see that the social dimension is important for two main reasons. First, we have to recognize that communication takes place in a social context, and that context will often have a very significant bearing on the success or otherwise of the communication and, indeed, on the very nature of that communication. Second, it is important to recognize that communication involves transmitting not only information from one person to another, but also in communicating a relationship. Scollon and Scollon (2001) refer to Gregory Bateson's notion of metamessages:

> The anthropologist Gregory Bateson (1972) pointed out some years ago that every communication must simultaneously communicate two messages, the basic message and the metamessage. The idea of the basic message we are familiar with. The metamessage is a second message, encoded and superimposed upon the basic, which indicates how we want someone to take the basic message. The prefix 'meta' is from Greek and carries the meaning of higher or more general. Bateson also pointed out that this was not just a case of human communication. When we play with a dog, the dog may pretend to bite us. We can tell from the basic message that the dog is biting. The metamessage is conveyed by the dog making its bite quite gentle and at the same time wagging its tail and other such gestures. (p. 77)

This passage illustrates that communication is not a simple mechanical matter of passing information from one person to one or more others but, rather, is a complex, multilevel event. One important extension of Bateson's notion of metamessages is the idea that communication involves the communication of a relationship. For example, if a person uses patronizing language in communicating with others, then the use of such demeaning language indicates a relationship based on a lack of respect. By contrast, a person using forms of language associated with deference will be communicating a relationship based on respect, status and hierarchy. The subtle ways in which such relationships are communicated in speech will be considered in Chapters 4 and 6 while the use of such communication in writing will be covered in Chapters 3 and 10.

The second word of Fiske's definition is also a key one, that of interaction. It perhaps goes without saying that communication involves interaction. One of the important implications of this is that communication can be highly problematic at times – that is, there can be a breakdown between individuals due to the complex dynamics of interaction which take place. This can relate to different perspectives or positions adopted by the people involved or it can arise due to aspects of the actual form of communication, as we shall see below. The third element of the definition through messages is also important. In particular, we should be wary of assuming that communication is only ever intentional. A message can be sent and received even if the person communicating had no intention to do so (see the quotation above from Moss, 2008). For example, if my tone of voice and nonverbal communication indicate nervousness, then it is likely that I will be communicating that nervousness, even though I may not wish to do so or even realize that I am doing so.

A further important point to recognize about communication is that it is not only a basic part of our everyday lives, but also an essential one, in the sense that we cannot *not* communicate, as Rosengren (2000) explains:

> we communicate also when, as helpless prisoners of our physiology, we blush for shame or sweat for nervousness. That is why it has been maintained that as human beings we 'cannot not communicate'. That is why the full study of man [*sic*] and of human society must always include both an objectivist and a subjectivist perspective, and must always include both science and scholarship. That is also why the study of human communication is such a fascinating subject. (p. 38)

Here again, there are echoes of the quotation from Moss (2008), in terms of the recognition of both the impossibility of not communicating and how this makes communication an important and fascinating topic of study.

This takes us away from the common-sense notion that communication is a discrete and separate aspect of social life – that is, something we engage in when we choose to, but do not when we would prefer not to. Rosengren's comments make it clear that the reality is far more complex than that. Simply being a member of society engaging with other people on a day-to-day basis involves communications of various kinds, whether we wish those communications to take place or not. While this may at first appear daunting or even a threatening point to accept, it can also be seen as a motivating and even inspiring one. This is because, if we recognize that communication takes place so widely and so frequently, it gives us the opportunity to raise our awareness of the complex nature of communication and to improve our social skills and effectiveness by enabling us to have a greater influence on what we communicate (and what we do not communicate).

Voice of experience 1.1
❝Spending so much time with children has really brought home to me the importance of 'unintentional' communication. They seem to pick up how you are feeling, even if you don't say anything about it. It was a bit unnerving at first, but it has given me the chance to learn a lot more about working with children.**❞** *Jo, a children's centre worker*

A further factor which makes the subject of communication even more complex is that of meaning. We can see that there are at least two dimensions to meaning. On one hand, we have meaning in the sense of intention. When I mean X, for example, this refers to the fact that I intend X; or I intend to convey X. On the other hand, meaning can refer to interpretation, for example, if I ask the question: What do you mean? This can be translated as: How should I interpret what you have said? These two aspects of meaning reflect two aspects of human existence: the subjective and the objective. Our actions and choices are based not simply on the objective world out there, but rather on our subjective interpretation of that objective world. In this way, we have an interaction between the subjectivity of the individual and his or her perception and the wider social world or objective dimension. Indeed, much of social life can be explained through this complex interaction between subjectivity and objectivity (Thompson, 1992; 2010). This emphasis on the interaction between subjectivity and objectivity is a feature of the theoretical approach known as existentialism and, in particular, one aspect of that, phenomenology. These are important terms that we shall examine in more depth below.

One of the implications of the importance of meaning is a reinforcement of my earlier point that communication is not just a mechanical process of passing on information. When I communicate with you, then there is the question of what I intend (that is, my meaning). There is also the question of how you interpret my communication to you. Your response will then depend on what you mean/intend and how I interpret that response. In addition, all this takes place in a social context which can also, as we shall look at in more detail below, influence the way communication takes place and its outcomes.

To say that communication is 'social interaction through messages' is helpful at one level. However, as we have already seen, this leads to immense complexities. Indeed, one of the aims of this book is to tackle those complexities, to begin to understand them so that we can learn how to communicate more effectively. In order to develop that understanding, it is necessary to look at how different theorists have approached the question of communication. This involves examining different models of communication, and it is to this that we now turn.

ACTIVITY 1.1

Think about the word 'communication'. What does it mean to you? What ideas does it conjure up in your mind? Make some notes about this and then use these as the basis of a discussion with colleagues. Think then about what conclusion you can draw from the activity, what lessons you might be able to learn.

Models of communication

Perhaps one of the simplest and best-known models of communication is that arising from Shannon and Weaver's (1949) classic text. Their approach is part of what has become known as the process school of communication. Put simply, their model involves three elements. First, there is the transmitter – for example, the person initiating the communication. Second, there is the receiver, the person being communicated with. In between these two elements is a third one which is referred to as 'noise'. This refers to any factor or set of

Figure 1.1 The basic model of communication

factors which can interfere with the communication – just as, in a literal sense, noise can prevent person B from hearing what person A is saying and therefore block communication. The term 'noise' can be used more widely to refer to any factor which interferes with or undermines the communication taking place. Noise factors can include distractions (communicating while driving a car, for example), emotional issues such as anger, or technical problems, such as poor-quality telephone lines.

PRACTICE FOCUS 1.1

Viv was concerned that there had been too many communication problems occurring. He therefore decided to hold a teambuilding session in which the team members were given the task of identifying what was getting in the way of effective communication (the 'noise' factors). He was surprised by how many issues were raised. In particular, though, he was concerned about how many of them seemed to be connected with issues relating to levels of workload. He was therefore able to realize that a vicious circle had developed. Workload pressures had got in the way of effective communication, and that, in turn, had led to even greater workload pressures as the team were not working together as much as they should. He therefore decided to look closely at how he could improve communication by addressing workload management issues.

Although this model has been quite influential and has a number of advantages, it has also been heavily criticized, mainly for being oversimplified. This is because it fails to take account of a wide range of other factors, and also presents communication as a fairly simplistic process of passing information. In this respect, it fails to take account of some of the issues discussed above – for example, the social context of communication and the importance of meaning.

The basic process approach can be extended and developed to take account of complex networks of interaction (for example, communication across multidisciplinary teams or networks). However, even a more sophisticated version of the process approach still leaves out very important issues. Communication clearly does involve a set of interacting processes. My argument is not that the process approach is 'wrong', but rather that it does not go far enough. It is a good beginning to our understanding, but is not enough on its own.

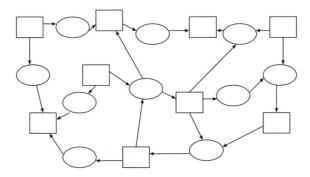

Figure 1.2 Networks of communication

An alternative approach to the process model is that of semiotics. Here the emphasis is on signs and the powerful symbolism associated with them. The term 'semiotics' derives from the word 'semiosis', which means the action of signs. Clearly, then, here the emphasis is on how signs are used and combined in systems to form the basis of communication. As Cobley (2001a) explains:

> *Communication* is a form of semiosis which is concerned with the exchange of any messages whatsoever: from the molecular code and the immunological properties of cells all the way through to vocal sentences. Signification is that aspect of semiosis which is concerned with the value or outcome of message exchange and is sometimes given the name 'meaning'. (p. 5)

Words themselves can be seen as forms of signs, and so the question of sign systems is a very relevant one to the study of language. This is therefore a topic to which we shall return in Chapter 2. However, for present purposes, we can note that semiotics goes far beyond the simple mechanical basis of the process model of communication. The major advantage of semiotics, with its emphasis on signs, is that it enables us to take account of meaning, in so far as meaning can be seen to arise from the use of signs and the combination of signs in sign systems.

The notion of sign systems introduces a very important concept in the study of communication, namely culture, as culture can be seen as a set of sign systems. Kendall and Wickham (2001) explain culture in the following terms:

> 'culture' refers to the way of life of a group (including, possibly, a society), including the meanings, the transmission, communication and alteration of those meanings, and the circuits of power by which the meanings are valorised or derogated. (p. 14)

This passage is important in a number of ways. First, it refers to the way of life of a group. This means that culture is not just an abstract entity, but rather forms a basic part of our everyday social experience. Second, it shows that meanings can be 'valorised or derogated'. This means that not all meanings and communications have equal value or validity. Indeed, we can recognize a hierarchy in which certain meanings are given higher status and importance than others. Here we are in the realm of power, a concept which plays such a crucial part not only in communication in particular, but also in social life more broadly. Power will be discussed in more detail in Chapter 5, but here we should note that power is a basic ingredient in understanding culture and semiosis.

At its simplest, culture can be defined as shared ways of seeing, thinking and doing, or, as Guirdham (1999) puts it: 'a historically transmitted system of symbols, meanings and norms' (p. 61). However, this is very much a basic definition and only gives a beginning to developing an understanding of this complex and wide-ranging term. Kendall and Wickham (2001) make an important point when they argue that: '"Culture" is one of the names given to the different ways people go about ordering the world and the different ways the world goes about ordering people' (p. 24). Culture gives us a framework for making sense of our experiences. It gives us an interconnected set of shared ideas, assumptions, beliefs, values and unwritten rules. It is in this sense that culture provides a major part of the framework from which we make sense of our lives and our interactions with others.

Of course, human culture as a whole can be subdivided into the vast array of particular cultures that apply in different countries, different religious groups, different interest groups and so on. Indeed, the term culture can be used to describe any shared set of meanings – for example, as when an organization develops its own distinctive organizational culture. The significance of this for communication is twofold. First, it is through cultural signs and symbols that we are so often able to communicate with one another and, second, each communication has to be understood in the context of the particular culture or intercultural network in which it occurs. For example, particular words and/or gestures can have different meanings in different cultural contexts.

PRACTICE FOCUS 1.2

Peter had worked in the same office since leaving school and had become very familiar with the organization and how it worked. However, when he took up a new post in another organization, he was amazed to find out just how different the culture was – even though he was still working in the same service sector. He had not appreciated how immersed in the culture of his previous workplace he had become. It was only now, after making the change of employer, that he realized that so much of what he regarded as the 'realities of the workplace' were largely only the realities of that particular workplace, with its distinctive organizational culture.

The emphasis on culture has led to the development of what has come to be known as cultural studies, which Kendall and Wickham (2001) define as follows:

> 'Cultural Studies' involves the study of a group's way of life, particularly its meanings (including its morals and its beliefs), with an emphasis on the politics of the ways those meanings are communicated. Cultural Studies must concern itself with the control of meanings and their dissemination, that is with circuits of power and with forms of resistance. (p. 14)

Cultural studies as an academic discipline is closely associated with the work of Stuart Hall and his colleagues (Morley and Chen, 1996). One basic starting point for this school of thought is the critique of marxist ideas which emphasize the importance of structural factors such as the economic base. While not wishing to dismiss the importance of such broad structural factors, the cultural studies approach has pointed out that, in addition to these, it is important to take account of cultural factors in making sense of social formations and processes. Individuals as social actors do not operate simply within a broader network of social, political and economic factors, but also within a context of cultural assumptions, formations and practices. Cultural studies has proven to be a very influential approach and has also tended to be very wide-ranging. For example, its influence can be seen not only in sociology and the social sciences generally, but also in the arts, humanities and media studies more broadly.

A key concept in cultural studies is that of ideology. This refers to sets of ideas which become very powerful in their ability to influence the thoughts and actions of individuals and groups of people. Berger and Luckmann (1967) define ideology as 'ideas serving as weapons of social interest' (p. 18). This refers to the fact that those who remain in positions of power do so not primarily as the result of the use of physical force, but because of more subtle means through the power of ideas. That is, an ideology is a set of ideas which help to maintain the status quo in terms of existing power relations. For example, it has been shown that patriarchal ideology is an important factor in the maintenance of relationships between the sexes (Bryson, 1999). Ideas based on the notion that 'it's a man's world' can be shown to have a very subtle and pervasive influence on social actions and attitudes. Even in this day and age, assumptions about the respective roles of men and women in society can easily be detected. This ideology will therefore influence not only society as a whole but also, more specifically, interactions between men and women.

The concept of ideology is also closely linked with that of discourse. Literally, discourse refers to a conversation or a portion of text. However, it has been developed within social science theory to refer to forms of text which affect how we think and act. For example, medical discourse refers to the ideas and assumptions that are associated with the medical world. Authors such as Michel Foucault have pointed out that discourses bring with them power relations or, more accurately, power relations are embedded within discourses. For example, in the case of medical discourse the notion that 'doctor knows best' or 'doctor's orders' can be seen to assign considerable power and authority to doctors within our society (Foucault, 1977; 1979). 'Ideology' and 'discourse', then, are terms which have a lot in common. Indeed, some authors use them more or less interchangeably. However, one significant difference is that discourse can be seen to be much more closely focused on language (Thompson, 2011).

From this approach based on discourse, we can recognize at least two major issues. First, we can see that communication is once again closely linked with power through the medium of discourse. For example, in using a particular form of communication, I may be reflecting and reinforcing a particular discourse. If I refer to someone as being mentally ill, then, in so doing, I am drawing on a discourse of madness as a form of illness rather than the various other interpretations of madness that have existed over the centuries, or the competing explanations of madness which exist today (for example, anti-psychiatry and critical alternatives to the medical model). I have deliberately chosen the example of madness as this is a theme in the work of Foucault where he examines the significance of discourse in shaping social responses to mental distress. Second, we can see that communication problems or mismatches can arise when the different people involved in an attempt to communicate have their starting points in different discourses.

Maintaining the theme of madness and mental distress, imagine the situation in which somebody with mental health problems is arrested. To the police officer making the arrest, the person arrested is likely to be seen as a threat to law and order and, indeed, possibly a threat to him- or herself. To a psychiatrist called to the police station to attend to the person arrested, however, he or she may be seen as somebody in need of help and treatment rather than as a threat. This disparity in perception can be explained by reference to the concept of discourse, in so far as it is likely that the police officer will be operating from what could be referred to as a law and order discourse, while the psychiatrist is likely to be operating from a medical discourse. It is no coincidence that differences in discourse are often signalled by differences in language. This is because discourses are maintained in and through language. The power relations inherent in the use of discourse will be discussed in more depth and detail in Chapter 5 (see also Thompson, 2007).

The emphasis on discourse in the work of some theorists has led us to appreciate the fact that language not only reflects reality, but also, in many ways, constructs that reality, as Shotter (1993) comments:

language is no longer seen as serving solely a representative function, but as also being *formative*, that is, rather than being of use merely to refer to circumstances within a situation, it functions to formulate the functions in which we are involved *as* situations, *as* states of affairs. (p. 33)

For example, in using the term 'chairman', we are not only reflecting the fact that the majority of positions of power are held by men, but also contributing to that state of affairs by reinforcing the discourse which makes it legitimate for men to be seen as the powerholders in society. Similarly, we should not be surprised to find that, in many situations, the use of terminology which reflects guilt or blame actually generates feelings of guilt in the person concerned.

PRACTICE FOCUS 1.3

When Peter took up his new post, he was pleased to discover that many aspects of his new employing organization were much better than he had been used to in his previous post. However, some things were not quite so good. In particular, he was concerned that there seemed to be a culture of blame and guilt. When things went wrong, even very minor things, senior managers wanted to know who was the person responsible – in other words, who was to blame. The language used was a major contributor to this culture. For example, in his previous job, people would ask: 'What went wrong?', whereas in the new job, the focus was very much on: 'Who fouled up?' This type of terminology created a lot of tension, as it implied that there was always someone personally responsible when something went wrong, even though the reality was that mistakes were often the result of a combination of factors (some beyond people's control), rather than one individual's specific error.

Maybin (2001) writes of the way in which language inevitably passes judgement on the world. Referring to the work of Volosinov and Bakhtin, she comments as follows:

Because of the way language inevitably passes judgement on the world, even as it describes it, Volosinov argues that rather than reflecting reality, language should be seen as 'refracting' it through the lens of social struggle. For Bakhtin and Volosinov, this ideological aspect of language does not only apply to its use within the grand social edifices of politics, education and religion, but is just as important in the apparently trivial, casual conversations of daily life. Comments about experience, other people, relationships or everyday activities are also at some level an evaluation of what is being talked about and will include assigning evaluative accenting to specific words and phrases. (p. 65)

Clearly, these are complex and wide-ranging issues which draw on very subtle sociological and philosophical analyses. However, a more pragmatic approach to the notion of language as formative or constitutive of reality is to be found in what has come to be known as speech act theory. Based on the work of Austin (1955), Searle (1969) and Bales (1976), speech act theory argues that different forms of language serve different functions. For example, while some utterances are a description of an action, others actually constitute an action in their own right. If I say, 'Steve promised to behave', then I am describing what Steve did. However, if I state: 'I promise to behave', then it is not so much a case of description but actual action. That is, in stating that I promise to behave, I am in fact promising to behave. Other examples would be, 'I resign', 'I now pronounce you man and wife', or 'I declare this meeting closed'. Such utterances are referred to as 'performatives' because they perform the act to which they refer, rather than simply describe it. Speech act theory is something that is very relevant to the discussions in Part II of the book where I look at the implications of communication theory for practice in a variety of settings. An understanding of speech act theory can be very helpful in ensuring that miscommunications are kept to a minimum and communications are as effective and appropriate as possible.

What I have presented here are just some of the approaches to communication, and this is by no means a comprehensive or exhaustive account. However, from what we have covered here, it should be apparent that, while some approaches overlap with others, there is also considerable difference and disparity amongst them. We are a long way from a unified theory of communication and it seems unlikely that we will ever achieve that. However, given the complexity and significance of communication, it is also questionable as to whether it would be desirable to have a single unified theory which attempts to account for such a wide-ranging and intricate subject matter.

ACTIVITY 1.2

Think of a piece of work (or other form of interaction) you have dealt with at some point – anything that has stuck in your mind. Using some of the ideas you have just been reading about in the last few pages, think about how one or more of them might have applied in the situation concerned.

The role of culture

I have already made reference to the importance of culture as a factor underpinning communication. Here I want to explore these issues in more depth, developing a slightly fuller picture of what culture is and how it relates to communication.

It has been explained that culture involves signs, symbols and meanings. Indeed, Berger (1991) defines culture as 'the realm of symbols and meanings' (p. 5). Scollon and Scollon (2001) explain the term more fully when they propose:

> When we use the word 'culture' in its anthropological sense, we mean to say that culture is any of the customs, worldview, language, kinship system, social organization, and other taken-for-granted day-to-day practices of a people which set that group apart as a distinctive group. By using the anthropological sense of the word 'culture', we mean to consider any aspect of the ideas, communications, or behaviors of a group of people which gives to them a distinctive identity and which is used to organize their internal sense of cohesion and membership. (pp. 139–40)

Clearly, culture is not being used to refer simply to what might be called 'highbrow culture' – for example, fine art, opera, ballet and so on. Rather, the term is used much more widely to refer to sets of symbols and meanings. Culture is, in effect, a system of symbolic representation. However, it is not simply symbols that are representations themselves, but rather, the whole framework of meanings and actions that flow from the use of such symbols.

Jenks (1993) makes interesting comment when he compares culture with nature:

> Animals, even the chattering dolphins, 'do' nature, while human beings inevitably transform their world into, and by way of, a series of symbolic representations. The symbolic, then, satisfies and absorbs the projections of human beings into objects and states of affairs that are different, and it also acts as a mediator between these two provinces. We no longer confront the natural, as if we were continuous with it, as it is supposed that animals do. We now meet with the natural and, indeed, experience it as performed through our vocabulary of symbols which are primarily linguistic but increasingly elaborate out into other forms like custom, convention, habit and even artefact. The symbolic representations that constitute human knowing are, in their various groupings, classifications and manifestations, the *cultural*. (p. 8)

A good example of culture as a system of symbolic representation would be newspapers. Newspapers are not only different in terms of which news they report and how they report it, but also in terms of what each particular newspaper symbolizes in terms of its values, standards, approaches to social life and so on (see McQuail, 2000).

One particular approach to culture which can be particularly helpful in trying to understand communication stems from the work of the French theorist, Pierre Bourdieu. Bourdieu introduced the important concept of 'habitus' which Lovell (2000) explains as follows:

By *habitus* Bourdieu understands ways of doing and being which social subjects acquire during their socialization. Their *habitus* is not a matter of conscious learning, or of ideological imposition, but is acquired through practice. Bourdieu's sociology rests on an account of lived 'practice', and what he terms 'the practical sense' – the ability to function effectively within a given social field, an ability which cannot necessarily be articulated as conscious knowledge: 'knowing how' rather than 'knowing that'. *Habitus* names the characteristic dispositions of the social subject. It is indicated in the bearing of the body ('hexis'), and in deeply ingrained habits of behaviour, feeling and thought. (p. 27)

And perhaps to this we can add deep and ingrained habits of communication. We can perhaps best understand Bourdieu's concept of habitus by thinking of the way aspects of culture become like wallpaper – that is, they fade into the background and, although we may be in contact with them on a daily basis, we forget that they are there and they have little direct bearing on our conscious decisions or actions. It is for this reason that we can experience what is known as 'culture shock' when we find ourselves in a cultural setting that we are not familiar with. That is, the differences in taken-for-granted assumptions can make us feel very uneasy and unsure of ourselves. Matters that we have tended to take for granted can suddenly become problematic and not quite so clear cut. This can be an unnerving and even threatening experience (see the discussion of ontological security in Thompson, 2011).

PRACTICE FOCUS 1.4

Sandra had worked in a number of settings since she registered with the employment agency as a temporary worker. However, all of these had been in the private sector, with a strong focus on business and commerce. When she was placed in a local authority Social Care and Housing Department, she was therefore very surprised to find such a different atmosphere and ethos. She had never worked in a public service setting before and she experienced a form of culture shock when she realized just how different it was in so many different ways. At first, she felt very uncomfortable, like a 'fish out of water', and wanted to go back to an environment that she was more familiar with. However, after a little while she started to adjust to the new culture and began to get over her shock and the very uneasy feelings the change had brought out in her.

This is particularly relevant to our understanding of communication, because habitus forms a powerful backdrop to our actions and interactions. Therefore, when we enter into communication with others, intentionally or otherwise, we are likely to be influenced by the many taken-for-granted assumptions that form the habitus. Once again, power is relevant to this discussion. In fact, Bourdieu introduces the concept of 'symbolic violence'. This refers to an acceptance of domination. The habitus can be so powerful in its influence over us that it can impose meanings which obscure the truth about social relations. This is similar to Marx's notion of false consciousness, but is a much more sophisticated concept. Whilst Marx linked false consciousness primarily, if not exclusively, to economic factors and relations of production, Bourdieu goes much further than this in ascribing a complex array of cultural meanings to the term 'habitus'. Also, Marx's notion can be criticized for being essentialist, in the sense that it seems to assume that there is a 'false' consciousness and a 'true' consciousness. Bourdieu, by contrast, recognizes the fluidity, flexibility and diversity of the cultural domain. That is, habitus is a generalized concept used to refer to a whole host of taken-for-granted assumptions and shared meanings and is not simply one dominant ideology, as per the marxist version of events.

The point was made earlier that communication is not simply a matter of transmitting information, but also involves transmitting a relationship. Bourdieu's theory is an extension of that notion. He is, in effect, arguing that the habitus incorporates a set of power relations, relations based on dominance and subordination. What this means is that ideas are not presented to us through our culture in an objective or impartial way; rather, they represent the interests of dominant groups. According to Bourdieu, then, it is no surprise that, in a male-dominated society, the dominant ideas within the habitus reflect and reinforce the interests of men. In effect, Bourdieu is arguing that power relations operate through symbolism and that symbolism is what constitutes the habitus. This is an important point, as it helps to explain the persistence of power relationships. As Poupeau (2000) explains: 'Domination is not merely power *over* a particular group, it is also a relationship of meaning *between* individuals in which recognition of legitimacy ensures the persistence of power' (p. 72). This is another point which helps to emphasize that power and communication are closely intertwined.

A further concept from Bourdieu which helps us to understand this complex interrelationship is that of 'cultural capital'. Bourdieu argues that different people have different amounts of 'cultural capital'. By this he means that certain people, depending on their position of power and status within the social hierarchy, will have greater cultural resources to draw upon in terms of influencing others – in other words, in terms of exercising power. For example, someone who, through their education and upbringing, has developed greater knowledge and understanding of a range of social circumstances, will be in a stronger position to operate within those circumstances to influence people and to communicate with them. Someone with less cultural capital – that is, someone with a lower level of education, less exposure to a wide range of social events and cultural circumstances – will be in a much weaker position to have their say in what happens. Their voice will be a much less powerful one than that of the person with the higher level of cultural capital. Bourdieu is once again drawing on marxist notions, but extending them in a more sophisticated way. Just as Marx argued that capital in the economic sense is a key factor in determining life chances and opportunities to exercise power, Bourdieu presents the notion of cultural capital in a parallel way – that is, it is not simply a matter of how much money or access to financial resources one has; other factors relating to cultural knowledge, ability and skills will also play a part in how we fit into society, what opportunities we have and the power that we can exercise in social situations.

Voice of experience 1.2

❝Most of the people we support in the community are very isolated. They tend to have few if any relatives, few social contacts and little by way of any involvement in clubs or societies. I have been convinced for some time that this is a big part of why there is so much depression among this group of people.**❞** *Mair, manager of a multidisciplinary community mental health team for older people*

One fundamental implication of Bourdieu's theory is that, in approaching a communicative encounter, participants do not start with a level playing field. That is, when person A communicates with person B, differences in cultural capital are likely to have a major influence on not only the nature of the communication itself but also its outcome. For example, if you are more culturally sophisticated than I am, then this means that you will be able to put me down, block my progress and limit my access to certain circumstances in ways which would not apply in reverse. In particular, Bourdieu linked this to the power and symbolism of such things as accent and dialect, important points to which we shall return in Chapter 2.

This brief outline of Bourdieu's theory should be sufficient to establish why it is important to consider communication theory when looking at issues of the practice of communication. It should be clear that attempts to tackle the complexities of the practicalities of communication without at least a basic understanding of some of these complexities is doomed to oversimplification and, in many cases, will not only fail, but may also be counterproductive.

Reference has already been made to the development of cultural studies as an intellectual discipline. One of the major contributions that this school of thought has made is the emphasis on the fact that culture can be seen as autonomous from other social spheres. For example, there is a wealth of sociological and political science literature which focuses on the economic and

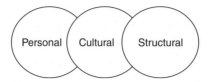

Figure 1.3 Culture mediates the personal and the structural

political structures of society which pay little or no regard to the role of culture. Cultural studies theorists would argue that culture is in itself constitutive of society. That is, culture is not simply a reflection of broader economic or political processes but, rather, is a set of processes in its own right which have the effect of forming the social base. This approach to culture emphasizes its role in society, but also places great stress on the significance of language and communication. It is for this reason that cultural studies will be an important feature underpinning many of the chapters of this book. What should be more than apparent by now is that culture and communication are closely interlinked and that any adequate account of communication processes must take into consideration the significance of culture.

Identity and communication

The subject of identity is one that has received extensive attention in the social sciences in recent years. This is largely, but not exclusively, due to the development of poststructuralism and postmodernism as theoretical perspectives on society.

For many decades, the study of identity was closely associated with psychological studies of personality. This approach has now been heavily criticized for two main reasons. First, it tends to have a narrow focus on individual/psychological factors and pays little attention to wider social concerns. Second, much of the research and theory relating to this approach has given the impression that personality is a fixed, enduring characteristic of the individual, something that allows for little or no change over time. Contemporary approaches to the study of identity challenge both of these assumptions. That is, they emphasize the social (and cultural) dimensions of identity and the fluid or changing nature of identity over time.

The traditional approach to personality can be seen to have little connection with the study of communication, except perhaps as a minor issue in relation to how the personality of individuals involved in communication may influence their style of communication and so on. By contrast, more recent approaches to identity emphasize the significance of communication, in so far as identity is not seen as a fixed entity, but rather as a developing process influenced by the communications and interactions in which the individual becomes engaged.

One long-established approach to identity which has influenced contemporary perspectives is that of Charles Horton Cooley and his notion of the looking-glass self (Cooley, 1902). This term refers to the way in which our actions and communications are mirrored back to us through the responses of other people. That is, if I project a particular image to other people, that image will either be reinforced or challenged by the ways in which people respond to me in their interactions. Cooley's approach has established itself as quite significant and influential, in so far as it has helped other theorists to appreciate the interactive nature of the self and thus to move away from deterministic notions of personality as being relatively fixed. Recent approaches to identity have built on this notion, although not always acknowledging the important foundations laid by Cooley.

Another long-established approach to identity and related matters, which is influential today, is that of existentialism. Existentialism is a philosophy which has proven immensely influential in both the philosophical world and the wider world of day-to-day popular consciousness (Panza and Gale, 2008). However, the influence of existentialism on the social sciences has tended to be patchy. We therefore have a strange situation in which dominant notions of personality in social sciences have been out of keeping with more flexible notions of identity in philosophy. These schools of thought have existed side by side for a long, long time and it is only relatively recently that philosophical ideas have started to influence the study of identity in a major way.

The basic starting point for existentialism is the *radical* freedom of the individual – that is, freedom to choose as the basis of human existence. What this means is that each individual is perceived as a person who not only *can* choose, but *must* choose, in the sense that, if we have no fixed personality, no biologically given need to behave in a particular way, then how we behave is a matter of choice. In making choices, the existentialists, such as Sartre, would argue we are constructing our self (Sartre, 1948; 1958). An individual sense of self can therefore be seen as a historical process built up over the years, based on the series of choices that the person concerned has made. A common misunderstanding or oversimplification of the existentialist approach is to assume that Sartre and his colleagues are arguing that there are no constraints on our ability to choose. This is clearly not the case. We are constrained by a wide range of factors, including biological (for example, I cannot 'choose' to be 6 foot 6 inches tall) and the constraints of other people – that is, other people's choices can get in the way of my choices. A traffic jam would be a good example of this, where my choice to travel to a particular area is hampered by the choice of other people trying to get to the same destination. However, despite these constraints, the existentialist conception of self is a powerful one, in so far as it places the responsibility for choice on the individual. To a large extent, I choose who I am through my actions and interactions.

This clearly has major implications for communication, as so many of the choices individuals make will depend on matters relating to communication and interaction. In fact, we could say that, in communicating, I am communicating my self. That is, my sense of self is created in and through my communications and interactions with others and the choices involved in that process.

Clearly, this school of thought is once again a long way away from the mechanical process approach to communication. Communication is not simply passing on information, but is actually a process through which an individual's identity is constituted. This means that communication has an even more important and far-ranging role than most people would generally realize.

A more contemporary development in social thought which has much to say about identity and which also has a lot in common with existentialism is that of postmodernism (although, once again, its debt to former theoretical developments is rarely, if ever, acknowledged). Postmodernism has developed as a broad theoretical movement in the social sciences, philosophy and the humanities more broadly. It is characterized by a critique of established enlightenment ideals – that is, the notion that science and progress are inevitable features of the modern world, or 'modernity' as postmodernists refer to it. Postmodernism is an approach which is suspicious of overarching grand theories (or 'metanarratives', as they call them). It is an approach which emphasizes fragmentation – that is, the relative lack of unity and coherence, in contrast to the enlightenment ideal of science providing a rational, unifying basis for social thought and human development. It is a highly complex and rapidly developing school of thought, and so it is beyond the scope of this book to examine it in any great detail. However, we should note that the thinking of many postmodernists has been very influential in contemporary developments in our understanding of communication and language and, in particular, of identity.

Sarup (1996) is one postmodernist thinker who has written about identity. He draws an important link between identity and boundaries:

> identity is a construction, a consequence of a process of interaction between people, institutions and practices and that, because the range of human behaviour is so wide, groups maintain boundaries to limit the type of behaviour within a defined cultural territory. Boundaries are an important point of reference for those participating in any system. Boundaries may refer to, or consist of, geographical areas, political or religious viewpoints, occupational categories, or linguistic and cultural traditions. (p. 11)

This passage illustrates that, in the postmodernist conception, identity is largely shaped by the social context in which we operate. However, this is not a narrowly defined or fixed social context, but rather a fluid and developing social context, just as the boundaries to which Sarup refers change and develop over time. For postmodernists, there is no core self, no essential 'I' at the centre of our being. Instead, what we have is a flow of activity, interactions and communications.

One important concept which has developed within postmodernism which casts much light on identity is that of narrative. In essence, a narrative is a story. However, it is used in a more specialist sense within postmodernist thinking to refer to the process by which we make sense of our existence, by which we develop a story which enables us to live our lives in as coherent a way as we can. In this sense, identity can be seen as the process by which I live my life through the narrative of my biography. Unlike traditional approaches to personality which would see identity as relating to the individual that the story is about, the individual *is* the story in the sense that the narrative that is constructed through my day-to-day experiences is the unifying thread that enables me to have a sense of who I am.

A further important concept within postmodernist thought is that of difference. Postmodernism, with its rejection of overarching grand theories and its emphasis on fragmentation, attaches considerable significance to the notion of difference, in the sense that diversity and the range of differences between people, between aspects of society and so on, are seen as important parts of the social sphere. However, this creates an apparent contradiction, as 'identity' is a word that is generally associated with the opposite of difference (consider the related word of 'identical'), but once we look more closely at the situation, we can see that contradiction is superficial, as we can understand identity in terms of differences – that is, what makes an individual a unique individual are the ways in which he or she is different from other people. Woodward (1997) explains this in the following passage:

> Identity gives us a sense of who we are and of how we relate to others and to the world in which we live. Identity marks the ways in which we are the same as others who share that position, and the ways in which we are different from those who do not. Often, identity is most clearly defined by difference, that is, by what it is not. Identities may be marked by polarization, for example, in the most extreme forms of national or ethnic conflict, and by the marking of inclusion or exclusion – insiders and outsiders, 'us' and 'them'. Identities are frequently constructed in terms of oppositions such as man/woman, black/white, straight/gay, healthy/unhealthy, normal/deviant. (pp. 1–2)

I earlier made reference to Sarup's notion of boundaries as defining features of identity. This can be seen to relate closely to Woodward's notion of difference. In identifying a difference, we are establishing a boundary. That is, in establishing that chalk is different from cheese, we are drawing a boundary between the two. My sense of who I am therefore owes much to the differences I recognize, the boundaries that I draw and the significance that I attach to them. However, identity is not simply a matter of how I see myself or how I locate myself within these differences, but also how other people locate me in terms of such differences. Racism would be a good example of this. How an individual identifies him- or herself in terms of ethnicity is largely a subjective matter. However, racism is something that is generally imposed from outside – that is, it is other people's definition of who should be seen as inferior or unworthy that attracts the negative attentions of racism. Again, we are recognizing that communication is a complex social matter, as it is through such subtle and intricate interactions that identity is established, maintained and/or changed.

PRACTICE FOCUS 1.5

Simon was born in Manchester but moved to Ireland when he was five years old as a result of his father being transferred to work in his employer's Dublin office. When the time came for Simon to go to university, he applied to universities in the Manchester area to return to his 'roots', as he still saw himself as English, even though he had lived in Ireland for thirteen years. However, when he moved to Manchester to begin his degree studies he was surprised to find that his Irish accent led many people to treat him quite badly. In particular, he found himself the butt of many jokes that implied that he was less than intelligent. He was very disappointed to find that he was being discriminated against by English people, especially as he regarded himself as English.

The relationship between identity and communication is in many ways a difficult one. However, we should not lose sight of the fact that it is also a very important one. Its particular significance should become apparent in subsequent chapters, particularly when I address the practicalities of ensuring that communication is as effective as possible.

Intercultural communication

The area of intercultural communication is potentially a minefield of difficulties and complications at both a theoretical and a practical level. This is partly because no one can enter into a communication without also being part of a culture and, as we have seen, culture is a complex and multifaceted entity. What this means is that, even when I am communicating with somebody who has much in common with me culturally, there is still the potential for misunderstanding and breakdown of communication because of the different assumptions or unwritten rules which can come into play as a result of any minor cultural differences between us. When we then look at the nature of communication between people of widely different cultural backgrounds, we should easily be able to recognize that there is immense potential for difficulties to arise.

These difficulties can be seen to apply in three main ways. First, we have already noted that cultures comprise sets of taken-for-granted assumptions, therefore it is quite feasible that a person from one culture communicating with a person from a different culture will become embroiled in complications relating to the incompatibility of the assumption that each person is drawing upon in forming the basis of their communication. For example, my own cultural background has taught me that it is polite to smile when meeting somebody for the first time. However, on more than one occasion I have met people from other cultures which do not have such an unwritten rule. I have therefore had to resist the temptation of assuming that the person concerned is being rude because he or she does not reflect the cultural norms on which I base my behaviour. Second, it is important to recognize that different cultures have different approaches to communication. For example, Guirdham (1999) draws the distinction between high-context and low-context cultures. In a high-context culture, as often found in the East, there is much reliance on contextual factors to provide meaning to the communication. In the low-context cultures more closely associated with the West, there is more of an emphasis on the explicit verbal content of the communication. As Guirdham (1999) explains:

> In high-context cultures (HCCs), people rely heavily on the overall situation to interpret messages – and so the messages which are explicitly spoken can be elliptical; in low-context cultures (LCCs) people rely more on the explicit verbal content of messages. Members of HCCs, for instance, Japanese people, use non-verbal cues and information about a person's background to a greater extent than members of LCCs, such as the British. (p. 60)

One way in which high-context and low-context cultures can be differentiated is in terms of the use of roles. In high-context cultures, roles tend to be more formal and are characterized by much more of an emphasis on ritualistic behaviour. In low-context cultures, by contrast, there is more emphasis on personal style, and communication therefore tends to be less formal. That is, in a high-context culture the role itself is intended to communicate much about the interaction, whereas in a low-context culture, the specific roles played by participants have less significance, with a greater emphasis on how in particular those roles are carried out by the individuals concerned. Third, problems can arise because of discrimination, in the sense that someone from one culture may look down upon someone from a different cultural background. From our understanding of how discrimination operates in society (Thompson, 2011) we know that cultures do not operate side by side on a level playing field. Unfortunately, the situation is far more problematic than that, with many cultures being seen as inferior to others. Indeed, this is the basis of racism as, in this ideology, certain cultural ethnic or racial groups are deemed to be automatically inferior to others. It is sad, but none the less important, to note that cultures so often exist in a relationship of domination and subordination rather than one of equality and mutual respect. It therefore takes little imagination to recognize that communication between members of cultures perceived to be in a hierarchy of dominance are likely to be influenced by the power relations involved.

Voice of experience 1.3

❝I learned so much on my placement in India. It was like a different world, not just a different country. It was incredible to see all the cultural differences. Everyone seemed so formal to begin with and I thought they were quite unfriendly, but I soon realized that they were being friendly, but in their own way. I learned so much from that sort of thing.**❞** *Derek, a social work student*

One factor that we can identify which clearly has an important bearing on intercultural communication is that of stereotyping. Unfortunately, stereotypes have the effect of distorting communication. This is particularly significant in relation to intercultural communication, because stereotypes commonly apply to members of particular cultures. Often such stereotypes are derogatory or unduly negative and can reinforce or cause some of the difficulties outlined above.

In our day-to-day lives, we have to rely on what are known as 'typifications' – that is, we have to see certain things as being typical. For example, if I go into a shop that I have never been into before, I will begin by assuming that it is a typical shop and that it operates according to the general rules of commercial interactions within my culture. However, if I were to go into a shop which is not typical – for example, if it is run by somebody from a different cultural background from myself, or if I am in a foreign country, then I would quickly learn that this is not a typical shop and I would seek to adjust my assumptions and my behaviour accordingly. The use of typifications in this way is a very helpful and constructive part of day-to-day social interaction. However, stereotypes go a step beyond this, in so far as what happens in the process of stereotyping is that typifications become rigid and resistant to change, amendment or renegotiation. A stereotype is a typification that is maintained despite evidence to the contrary – that is, we continue to treat the person concerned as if he or she were typical of a particular category, when in fact this is not the case or, indeed, when the typification itself is inaccurate and based on derogatory assumptions. In short, typifications are helpful, stereotypes are not. As Scollon and Scollon (2001) argue:

Stereotyping is simply another word for overgeneralization. The difference, however, is that stereotyping carries with it an ideological position. Characteristics of the group are not only overgeneralized to apply to each member of the group, but they are also taken to have some exaggerated negative or positive value. These values are then taken as arguments to support social or political relationships in regard to members of those groups. (p. 168)

They go on to make the important point that:

Stereotypes limit our understanding of human behaviour and of intercultural discourse because they limit our view of human activity to just one or two salient dimensions and consider those to be the whole picture. Furthermore, they go on ideologically to use that limited view of individuals and of groups to justify preferential or discriminatory treatment by others who hold greater political power. (p. 169)

Effective intercultural communication is therefore premised on an awareness of the dangers of stereotyping and a commitment to doing something about ensuring that these are not allowed to influence our actions and interactions.

PRACTICE FOCUS 1.6

When Simon had begun his university studies in Manchester he had realized how his Irish accent led many people to stereotype him. This made him very aware of the dangers of stereotyping in general, and he became very sensitive to the various ways in which stereotypes tend to be used. What he found particularly interesting was how the people who used these stereotypes were generally unaware that they were doing so. However, he was not only interested in the prevalence of stereotyping, but also quite concerned by it. He was able to see how people who were regarded as culturally different were likely to be treated as members of a particular category or classification, rather than as unique individuals in their own right.

One important way in which cultures differ is the ways in which they handle 'face'. Face is a technical term used in psychology and sociology to refer to the status and esteem of individuals within social interactions (Goffman, 1990). This is exemplified by phrases such as 'saving face' or 'losing face'. Individuals will behave in particular ways which seek to maintain their face (that is, their status and sense of esteem) and will seek to avoid situations in which they lose face. Societies have complex systems of rules and rituals for maintaining face, and these will be different in different societies and cultures. It can therefore be seen as very important to understand the rules relating to face as they relate to a particular culture, as these may be different from those applying in our own. Scollon and Scollon (2001) argue that any communication involves the risk of a person losing face. In particular, they relate this to maintaining a balance of independence and involvement between two persons in a communicative encounter. They comment as follows:

> Any communication is a risk to face; it is a risk to one's own face at the same time as it is a risk to the other person's. We have to carefully project a face for ourselves and to respect the face rights and claims of other participants. We risk our own involvement face if we do not include other participants in our relationship. That is, if we exclude others, while that may increase our own independence, it at the same time decreases our own involvement. At the same time, if we include others, we risk our own independence face. (p. 48)

One theoretical approach which can help us to understand the complex interaction of face relationships is that of frame analysis. This is an approach developed by the sociologist Erving Goffman (1922–1982). He uses the term 'frame' to refer to the way in which particular activities or sets of activities are framed – that is, the way they are understood. For example, the various activities in between waking up and leaving the house to head for work could be included under the frame of 'getting ready for work'. The significance of frame analysis is that it is through frames that we make sense of what we are doing and what is happening around us. That is, we do not interpret events as unique individual occurrences each time they happen but, rather, see them as examples of aspects of a particular frame of reference. The important point to recognize here is that frames may differ from culture to culture, whether this is in relation to face or any other aspect of social life.

One final point to note in relation to intercultural communication is the significance of discrimination as a barrier to effective communication. The point has already been made that some cultures are perceived to be inferior to others within, for example, racist discourses. However, we can generalize this point to recognize that various forms of unfair or unjust discrimination can be seen to act as a barrier to effective or appropriate communication taking place. As Guirdham (1999) comments:

> any kind of harassing or discriminatory behaviour is not only wrong and unacceptable in itself, it also creates barriers to communication, not only with its victims but with all who perceive and condemn it. (p. 248)

Indeed, discrimination is such an important issue in relation to communication that it will feature in a number of chapters that follow.

ACTIVITY 1.3

Think about your own identity, your own sense of self or who you are. What do you see as the key features of your identity? How do you think these might influence your interactions with other people?

Communicative sensitivity

This chapter has explored a number of important ideas which form part of the underpinning theory base of communication. It has painted a picture of the complex web of interacting factors which contribute to our understanding of communication. However, one further important issue which needs to be raised is what I shall refer to as 'communicative sensitivity'. By this I mean the ability to identify the circumstances in which communication is required, the nature of that communication, the persons or organizations that should be communicated with, and so on.

There is a great irony that it is so often the case that people who have excellent communication skills play a significant part in serious problems arising from communication breakdowns. This is because, in such situations, advanced-level communication skills are of little or no value if they are not put into practice. That is, if the person concerned fails to realize that communication is needed, problems will still arise, despite the high level of communication that he or she is capable of.

A significant part of understanding communication, therefore, is to understand when communication is required. Of course, this is not a simple skill, but rather relies on a range of social, interpersonal and organizational skills (Thompson, 2009b) which combine to give us what can be summarized under the heading of 'communicative sensitivity'. Two major factors in this are:

(i) being able to 'read' situations in such a way as to be able to determine what communicative response is required; and

(ii) being aware of how excessive work pressures can often lead us into situations where we lose sight of the need to communicate.

Communicative sensitivity is an issue that remains underdeveloped. It is beyond the scope of this book to contribute to that development here, but the point that communicative sensitivity is an important issue remains one worth emphasizing.

Conclusion

In this first of two introductory or scene-setting chapters I have sought to map out the range of communicative matters that I wish to examine in the book as a whole. In doing so, I have raised a number of issues about the nature of communication, various approaches to, or models of, communication and have emphasized the broad social basis of communication. In particular, I have concentrated on the role of culture and discourse as factors which have a considerable bearing on shaping the nature and effectiveness of communication. Culture as a broad theme was also extended to include discussion of identity and the significance of intercultural communication and the complexities that can arise in circumstances where people's cultural backgrounds differ in one or more respects.

A number of themes and issues can be identified through the various topics covered in this chapter. However, I wish to concentrate on three in particular. First, we can see that communication is a very wide-ranging topic that intertwines with so many different aspects of social life. It is certainly a much bigger and broader issue than the simple matter of one person passing on information to one or more others. Second, communication is profoundly social in its nature. Although much of the early research on communication was psychological in its focus and concentrated on individuals, more recent developments have emphasized the immense influence of sociological factors. Third, we can recognize that meaning and interpretation are basic elements of communication, and that these too are linked to the social base, in particular in terms of power and power relations. These three themes will underpin the chapters that follow and will be developed in various ways throughout.

It is also important to note that much of what has been discussed in this chapter relates to language. That is, although communication is not purely a matter of linguistic communication, it is clear that language is the primary form of communication. What has been discussed in this chapter therefore has to be closely linked with our understanding of language, and this is what forms the basis of Chapter 2.

POINTS TO PONDER

- How has this chapter helped you to develop your understanding of communication?
- What are the main reasons for developing a good understanding of communication?
- How might a better understanding of communication help to improve your practice?

Understanding language

Introduction

Montgomery (1995) is not the only author to emphasize the importance of language when he comments that:

> Language informs the way we think, the way we experience, and the way we interact with each other. Language provides the basis of community, but also the grounds for division. Systematic knowledge about language and practical awareness of how it works is fundamental to the process of building mature communities. (p. 251)

Indeed, language can be seen as the basis of interpersonal and social interaction at a variety of levels. Its importance in understanding people and their problems therefore cannot be overemphasized. It is no exaggeration to say that language is in many ways the basis of thought, feeling, action and interaction. It is also a primary factor in terms of the make-up of society in relation to both cultural and structural factors.

Perhaps it is because language is so important and such an ingrained part of our everyday life – both in the workplace and outside it – that it is very common for people to take it for granted and not realize just how significant a role it plays. We should also be aware that language is a very complex phenomenon, and it is not uncommon for people to oversimplify it. This is no doubt also due to its familiarity. We feel so comfortable with language that we perhaps make assumptions about it being simple and straightforward when, in reality, as this chapter will illustrate, language matters are very far from being at all simple or straightforward.

The basic aim of this chapter is to provide an introductory overview of the nature of language, its role in society and its significance in so many aspects of our day-to-day lives. I begin by asking the basic, but none the less important, question: What is language? This leads into a discussion about myths relating to language, as unfortunately there are many such misapprehensions about the nature and role of language in society. From this I proceed to look at the relationship between language and the individual, before then moving on to consider language and society. Finally, I explore issues relating to language in use – or, to use the technical term, pragmatics.

What is language?

The term 'language' can be used in a very broad metaphorical sense to refer to any system of communication. For example, many people refer to the language of mathematics or the language of music. Similarly, computer programming systems are generally referred to as languages. However, it is important to be clear right from the start that our focus here is on human language – that is, the use of linguistic forms as the basis of interpersonal and social communication ('interpersonal' meaning specifically between individuals or groups of individuals, and 'social' meaning across whole societies and cultures or significant proportions of them).

Montgomery (1995) offers the following definition:

> Language, indeed, is best understood as a set of interlocking relationships in which a linguistic form takes on the meaning it does by virtue of its place within the total system of signs. (p. xxv)

In my view, there are three key issues arising from this definition. First, Montgomery refers to interlocking relationships. It is important to be aware that language is not simply the ability to use words to get across a particular message. Language actually runs much more deeply than this and refers to the complex array of interlocking relationships which form the basis of communication and social interaction. Language is also a set of interlocking relationships in its own right, in the sense that meaning arises from the way in which particular language forms are combined and interact with one another. This introduces the second important concept from Montgomery's definition, namely that of meaning. As we noted in the previous chapter, the concept of meaning is a very complex one. It is a concept I shall explore in more detail below. However, at present we should note that meaning is a primary aspect of language, and so we have to acknowledge the important role of interpretation. Third, Montgomery refers to language as a system. This further emphasizes the point about interlocking relationships. Language is not simply a naturally occurring phenomenon, but rather is a complex system or, indeed, a set of systems which interlink with a range of social and psychological factors.

Language, then, refers to the use of a system of units which, in combination, provide meaningful communication. Such units may be words, sentences or whole texts. We should also note that we are referring to not simply using these words and so on for the sake of it, but rather as part of a system of human communication.

The next important question to address is that of: What is *a* language? Clearly, in the discussion of what is language, we are looking at an abstract entity, the concrete manifestation of which is very diverse indeed: French, Portuguese, Arabic, Urdu, Punjabi, Xhosa, Chinese, Japanese, Breton, Norwegian and so on. That is, we are not talking about a single language, but rather a multiplicity of different languages. Indeed, Aitchison (2001) suggests that there are approximately 6000 languages currently in use. Given the political and social dominance of the English language, it is a very easy mistake for English speakers to make to assume that the study of language is the study primarily of the English language. The reality, of course, is far more complex than this, and the various assumptions implicit in the idea that the study of language should be equated with the study of the English language are a fascinating topic of study in their own right and one to which I shall return below.

In looking at what constitutes a language, we need to draw a distinction between language and dialect. If we take the English language as an example, we see that it can be divided up into a number of different dialects or sub-forms of the overall language of English. For example, we have Cockney English and Geordie English which, as many people will readily recognize, are very different. In fact, there can be many occasions when people speaking the respective dialects may have difficulty communicating with one another, even though they are, in effect, speaking the same language. This example relates specifically to England but we can broaden this out to the rest of the UK and note that, for example, there are Welsh, Scottish and Northern Irish dialects of English which are significantly different in many respects from English dialects spoken within England itself. For example, there are many words used in Scotland which rarely, if ever, feature in English conversations south of the border (Elmes, 2005).

PRACTICE FOCUS 2.1

Signe received a grant from her university in Latvia to study teaching methods in British universities over a ten-week period. Her English was excellent and she had no difficulty in expressing herself clearly and fluently in English. However, when it came to understanding others speaking English, the situation was more mixed. At the university where she was temporarily based she had little difficulty in understanding what was being said to her. However, as part of her study programme she visited other universities in Britain. What she found was that, in some areas, she really struggled to understand what was being said to her as the accents being used were so different from what she was used to. At times she required her British host to act as an interpreter for her.

We can also extend the issue beyond the UK to look at, for example, American varieties of the use of the English language, as well as Australian and so on. An interesting development in this regard in recent years has been the development of call centres based in India. The use of 'Indian English' can present complications at times where such usage differs from the form of

English spoken by the enquirer (see John, 2007, for an interesting discussion of this). What we have to recognize, then, is that there is huge diversity within what is labelled as a single language.

The situation becomes more complex when we look at other languages. This is because drawing a line between where one language ends and another one begins can be a very difficult process. Consider the example given by Downes (1998):

> Linguistic relatedness and difference is a matter of degree ... One could proceed, village by village, from the Dutch coast to Vienna and always find mutual intelligibility between adjacent communities, although unintelligibility obviously occurs when the varieties are remote from each other in the continuum. But the Dutch and Germans consider that they speak distinct languages. (p. 25)

A major implication of what Downes is saying is that the boundary between one language and another has more to do with social and political factors than with linguistic ones. The reason for this situation is mainly historical. That is, in the example of Dutch and German, we can see that these two languages both stem from an earlier common Germanic language. A parallel example would be the 'merging' of French and Spanish in parts of southern France, as both of these languages have their roots in Latin. The fact that French and Spanish are seen as distinct languages, rather than dialects of Latin, is a reflection of the political, economic and social development of the respective states, and it is for this reason rather than purely linguistic ones that they are regarded as separate languages.

Dutch-speaking area	Intermediate zone	German-speaking area

Figure 2.1 Language merging

> Aitchison (1999) makes a related point when she argues that:

> a Glaswegian and a cockney are likely to find it harder to understand one another than a Dutchman and a German who are considered to be speaking distinct languages. And there is no objective linguistic criterion which can be applied. Dutch and German are not only mutually intelligible, they are also structurally more alike than some of the so-called dialects of Chinese. (p. 107)

And the point is further emphasized with the following comment from Pinker (1994): 'The best definition comes from the linguist Max Weinreich: a language is a dialect with an army and a navy' (p. 28). Cameron (1998b) is critical of comments made by Doyle (1995) to the effect that the English language has survived due to its adaptability, pointing out that it would be more accurate to attribute its success to 'the historical power and current political dominance of some of the nation-states in which it is the majority language' (p. 157).

In effect, what we have is a situation whereby there is a huge diversity of linguistic systems, some of which achieve the formal title of language, while others are assigned the lower status of a dialect. The boundaries are drawn for partly linguistic, but predominantly social and political reasons.

In order to develop a better understanding of the significance of language, it is important to understand the component parts of language. Perhaps the most important term in this regard is grammar. It is often (misleadingly) assumed that grammar refers to how language *should* be spoken or written. However, in the study of linguistics, grammar refers to the sets of rules which govern how linguistic utterances are organized. In a sense, grammar refers to the logic of language. As Waismann (1997) puts it:

> The relationship between grammar and language is similar to that between deciding upon the metre as the unit of length and carrying out a measurement, or indeed between the adjustment of a telescope and an observation made through it. Grammar is, as it were, the installation and adjustment of a system of signs, in preparation for their use. (pp. 13–14)

In this regard, Aitchison (2000) draws an important distinction between prescriptive and descriptive grammar. Prescriptive refers to the popular view of

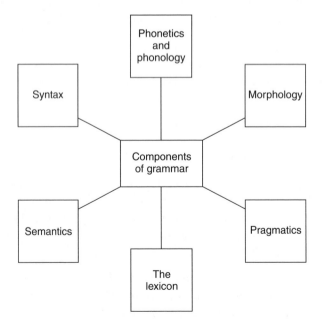

Figure 2.2 The components of grammar

grammar as a set of rules concerning what is regarded as 'correct' language to use. Descriptive grammar, by contrast, is one which is used to describe (and, to a certain extent, explain) the rules which have a bearing on how words are combined into sentences, how meaning is attributed, how sound systems work to produce language and so on. We shall return to this point below when we look at a number of myths relating to language.

While grammar can be seen as a term which refers to the overall set of linguistic rules, this in itself can be subdivided into a variety of linguistic systems. I shall briefly outline the basics of each of the main ones.

Syntax

Syntax refers to the set of rules which govern how we can combine words in a way which is recognized by first-language speakers to be acceptable or 'grammatically correct'. For example, 'Who is the boss?'; 'Who the boss is'; 'The boss is who?' are all meaningful, syntactically acceptable combinations of these four words. However, 'who boss is the', involves the same four words but in an order which is not syntactically acceptable as it stands within the rules of English syntax. Syntax refers to such matters as the need to ensure that a verb matches its noun in terms of singular versus plural. For example, a singular noun requires a singular verb, while a plural noun requires a plural verb ('the child *is* asleep' versus 'the children *are* asleep'). Montgomery (1995) makes apt comment when he argues that:

> What the syntax does ... is to specify a set of possibilities for sentence construction, the adherence to which ensures some degree of mutual interpretability. Indeed, from the basic core patterns of the syntax an indefinite variety of sentences can be composed. And as long as they conform to the patterns, the sentences will be interpretable even though they stand as 'one-off' creations – unique events. (pp. xxiii–iv)

Phonetics and phonology

Phonetics refers to the study of pronunciation, while phonology refers to the set of rules which govern how sounds can be combined in particular patterns. The former involves trying to understand the subtleties and complexities of pronouncing individual words and their combination in sentences or utterances. This involves recognizing differences between the way words are spelled and the way in which they are pronounced. For example, the word 'spin' is spelled with 'p' as its second letter. However, if we listen carefully to how it is generally pronounced, we will realize that it tends to be pronounced as a 'b'. Phoneticians distinguish between *voiced* and *unvoiced* sounds, a distinction based on whether or not the vocal cords vibrate during the pronunciation. 'P' and 'b' are generally identical sounds in terms of the shape made by the oral cavity, the lips and the position of the tongue. What distinguishes the two sounds is the vibration or otherwise of the vocal cords. That is, 'b' is voiced (the vocal cords vibrate) while 'p' is unvoiced (the vocal cords do not vibrate).

Phonology is closely linked to phonetics, but is concerned with how the use of sounds affects meaning and syntax. For example, in the word 'spin', the fact that the letter 'p' is pronounced as if it were a 'b' makes no difference to the meaning of the word. However, if the 's' is not present, then the difference between 'pin' and 'bin' is a meaningful distinction and therefore affects the way English operates as a language. Phonology therefore involves studying which sound differences are meaningful and which are not. Consider, for example, the case of Chinese, in which the 'l' and 'r' sounds are used interchangeably. Many Chinese people speaking English often confuse 'l' and 'r' sounds because, within their own language, the two are distinguished phonetically, but they are not distinguished phonologically – that is, they are not seen as sufficiently different to ascribe meaning to them (just like the difference between 'p' and 'b' sounds in the word 'spin'). This is an example of how different languages tend to have different phonological rules.

Morphology

Morphology is the study of how parts of words are combined to make whole words. Again, this differs from language to language. For example, in English, we combine parts of words or syllables in certain ways which would not necessarily apply in other languages. We commonly add 'ed' to the end of verbs to indicate past tense, but this does not apply in languages such as French, Welsh or Spanish, for example. Another example would be the way in which, in English, we commonly form plurals by adding an 's' to the singular noun (singular 'dog', plural 'dogs'). An example of a difference between languages would be the way in which we indicate repetition or recursion. In English, we do this by adding 're' to the beginning of a word (*re*position, *re*consider, *re*visit and so on). If we contrast this with Welsh, we realize that the recursion is indicated not by a change to the existing word but by the use of an additional word. For example, the word for 'to establish' is 'sefydlu'. To re-establish is 'ail sefydlu' (literally 'second establish'). In other words, this recursion is indicated through syntax (that is, the combination of words) rather than morphology (the combination of elements within a word).

Semantics

This refers to the way in which systems of meaning are established through language. Speakers of a particular language are able to recognize which combinations of words have meaning and which do not, as it is not a simple case of putting words together in any combination and finding that they automatically have meaning. A well-known example of this comes from the work of the famous linguist Noam Chomsky. He used the sentence: 'colourless green ideas sleep furiously' to indicate the difference between syntax and semantics (see Cook and Newsom, 1996). This sentence is grammatically acceptable in terms of syntax – that is, the combination of words does not involve breaking any syntactic rules. However, the combination remains meaningless at a semantic level – that is, it breaks the rules of semantics in terms of how words can be combined into meaningful utterances. Semantics is a very complex topic, as it interrelates with many issues around culture, power and other social factors. I shall therefore return to this topic in Chapter 5.

The lexicon

This refers to the set of words used in a language – its vocabulary. Languages can differ significantly in terms of the size of their lexicon. For example, English has a particularly large lexicon, partly a reflection of its relative position of global dominance (many other languages will use English technical terms in relation to computers, for example), and partly because English has assimilated so many words from other languages as a result of Britain's colonial history.

Voice of experience 2.1

"When I started at the hospital I was totally confused by all the technical terminology – it was like having to learn a new language. It made me wonder what it must be like for patients when staff speak in a way that is so alien to ordinary people.**"** *Lorna, an orthopaedic nurse*

Pragmatics

This refers to the study of how language forms are actually used in everyday social situations, and is therefore again a very complex topic which relates closely to sociolinguistic factors. When we learn a language as we grow up, we learn not only how to make utterances which are syntactically, phonologically, morphologically and semantically acceptable, we also learn in what social situations certain forms of language are acceptable and in what they are not. Consider, for example, the use of swearing. While some people may never use swear words and, at the other extreme, others may use swear words regardless of the social situation, there are significant numbers of people who have learned which social circumstances are acceptable in terms of swearing and which are not. That is, they have learned the pragmatic rules of when this particular form of language is socially acceptable.

While the study of semantics explores how words are combined to form meaningful utterances, pragmatics is concerned with how meanings are formed through the social use of language based on interpersonal interactions.

Pragmatics is therefore partly concerned with the context in which language use takes place (a topic to be explored in more detail in Chapter 5). The role

---

PRACTICE FOCUS 2.2

Richard was a very hardworking colleague who was well respected for his high work rate and his commitment to getting the job done. However, the downside was that he had only a very limited understanding of pragmatics. Often the comments he made would be highly inappropriate and caused considerable embarrassment to his colleagues (although he himself was often unaware of how insensitive he had been). He created a great deal of ill-feeling and gained a reputation for being grossly insensitive much of the time. Although he was quite skilled in many aspects of language use, the social skills involved in pragmatics were largely beyond him.

of the context in shaping meaning can be illustrated by the multiple meanings that some words have and the consequent need to determine the precise meaning of an utterance in the context in which it is to be found. For example, consider the word 'go'. It has a large number of meanings attached to it, and so its meaning in a particular utterance will depend very much on the contextual cues which accompany it at that particular time. Its meanings include:

- Move or travel: 'Go to the end of the street and turn right'.
- Turn: 'You've had your turn, so now it's my go'.
- Energy: 'She's a very energetic person, always full of go'.
- Depart: 'What time does your train go?'
- Try: 'I've given up, but you can have a go if you want'.
- Become: 'If I don't find out soon, I'll go mad'.

And, as if that were not confusing enough, it also has a number of other meanings when combined with other words:

- Continue: 'Go on, we haven't finished yet' or 'Go ahead, we've got plenty of time left'.
- Attack: 'Be careful what you say. If you upset him, he might go for you'.
- Fit or match: 'This nut goes with that bolt'.

These are not the only examples, and so it should be clear that determining meaning is a very skilful task that involves us in having a very good understanding of contextual factors in order to deal effectively with the ambiguity built into language use.

ACTIVITY 2.1

Can you think of any other terms you might use in your work that have different meanings in different contexts (referral, for example)? What implications might such ambiguity have for practice?

A further aspect of the importance of pragmatic factors in making sense of utterances is, in some ways, the converse of the above – that is, where one idea can be expressed in a bewildering number of ways. For example, as an exercise on training courses I have often asked groups of participants to identify words or phrases that refer to being drunk or inebriated. As you might imagine, this produces a very long list indeed – further testimony to our ability to wend our way through the complex avenues of communication and meaning making.

An important point to emphasize in relation to pragmatics is that an excellent grasp of language and its complexities will be of no use whatsoever in professional practice (or management) if we lack the skills of pragmatics, if we are not able to use language to appropriate effect in our dealings with other people – think of a highly skilled, very effective communicator you know and contrast him or her with the example of Richard above (in Practice Focus 2.2).

These then, are the main components or subsystems of language. This is not intended as a comprehensive account of these issues, but rather as a basic introduction to present a picture of the complexities of language. Each of these areas could be given a whole book in itself and still not be exhausted. Anyone who takes the study of language seriously is clearly embarking on an enormous project in terms of getting to grips with a range of factors and issues which have such an important bearing on how language operates and how it is used by actual speakers and writers.

Myths about language

Aitchison (1997) makes the important point that, while all humans are able to breathe, we do not assume that we are therefore experts on breathing and related matters. However, it is not uncommon for people to believe that because they are fluent in a particular language, they are therefore experts on that language:

> Yet because they talk, many *do* feel able to comment on linguistic matters, and often have surprising confidence in the rightness of their views. As a result, various entrenched beliefs circulate. Some of them are clear cut and wrong, such as the folk-myth that Eskimos have hundreds of words for snow. (p. x)

We have to recognize that there are very many myths indeed about language. For example, Bauer and Trudgill (1998) identify 21 such myths, although it is clear that this is far from an exhaustive list. Space does not permit a detailed discussion of myths about language. I shall therefore restrict myself to three in particular.

Language decay

Aitchison (2000) asks the important question: Is language change progress or decay? In this important book, she points out that languages are in a constant state of change, but she warns against the mistake of assuming that change in a language can be equated with decay or deterioration. Forms of language which at one time were considered incorrect or 'ungrammatical' gradually become established as acceptable forms of language. A relatively recent example of this is the gradual change in the use of the word 'impact'. Originally a noun only, it is now in the process of also becoming established as a verb. Its use as a noun ('This has had a significant impact on ...') has been regarded as an acceptable and grammatical form of language for some considerable time. However, its use as a verb ('This has impacted on ...') has been seen by many as an unacceptable or ungrammatical form of language. Despite this, in recent years, this usage has become so well established that it is now in the process of gradually becoming seen as an acceptable and 'correct' use of the word.

Aitchison is therefore drawing attention to the myth of assuming that changing language should be regarded as a weakening or deterioration of the language. It is a well-established pattern of linguistic change that new forms of language are often perceived as 'incorrect' or 'ungrammatical' in the early stages of their usage. It is only after a considerable period of established day-to-day usage that they achieve the status of 'acceptable' language.

This has significant implications in terms of the relationship between language and power. For example, who has the power to determine what is acceptable or unacceptable? Also, how can a person whose language is deemed to be unacceptable be disadvantaged through such false assumptions about language decay?

It is interesting to note that views about this myth are so well entrenched for so many people that, when Aitchison presented a series of lectures on the subject of language at the 1996 Reith lectures, she received a large and hostile mailbag objecting to her views on the subject (see the Afterword in Aitchison, 1997). This strong reaction once again emphasizes the power and significant role of language in society.

Superior and inferior languages

Just as the above myth presents some forms of language as superior to others, we can see that there is also an assumption that some languages in themselves are superior to other languages. Harlow (1998) argues that some languages are perceived to be 'just not good enough'. He notes that this is particularly the case in situations where a minority language exists alongside a much more powerful language – for example, the Maori language in New Zealand alongside the dominance of English, and similarly the Welsh language in Wales. Despite these views, it has to be recognized that all languages are sets of complex systems which operate at a variety of levels. The notion that some

languages are of a superior form to others can be seen to owe more to stereotypes than to actual linguistic fact.

Crystal (1997) once again points to the important relationship between language and power when he argues that:

> A language becomes an international language for one chief reason: the
> political power of its people – especially their military power. The explanation
> is the same throughout history. Why did Greek become a language of
> international communication in the Middle East over 2000 years ago? Not
> because of the intellect of Plato and Aristotle: the answer lies in the swords
> and spears wielded by the armies of Alexander the Great. (p. 7)

In a similar vein, Bryson (1990) tackles the myth that creole languages are
inferior to other forms of language. (A 'creole' is a language that has developed
from a 'pidgin' language, which is a simplified version of an established language used to facilitate trade between groups of people without a common
language.) He points out that many so-called fully-fledged languages were originally creoles – for example, Afrikaans in South Africa, Chinese in Macao and
Swahili in East Africa. He also makes the interesting point that creoles can
have subtleties not contained in other languages such as English:

> in English we are not very good at distinguishing desire from accomplishment
> in the past tense. In the sentence 'I went to the store to buy a shirt' we cannot
> tell whether the shirt was bought or not. But in all creoles such an ambiguity
> is impossible. In Hawaiian creole the person who bought a shirt would say, 'I
> bin go store go buy shirt', while the person who failed to buy a shirt would say,
> 'I bin go store for buy shirt'. The distinction is crucial. (p. 19)

PRACTICE FOCUS 2.3

Meinir was pleased to have the opportunity to attend an international
conference at which 17 different nations were represented. She found the
richness of cultural and linguistic diversity a very stimulating and enjoyable
aspect of the event. However, what was not so positive was the attitude of
one man towards Meinir's linguistic background. When he discovered that
her first language was Welsh, he found it difficult to accept that Welsh was
a language in its own right, distinct from English. 'But surely', he kept
saying, 'Welsh is really a dialect of English.' He seemed to have difficulty
taking on board that English is not the only official language used in the
UK. Once he realized that Meinir was becoming irritated by his failure to
grasp the nature of Welsh as a language in its own right, he changed tack
and commented that he assumed Welsh must be a simple language,
lacking the sophistication and complexity of English. Meinir did not know
whether to laugh or cry at this man's depth of ignorance and prejudice.

Thus, while languages may be seen to have different levels of status or prestige, we should recognize that this is to do with cultural, social and political factors, and is not a matter of linguistics. From a linguistic point of view, all languages are complex, sophisticated sets of systems and it makes little or no sense to argue that one is 'superior' to another.

Accent indicates intelligence

It is commonly assumed by many people that certain accents indicate a low level of intelligence. However, closer examination of this notion indicates that it is a myth and a dangerous and discriminatory one at that (Elmes, 2005). While there may well be links between accent and educational level (although here we cannot simply equate the two), it is certainly dangerous to equate education with intelligence.

Some areas seem to be particularly prone to this type of prejudice. For example, there is a close association between a Birmingham accent and the assumption that someone is of low intelligence or 'slow on the uptake'. Once again, this is a matter of social, cultural or political influences, rather than linguistic matters. Such false assumptions about what can be attributed to a particular accent can have very disadvantageous effects for certain people – for example, in terms of employment.

A related issue is the common assumption that speakers of Standard English (or Oxford English as it is sometimes known) are speaking a 'pure' form of English. It is assumed that there are those who speak 'proper' English and those who speak with an accent. However, as Esling (1998) points out, everyone has an accent, including speakers of so-called Standard English.

These, then, are just some of the prevalent myths about language. The fact that there are so many myths is no doubt due, partly at least, to the fact that language is such an ever-present and vitally important part of our personal and social lives. It is a hugely complex topic and, without an extensive period of specialist study, we cannot expect the general public to have a clear and unflawed understanding of how language works. We should therefore not be surprised to find that there are indeed many myths and misunderstandings relating to language and its use. We should also note that such misunderstandings are not reserved solely for the general public. For example, Bryson (1990), whose work I referred to earlier and which has much to commend it, also shows in places a degree of misunderstanding or oversimplification of matters. Consider, for example, the prejudice inherent in the following situation. On page 4 of his book, he refers to a highland Scottish word as 'monumentally unpronounceable'. On page 34, he quotes a Welsh phrase and then comments that it 'is about as unpronounceable as it looks'. However, on page 43 of the same book, in discussing Old English, he comments:

if you take twenty minutes to familiarize yourself with the differences in Old English spelling and pronunciation – learning that *i* corresponds to the modern 'ee' sound, that *e* sounds like 'ay' and so on – you can begin to pick your way through a great deal of abstruse-looking text.

It would seem that learning the pronunciation of Old English, a language no longer in direct use, is worth the effort, while we are left with the implication that learning the pronunciation of Scottish words or Welsh phrases is beyond our reach. Sadly, this sort of linguistic arrogance is not uncommon.

ACTIVITY 2.2

Think about the accents you are familiar with. What does each of them convey to you? For example, what do you associate with a Cockney accent or a Liverpool one? Make some notes about this and compare them with one or more colleagues. What does this tell us about the social signifi-cance we attach to how people pronounce what they say when they are talking?

Language and the individual

As noted in Chapter 1, language is very much a part of our sense of who we are – our identity. And, indeed, we shall return later in this chapter to that very subject. It is important to be clear, then, that language is an important matter in relation to the individual in society. This can be seen to have a number of dimensions, but here I am going to focus on three in particular: language and understanding of the world; idiolects; and language development.

Language and understanding of the world

There is a well-established and extensive literature base relating to the rela-tionship between language and thought. Much of this relates to what is known as the Sapir–Whorf hypothesis which presents thought as being largely shaped by language. In my view, this debate has proven to be largely unfruitful if not tedious. Without wishing to get bogged down in this argument, we can none the less note that there are significant ways in which language can be seen to influence our understanding of the world. For example, Pinker (1994) dis-cusses the differences between languages in terms of how they divide up the colour spectrum:

> [Whorf] noted that we see objects in different hues, depending on the wavelengths of the light they reflect, but that physicists tell us that wavelength is a continuous dimension with nothing delineating red, yellow, green, blue, and so on. Latin lacks generic 'gray' and 'brown'; Navajo

collapses blue and green into one word; Russian has distinct words for dark blue and sky blue; Shona speakers use one word for the yellower greens and the greener yellows, and a different one for the bluer greens and the non-purplish blues. You can fill in the rest of the argument. It is language that puts the frets in the spectrum. (pp. 61–2)

However, Pinker does go on to show that delineation between colour boundaries is not simply a linguistic matter, but also has its roots in physiology. Clearly, then, language is not the only factor in shaping how we construct our sense of reality. Given that so much of our understanding of the world derives from language (through conversations, reading, exposure to the media and so on), then it should not be surprising to learn that language has a significant bearing on how we experience the world and how we make sense of it. This is not to go as far as the Sapir–Whorf hypothesis and to argue that different languages construct reality in different ways, but rather to present language in general as a very influential factor in how individuals, groups, communities and whole societies make sense of their day-to-day reality.

Voice of experience 2.2

❝There are 49 languages spoken in this borough. One thing I have learned in working here over the past three years is that different languages means different cultures and different ways of seeing the world. It can seem over-whelming at times – the sheer complexity – but it is also very enriching. I find it fascinating.**❞** *Zafar, a community worker in a public health project*

Idiolects

Just as a dialect is a form of language shared by a group of people – for example, within a geographical area – an idiolect is a form or style of language associated with each specific individual. That is, each individual's use of language will reflect wider cultural, social, geographical and political factors, but will also, in some ways at least, be specific to that individual. This is something that is quite easy to spot. For example, consider the speech patterns of people that you know quite well. Can you identify differences between those individuals, perhaps styles or forms of language that are distinctive to that particular individual? This can be significant in relation to identity, a topic to which we shall return below.

A study of idiolects can be particularly interesting in bilingual communities. This is because bilingual speakers will tend not to speak entirely in one language or the other, but will frequently switch from one to the other according to the context and circumstances. Which language is used in what situation will often depend on social factors, the unwritten rules, as it were, of a particular culture or society. However, there will also be room for individual

---

PRACTICE FOCUS 2.4

Liz was a very articulate woman who had no difficulty in expressing herself clearly and effectively. However, she also had a number of speech mannerisms which made her use of language quite distinctive. For example, if she made a mistake in what she was trying to say, she would stop and then start the sentence again. Most people would tend to simply correct the word or phrase that was incorrect and then press on with the rest of what they were saying. Liz, however, clearly felt uncomfortable doing that and took the trouble of restarting if she got something wrong. Fortunately, she was such a skilful speaker that she did not need to stop and start again very often, as it is something that was not irritating when done occasionally, but would surely have been a problem if repeated frequently.

---

preference. That is, no two bilingual individuals will necessarily make the same choice of language in the same circumstances every time.

Language development

Of course, we are not born able to speak. However, many linguists would argue that we are born with the ability to learn how to use language. That is, it is claimed that the development of language in children is pre-programmed. This has been a highly contentious area of debate and has contributed a major literature base. Space does not permit a detailed analysis of this debate, but I would like to make some brief comments about some aspects of it.

Language is not a simple skill or set of skills that can be learned simply by copying others. In reality, the situation is far more complex than this. Theorists such as Noam Chomsky have long argued that what is needed in order for language to develop within a child is a predetermined understanding of how grammar works (see Cook and Newsom, 1996). That is, Chomsky argues that we have within our mental frameworks an inbuilt means of developing language.

The reason language cannot be learned simply by copying others is its 'generative' nature. By this, I mean that language is not a finite set of statements or sentences. We each have the ability to generate an infinite number of sentences. Our understanding of grammar (that is, syntax, semantics and so on) allows us to combine words in a wide variety of ways to produce meaningful utterances. In fact, the term 'wide' is something of an understatement for, as I have already indicated, it is in fact an infinite number that we can generate. This does not mean that we can combine words in any way we wish, as clearly that would produce a large number of meaningless and ungrammatical utterances. We are none the less capable of producing an infinite variety of sentences. Consider this very chapter as an example. How many of the sentences within it have ever been produced before in their precise form?

This emphasizes the important role of grammar in our understanding of language for, as was noted earlier, grammar is not to be understood as a prescriptive set of rules about how language should be used, but rather as a cognitive framework for being able to use linguistic rules to generate an infinite variety of language forms.

A particular feature of the debate about the development of language in children is the interrelationship between nature and nurture – in other words, the question of: To what extent is language development predetermined and to what extent does development depend on the way children are brought up? Aitchison (2007) explores these issues in some depth. She concludes that language development is 'innately guided'. By this she means that it is partly nature (innate) and partly nurture (guided). She sums up her views in the following passage:

> it would be wrong to think of language as something which is governed *only* by internal mechanisms. These mechanisms require external stimulation in order to work properly. The child needs a rich verbal environment during the acquisition period.
>
> This suggests the so-called nature–nurture controversy … may be misconceived. Both sides are right: nature triggers off the behaviour, and lays down the framework, but careful nurture is needed for it to reach its full potential. The dividing line between 'natural' and 'nurtured' behaviour is by no means as clear cut as was once thought. In other words, language is 'natural' behaviour – but it still has to be carefully 'nurtured' in order to reach its full potential. In modern terminology, the behaviour is *innately guided*. (p. 90)

One of the implications of Aitchison's work is that we should be careful not to oversimplify the complex relationship between nature and nurture, a view shared by Pinker (1994).

Language and society

Just as the relationship between language and the individual is complex, so too is the relationship between language and society. This is because language and society can be seen to influence and shape one another. As Montgomery (1995) argues, language not only reflects structural differences within society, it also shapes and reinforces those differences.

As an example of the relationship between language and society, we can explore the topic of prestige. Trudgill (2000) argues that, because language is closely associated with social structures and cultural value systems, there are differences in how particular dialects and/or accents are attributed with worth, value or status. In particular, he comments on the significance of standard English:

Because language as a social phenomenon is closely tied up with the social structure and value systems of society, different dialects and accents are evaluated in different ways. Standard English, for example, has much more status and prestige than any other English dialect. It is a dialect that is highly valued by many people, and certain economic, social and political benefits tend to accrue to those who speak and write it. (p. 8)

As noted earlier, the idea that Standard English is a superior form of language is a myth. What leads to it being seen as superior or indicating a higher level of intelligence or ability in a speaker is the social prestige attached to it. Prestige-related language systems are therefore part and parcel of the complex ways in which society distributes status and its associated rewards to various groups and individuals.

PRACTICE FOCUS 2.5

Darren was a well-respected employee who was keen to learn and to develop his knowledge and skills. He was praised by all who came into contact with him not only for the standards of his work but also for his friendliness and relaxed manner. However, when his success was rewarded by a period of secondment to headquarters for three months, Darren found that the new setting was not to his liking. He had been brought up on his local council estate and was proud of his roots. However, at headquarters he found himself among people with a variety of accents, but mainly ones he associated with middle-class backgrounds. He felt that he did not fit in and that his accent made him stand out as someone who lacked the university education so many of his new colleagues had received. His line manager reassured him that his accent was not an issue and that he should feel proud of the way he had worked his way up. None the less, Darren did not feel comfortable and he was glad when the three months were up and he could return to his base and be among people he felt he belonged with.

Even in relation to the distribution of prestige along language lines, the matter is not simple or straightforward. Aitchison (2000) points out that different forms of language have status in different circumstances. She refers to studies carried out by Cheshire (1978; 1982) in relation to the use of non-standard forms of English in the town of Reading. These studies reflect the finding of similar studies in showing that adolescent boys preferred to use non-standard forms and therefore attained covert prestige while adolescent girls preferred standard forms and this gave them overt prestige. The distinction between covert and overt prestige is an important one. This is because it shows just how complex and subtle both language and society are, especially when the two come together. Overt prestige is what gives us status and social standing within mainstream society and is generally regarded as a positive thing. Covert prestige, by contrast, is a form of prestige which gives status or standing only in certain subcultures. It would therefore be seen as a positive thing within a specific subculture but not within the broader society. These two forms of prestige can lead to situations of conflict. For example, language and behaviour which are given covert prestige within a subculture may be seen as disruptive or inappropriate within the wider mainstream society. On the other hand, language and behaviour which attract overt prestige within the mainstream society may be dismissed within a subculture as 'goody goody'.

The existence of cultures, subcultures and different contexts and settings for language introduces the notion of registers. A register is a particular form of style of speech which is geared towards a particular social context. For example, the type of language we would use while relaxing with friends may be of a very different kind from a type of language that we would use in more formal circumstances such as a job interview. This can also be seen to apply to wider social circumstances, for example, occupation. Technical jargon associated with particular groups can be seen as a form of register – that is, a particular form of speech which is applicable in certain contexts but not in others. The misuse of such registers can lead to significant social or interpersonal problems. For example, while the use of medical terminology between doctors, or indeed other health professionals, may be an appropriate use of language, where such jargon is used in speaking to patients who do not understand the terminology, the effect may be to leave the patient feeling alienated, excluded, uninformed and even, in some circumstances, frightened. The social skills involved in matching a particular register to the appropriate setting or context are therefore very important communication skills.

PRACTICE FOCUS 2.6

Sheila arrived at the hospital to find her mother very distressed. This had the effect of making Sheila feel worried as she quickly assumed that there was something seriously wrong, since she knew that her mother was not the sort of person to become distressed easily. However, Sheila soon realized that there was no major problem to worry about. What had happened was that the doctor had been to see her mother and had spoken to her in medical jargon, leaving her feeling very anxious and confused, a state of affairs that had led her to panic about being in hospital and just how serious her condition was. Sheila eventually managed to speak to the doctor and asked him to apologize to her mother for the distress he had caused. However, he refused to do so, as he could see nothing wrong with the language he had used.

A further aspect of the use of particular language forms in appropriate social circumstances is the concept of code-switching. This refers to the process of switching from one code to another. In this sense, a code refers to either a language, a dialect or some other linguistic form, such as a register. In bilingual communities, switching between languages is not uncommon. For example, in Wales bilingual speakers may hold conversations entirely in Welsh, entirely in English, or what is also very common is for conversations to take place partly in English, partly in Welsh, sometimes switching language in mid-sentence. This is a perfectly normal and well-established feature of bilingual communities. Many people who are not familiar with this process mistakenly assume that Welsh speakers are being 'rude' because they switch from English to Welsh in their presence.

Similar examples can be found within monoglot communities where the switching is perhaps between dialects. For example, children in a classroom awaiting the arrival of a teacher may speak to one another in the local dialect, but switch to more standard forms of English in the process of a formal lesson. When a child is asked by another child what they have in their lunch box, the reply may be 'butties' or 'sarnies'. However, when it is a teacher who is making the same enquiry, the response is much more likely to be the more formal term, 'sandwiches'.

As noted earlier in relation to language and the individual, these are not hard and fast rules. We are not, as Trudgill (2000) points out, 'sociolinguistic automata'. While the influence of the social context on individuals can be seen to be immense, this does not stop us from being individuals.

Trudgill shows that code-switching is not only a very common occurrence, it is also one which is closely linked to identity. As noted in Chapter 1, identity is not a simple monolithic entity, but rather a complex and fluid one. In this respect, there can be different aspects of identity which can be signalled by different aspects of language and the code-switching between them:

> *Code-switching*, as we can call this rapid form of language switching, also has the effect, as the British sociolinguist Le Page has pointed out, of enabling a speaker to signal two identities at once. For example, Chinese students at the University of Hong Kong often speak a dense mixture of English and Cantonese. If they spoke only English, they might be regarded as being disloyal to their community. If they spoke only Cantonese, they might be regarded, within the context of an English-language university, as uneducated and unsophisticated. Speaking both languages together overcomes both these problems. It is perhaps therefore not at all surprising that code-switching is a very widespread phenomenon. (Trudgill, 2000, p. 106)

A further major aspect of the relationship between language and society relates to the notion of gender. While the term 'sex' refers to biological differences between men and women, the term 'gender' refers to social differences between men and women. There is an extensive and growing public debate on the relationship between language and gender. This is a complex topic and one which will be explored in more depth in Chapter 5. However, one concept I would like to introduce here is that of a 'genderlect'. Parallel with the terms dialect and idiolect, a genderlect refers to a style of language associated with one or other gender. The use of this term in effect acknowledges that the speech patterns of men and women are characteristically different. Unfortunately, some of the theorizing in relation to language and gender has tended to be oversimplified and has relied on sexist assumptions and stereotypes. However, despite this, it remains the case that gender is a significant factor in terms of the relationship between language and society.

Language and ethnicity is also a complex area of study. In the 1970s Fishman argued that language is the most salient feature of ethnicity in symbolic terms (Fishman, 1977). Since that time, many others have emphasized the significance of the relationship between language and ethnic identity.

One well-established example of this relationship can be shown in the case of what is known as black English vernacular, or BEV for short. This is a term used to denote varieties of English used by black Americans. Some examples of differences in BEV compared with standard American English would be no final *s* in the third-person singular present tense – for example, 'he say', 'she do', or the use of the verb 'be' to indicate habitual meaning, 'sometime they be walking round here' (Crystal, 1987). The work of William Labov has been very helpful in assisting us in understanding how BEV works and, just as importantly, in appreciating that it is not to be seen as a substandard or inferior form of language (Labov, 1972).

We should note that ethnicity is not simply a matter of race or skin colour. Issues of language and ethnic identity can also apply – for example, in relation to the Welsh language within the UK. The Welsh language was spoken in Britain long before Anglo-Saxon settlements. However, the historical development of English as a global language has been a major factor in the decline of the Welsh language. But the development of English in its own right has not been the only factor. For a very long time, there was a specific and explicit policy of suppression of the Welsh language. For example, for many years children caught speaking Welsh in the school playground were punished for doing so. They were required to wear a sign indicating their misdemeanour. They had to continue to wear this until another person was caught speaking Welsh. This was known as the 'Welsh Not'.

Despite this linguistic imperialism, the language has continued to survive, and indeed there are now signs that it is beginning to flourish once again. As Crystal (1997) points out, in addition to the resurgence of Welsh in the UK, similar developments can be seen to be taking place in Hawaii, Ireland, New

Zealand and Quebec. The continued survival of Welsh and other minority languages despite attempts to eradicate them is therefore testimony not only to the resilience, commitment and resourcefulness of the peoples concerned, but also to the power and significance of linguistic and ethnic identity.

Language in use

In discussing the components of language earlier in this chapter, I have made reference to pragmatics which Rosengren (2000) defines as 'a system of rules for relating verbal symbols to the actions of the communicants' (p. 31). Language can be studied as a system of communication in its own right. However, what can be just as interesting, if not more so, is the study of language in use – that is, the various ways in which language interrelates with the real-life experiences of people in a variety of settings. It would be unrealistic in the extreme to attempt to discuss language in use in its entirety, as that could easily amount to a life's work. I shall therefore limit myself to a much smaller range of topics to consider, namely: bilingualism; influence and persuasion; discourse and narrative; and language games.

Bilingualism

Bilingualism is a much more common social phenomenon than people generally realize. As Drakeford and Morris (1998) point out: 'Almost every state in Europe is at least bilingual, in the sense of having more than one indigenous language, as well as languages spoken by migrants from other places' (p. 93). Not only is bilingualism more common than people generally realize, it is also more complex. It is not simply the case that bilingual speakers have two or more languages to choose from. There is a complex web of social and political rules which influence which language is spoken in what circumstances and with whom. For example, I have worked with many students in Wales who have preferred to converse through the medium of Welsh, but to submit their formal written assignments in English, as they associate English with the more formal world of law, business and public life. While this is not a view shared by all bilingual speakers, it is none the less an important one, in so far as it shows that there are complex influences which play a part in shaping the choice of which language is used in what circumstances.

In other circumstances, bilingualism can be correlated with class or other status. For example, Downes (1998) discusses French-English bilingualism in Canada and refers to a study which showed that there were significant income differences between language groups:

> Bilingualism correlated with the [occupational] status of the French group,
> but not with the British one. The number of bilingual individuals of the

French-mother-tongue group was 94 per cent for managerial positions, through 70 per cent to 80 per cent in sales positions, to 49 per cent for labourers. For the British group there was no such correlation. (p. 59)

The case of bilingualism shows that, in addressing the issue of language in use, we must in effect address languages in use. This is particularly so when we consider that it is rarely, if ever, the case that languages which exist in ailingual relationship are on a level playing field. That is, it is highly likely that there will be significant status and power differences between the languages.

ACTIVITY 2.3

Do you live or work in a bilingual community? If so, what implications does this have for you and your practice? If you do not, what difference do you think it would make if you found yourself in a blingual situation? What would you need to bear in mind?

Influence and persuasion

The point was made in Chapter 1 that communication involves communicating not only information but also a relationship and, of course, such relationships involve power. The same is true of communication through language. When we speak or write, we are not simply conveying information but also engaging in the use of power within one or more relationships (see Chapter 5 for a more detailed discussion of this). In so doing, we are often trying to influence or persuade others (is this book itself not an example of an attempt on my part to persuade you to share my belief in the value and fascination of language and communication?).

Aitchison (1997) argues that the use of metaphor can be very persuasive in influencing people. She comments: 'if you … want to influence anyone, use metaphor, though use it carefully' (p. 92). This is an example of 'interpellation', the way in which an ideology or discourse can seek to persuade us to adopt a particular view of a situation.

In a similar vein, Kitzinger and Frith (2001b) show that refusing, for example, sexual advances is not simply a matter of saying no. There are complex ways in which forms of refusal can be phrased either effectively or ineffectively. As they put it, 'conversation analysis shows that refusals are complex and finely organized interactional accomplishments' (p. 171). They show that the use of language to make a refusal is a far from simple matter. The skills involved in the effective use of language in influencing others can therefore be seen as very important indeed.

Sometimes we can also influence others without intending to. That is, the language we use may establish a frame of reference which proves influential, but which may actually run counter to our intentions or wishes. Parton and O'Byrne (2000) argue that therapeutic interventions can be hampered by the use of language which focuses on problems rather than solutions. They argue that it is necessary for us to 'mind our language'. They refer to the work of Weiner-Davis (1993) and O'Hanlon and Weiner-Davis (1989) which indicates the power of words to create a bias which can affect the expectations of others and thus shape the outcome of our interactions. They make the important point that:

> What we choose to talk about is crucial. If we ask about problems there will be more problems. If we choose to talk about solutions there will be more solutions. For example, if someone reports having a bad argument last night, we can wait for an opportunity and ask 'How did you end it?' Even if they can't tell you how it was ended the question conveys that they were capable of ending it. When questions about solutions are used consistently in a session the message about the potential for change is more powerful still. (p. 57)

The important implication of this approach is that, if we are not sensitive to the language we use, it may actually prove counterproductive by blocking the progress we are trying to make.

Voice of experience 2.3

❝The offenders I work with may well cause problems with their behaviour sometimes, but I generally find that they have more problems than they cause. My way of working is based on the idea of trying to focus on solutions to their problems and then there is a much greater chance of reducing their criminal activities.**❞** *Chris, a probation officer*

Discourse and narrative

Wetherell (2001) comments that 'the study of discourse is the study of human meaning making' (p. 3). Similarly, narrative refers to the use of stories to make sense of our lives or particular aspects of them. Once again, in using language, we are not simply conveying information, we are entering into discourses, creating and recreating narratives. Indeed, there is now a school of therapy and social intervention which goes by the name of narrative therapy. This approach involves helping people to review their life and experiences, particularly those aspects which they find problematic, and to carefully reconstruct the meaning of their experiences or, as narrative therapists would put it, to re-author their narratives (Payne, 2006). Language is therefore used as the basis for helping people solve problems in their lives or move beyond blockages which are holding them back in some way. Of course, narrative therapy is not the only approach which involves the use of language in this way, but it is one which makes the use of language, discourse and narrative more explicit. It is a helpful basis for empowering forms of practice (Thompson, 2007).

PRACTICE FOCUS 2.7

Louise had been subjected to persistent sexual abuse at the hands of her stepfather between the ages of 12 and 14. Now in her mid-twenties, she was taking steps to leave behind the trauma of her experiences. With the aid of a counsellor specially trained in narrative therapy, she was in the process of revisiting her childhood experiences and 'rewriting' her life story as one in which she was no longer a passive victim and was, instead, someone who was actively making choices about the direction of her life. She was being helped to make the transition from victim to survivor.

Language games

The term 'language games' is one that is closely associated with the philosopher Ludwig Wittgenstein. Wittgenstein argued that there was no single entity of game; rather, there are various games which have what he referred to as a 'family resemblance'. By this he meant that those things we refer to as games have certain themes in common but there will be no single defining feature that is common to all of them. It is as if there is a set of features of games and before we apply the label game to a particular activity, it needs to match a certain number of those characteristics. For example, many games involve an element of competition but not all do:

> you will not see something that is common to all, but similarities, relationships, and a whole series of them at that … Look for example at board games, with their multifarious relationships. Now pass to card-games; you find many correspondences with the first group but many common features drop out, and others appear. When we pass next to ball-games, much that is common is retained, but much is lost … And the result of this examination is: we see a complicated network of similarities overlapping and criss-crossing: sometimes overall similarities, sometimes similarities of detail. (Wittgenstein, 1953, pp. 31–2)

Wittgenstein's philosophy of language was based on the idea that concepts in general can be regarded in much the same way as a game. That is, when we use terms such as 'truth', 'beauty' or 'intelligence', we are in a similar situation as that relating to games. There will be certain features in common to the various interpretations or usages of these words, but there will be no single defining feature. This means that words will often be used by people in slightly different ways, leading to considerable potential for confusion, misunderstanding and even conflict.

This moves us away from the essentialist idea that there is one given, underlying truth for each concept. The reality is far more complex than this, with words and concepts being characterized by a variety of interpretations. However, these interpretations are not entirely unrelated, as they will share some of the characteristics (in the same way that there will be no single defining feature of games, but there will be unifying characteristics). Wittgenstein's notion of language games therefore tells us that the use of language will not be simple or straightforward. The very nature of the use of language leaves us with considerable potential for confusion and break-down of communication.

Conclusion

This chapter has been nothing more than a brief visit to the vast and very complex world of language. However, it should be enough to show that language is an extreme topic – extremely large and extensive, extremely subtle and complicated, and extremely fascinating. Of course, language is also extremely important. It does not take much thought to realize just how significant a role language plays in our day-to-day lives. If we think of topics that are very important in our lives, then for many of them we can realize that language is also important within them. For example, work is a very significant feature of human life, and so much work takes place with the medium of language. But it is not just work: friendships, love affairs, loving relationships of all kinds, pleasure and entertainment, education and learning – these all owe a great deal to language.

We should also remember that language is closely associated with power, with the way we make sense of our lives and of the social world, and even how we make sense of ourselves – that is, our identity. Language, then, is in many ways our window on the world, as well as a set of tools that we use to live our lives. Language can be used to solve problems, to build positive and constructive relationships, to inspire and motivate and to liberate. However, it can also be used to attack and destroy, to belittle, undermine and oppress. It can also be used to create problems as well as solve them, to incite hatred and to create great pain and suffering.

It is therefore vitally important that we have at least a basic understanding of language in particular and communication in general, so that we are better equipped to make use of the positives and to avoid, wherever possible, the negatives. This is no easy task, but it is to be hoped that the remaining chapters in Part I of this book will help to deepen that understanding and that Part II will help to pave the way for making use of that understanding in practice.

POINTS TO PONDER

- What are the key points about language you have learned from this chapter?
- Why is it important to understand language?
- How can a knowledge of language be useful in practice?

CHAPTER 3

The written word

Introduction

In a book on communication, writing is clearly an important topic to examine. While we can draw a distinction between verbal and written uses of language and, indeed, between written communication and other forms of communication more broadly, it remains the case that the written word is a very common and widely established form of communication. We can see writing as the basis of learning and, indeed, even of civilization itself. This is because, for the most part, so much of our learning depends on the use of the written word. Even in the technologically advanced twenty-first century, so much of our learning depends on writing, even if this writing is in the form of words on a computer screen rather than on paper. While it would certainly not be true to argue that learning is dependent upon writing, it is clear that someone who does not have the benefit of being able to read and write is at a serious disadvantage when it comes to education and learning.

The written word is not a simple matter. As we shall see, it is not simply the case that writing is a written version of speech. The rules that govern writing are in many ways very different from the rules that govern spoken language. The point has already been made that the term grammar, as used by linguists, refers to the rules which govern how a language *is* used rather than how it *should* be used. That is, grammar is descriptive or explanatory rather than prescriptive. This also applies to the rules of written language – that is, the grammatical rules referred to are those sets of rules which seek to explain or account for how correct or acceptable language forms are used in writing, rather than how they should be according to someone's predefined notion of what constitutes correct or acceptable language.

These rules are far from simple. Consider, for example, the rules which govern the use of punctuation. Many textbooks on the appropriate use of English go to great lengths to try and explain how punctuation should be used. However, despite these extensive efforts, we remain far from a comprehensive understanding or set of guidelines on the use of punctuation (even the best-selling 'Eats, Shoots and Leaves' – Truss, 2003, does not answer all the questions about punctuation use). This is because punctuation is, in effect, a relatively crude attempt for written language to mimic the complex use of intonation, pitch and various other factors in the spoken word.

The written word exists in a diverse range of forms and operates at a number of levels. We cannot hope to cover every aspect of this enormous topic, but what I do intend to cover is the importance of writing, a brief historical background of the written word and an overview of the various forms writing can take, as well as an examination of the relationship between writing and what has come to be known as 'power/knowledge'. I begin, then, with a discussion of whether writing should be seen as secondary to the spoken word.

The primacy of writing

It is interesting to note that prescriptive approaches to grammar have generally tended to concentrate on the written word. In such approaches, spoken language is often seen as secondary to writing, with the expectation that speakers should try and make their language as close to the written form as reasonably possible – that is, the written form of language is seen as the form which should be aspired to. For example, the phrase 'with whom' is often used in writing, particularly formal styles of writing. However, it is increasingly rare in most forms of spoken English for this term to be used in speech or conversation. However, many supporters of the prescriptive grammar school would argue that *with whom* is the 'correct' form, even in spoken English. Indeed, Milroy (1998) argues that the use of such terminology in spoken English would be a sign of social distance:

> Not only are prescriptive arguments difficult to sustain, but if taken seriously they are likely to create problems. For example, 'Who am I speaking to?' is normal in most contexts, while 'To whom am I speaking?' will generally be interpreted as marking social distance. (p. 95)

This is an important point, as it shows that the use of language involves far more than following a set of prescriptive rules about what is considered 'correct' or 'appropriate' language usage.

Significantly, however, as the move away from prescriptive grammar has developed into modern linguistics, the focus has shifted largely towards the spoken word. Written language has come to be seen as secondary to actual speech. This is an approach which has come to be criticized by a number of thinkers, not least the French theorist Jacques Derrida. Derrida's argument is that it is in fact the written word which should be seen to have primacy (Derrida, 1976). One important reason for seeing the written word as primary is its relative permanence. That is, while speech can be recorded and, indeed, often is, the vast majority of spoken utterances are not kept on record for posterity. The written word, by contrast, is by its very nature, more of a permanent record.

┌─ PRACTICE FOCUS 3.1 ──────────────────────────────────────┐

Ralph was the last member to join the newly formed team and he was
keen to be part of the team set-up, as he had mainly worked on his own in
the past. As the team settled down and began to establish its own patterns of work and its own culture, everything was going well except for one
thing. Ralph had been brought up by parents who set great store by
'correct' grammar and they had instilled in him a strong need to be seen
as 'well-spoken'. This created a certain amount of tension, as Ralph's
speech and conversation came across as very formal and distant. It
seemed to contradict his attempts to be fully part and parcel of the team.
The other team members just hoped that they would get used to it, as
they too were keen to have an inclusive team.

└───┘

We have many examples of writing which date back many centuries, and it is
feasible that much of today's writing will be available in future centuries.
Speech by its very nature is far more ephemeral. Derrida would accuse contemporary linguists and others of 'phonocentrism'. By this he means making
the spoken word primary rather than the written word.

Of course, the danger here is that we can get embroiled in a sterile debate
about which is primary, speech or writing, rather than embrace the fact that
both are of major significance. As Foucault (1999) comments: 'What is interesting is always interconnection, not the primacy of this over that, which never
has any meaning' (p. 141). We therefore have to be careful not to attach more
significance to this debate than it deserves, as this could so easily distract
attention from other, more important issues. My aim, then, in this chapter is
not to argue that writing is more important than speech, but simply to put
forward the view that writing is not simply a version of spoken language and
is an important form of language in itself which should not be neglected.

Without doubt, Derrida and others are correct in arguing the case for paying
greater attention to writing. Consider, for example, the role of writing in establishing formal records. Anyone who has been involved in any form of legal proceedings will know just how significant written records are. Even without
getting as far as court proceedings, the written word can be crucial in determining the outcome of complaints and grievances, disciplinary proceedings,
inquiries and other such forms of formal investigation. Evidence in writing
carries considerable weight which other forms of communication do not.

As a result of data protection and human rights legislation, major problems
can arise as a consequence of false, inaccurate or misleading written records.
Consider, for example, the difficulties that could arise from information being
recorded inaccurately or inappropriately. Such difficulties can be seen to fall
into (at least) three categories:

- *Inappropriate actions*   Incorrect information recorded in a file, for example, could lead to actions being taken which are not appropriate to the situation. For example, somebody may be offered a service of some kind which is not in keeping with their needs or wishes.
- *Failure to act*   Inaccurate or misleading information could lead to a situation where an action needs to be taken but is not. For example, someone may not receive what they require because their requirements were not accurately recorded (or were not recorded at all).
- *Complaints or litigation*   If someone becomes aware that inappropriate records have been kept and can show that this has led to some harm or disadvantage being experienced, they may be in a position to make a formal complaint or even commence legal action.

Consider also the importance of writing in terms of job application procedures. While so much may depend on one's verbal performance at interview, it is unlikely that the interview stage will be reached without first submitting a high-quality written application. Indeed, it is often through the written word that important judgements are made in a variety of circumstances and settings.

PRACTICE FOCUS 3.2

Lena had been a student on placement in the team the previous year and had been well liked and well respected as a competent practitioner. So, when a vacancy arose in the team and Lena applied for it, she was confident that she stood a very good chance of being successful. The team members too were keen that she should get the job because they had got on well with her and knew that she was a very capable worker. However, when the shortlisting meeting was held, the team manager had a problem. This was because Lena's written application was of a very poor quality. It looked as though very little care had been taken in writing it. This gave the team manager a dilemma, as he wanted to shortlist Lena but found this hard to justify on the basis of the inadequate written application. His dilemma was resolved by the service manager who had not met Lena, as he felt he could not possibly agree to someone being shortlisted after submitting such a substandard application form.

We can see that the role of writing has become more important over time due to developments in technology. It has been argued that the invention of the printing press made a significant difference to society. In fact, Man (2002) argues that the ability to produce quantities of printed material shaped history significantly, particularly in relation to the development of education for children. Prior to the availability of printed material on a large scale, education was seen primarily as a family matter. However, the arrival of the printing press changed all this. Indeed, it can be seen that today's education system owes much to the versatility of printing methods. Without ready access to printed matter, our contemporary education system would not have been able to emerge as it has and, of course, this is not the only way in which writing has played a significant part in shaping history.

ACTIVITY 3.1

Consider the various ways in which your work relies on the use of the printed word. What skills do you need to have to make the most of the use of the printed word in your work?

Man (2002) captures the situation well when he comments, in describing the emergence of the printing press:

> The result, of course, was a new world of communication. Suddenly in a historical eye-blink, scribes were redundant. One year, it took a month or two to produce a single copy of a text; the next, you could have 500 copies in a week (500 was an average print run in the early days). Distribution was still by foot or hoof, but that didn't matter. A copied book just sits there, waiting for readers, one by one; a successful printed book is a stone dropped in water, its message rippling outwards to hundreds, thousands, millions.
>
> Hardly an aspect of life remained untouched. If rulers could bind their subjects better, with taxes and standardised laws, subjects now had a lever with which to organise revolts. Scholars could compare findings, stand on each other's shoulders and make better and faster sense of the universe. Gutenberg's invention made the soil from which sprang modern history, science, popular literature, the emergence of the nation-state, so much of everything by which we define modernity. (p. 2)

This is an important passage which makes reference to a number of key issues. It is worth exploring each of these in a little more detail:

- *Laws and taxes*   The social order depends very much on the regulation provided through legal statutes and the revenue gained from taxation to police those laws. While the printing press was not necessary for the development of laws and taxes (consider Ancient Greece and Rome, for example), clearly it has played a part in making the study and use of law a more widely available possibility.
- *Political revolt*   As Man indicates, the printing press has also made it possible for a much wider constituency of people to challenge legal,

political and economic structures and practices and to play an active part in developing them.

- *Scholarship* The widespread availability of books, journals and other printed materials has, of course, been a major factor in the development of a wide range of academic subjects in terms of the research and theory base on which they depend. Each new generation of scholars depends, of course, on the printed output of their predecessors.

- *Understanding the universe* The widespread availability of printed materials contributes not only to the depth of scholarship but also to the breadth of learning. That is, it is not only scholars who benefit in learning from the written word, but also the general public who have the opportunity to learn about the world in which we live.

- *Modern history* With the development of the printing press the study of history ceased to be a specialist subject and became more widely available. At the same time, the publication of various texts has in itself contributed to modern history, especially those books which have proven influential in shaping modern thought.

- *Science* Just as scholarship in general owes a great deal to printed materials, science in particular has benefited from its practitioners having access to the findings of the research of others and the theoretical understandings on which such research is based.

- *Popular literature* The development of cultural understandings of various issues has been influenced by the ready availability of popular literature. This would not have been possible without the printing press.

- *The nation-state* Nation-states on the complex scale of today can also be seen to owe much to the printed word, in so far as the day-to-day running of administrative systems relies heavily on printed materials.

Added together these factors combine to paint a picture of a major revolution in communication (and therefore in society, given the central role of communication in social life, as discussed in Chapter 1), one that has had profound and far-reaching effects in so many different ways.

It can also be seen that the very notion of childhood owes much to the development of writing through the printing press. This is because the evolution of the education system played a significant part in separating children from adults. Prior to the emergence of the printing press, children were seen simply as small adults. Consider, for example, the practice of children being used as chimney sweeps in the Victorian era and, indeed, acting almost identically to adults in so many different ways. The social construction of childhood as a stage in life separate from adulthood therefore owes much to the development of writing and its widespread dissemination in print. In this regard, John (1988) discusses the work of Postman (1983) who argued that the development of print media helped create a 'symbolic world' in so far as it was now possible to learn from more than just one's immediate physical environment and the oral folk tradition of one's culture. She comments:

> Adulthood became a 'symbolic not a biological achievement' and the child was excluded from this symbolic world until he/she could read. Education was necessary to enter this world so schools were reinvented (they had existed in Greek and Roman times) and childhood became a necessity. In a predominantly oral culture, the child had had equal access to the world of adults once he/she had mastered speech ... Now education became a significant way into the world of adults and a significant form of social control: it became an institutionalized intervention based on a view of the adult which was a product of technological change. Power relations between the child and the adult changed. 'The mastery of the alphabet and then mastery of all skills and knowledge that were arranged to follow constituted not merely a curriculum but a definition of child development' (Postman, 1983, pp. 45–6). (p. 9)

Voice of experience 3.1

❝It took me a long time to take on board the idea that childhood is not something natural or in some sense God-given. Learning about how it has developed in society over time, that it is a historical thing ... well, what I can I say? It really made me look differently at how society works. I hadn't expected my degree to make such an impact on how I saw the world.**❞**
Lisa, a newly qualified social worker

We can go a step further than this to argue that writing is not only a significant foundation of our education system and therefore the social construction of childhood, it is also a very strong feature in the foundation of our culture itself. This is because culture is transmitted from generation to generation in a variety of ways, not least those that involve the written word. While at one time the transmission of culture was exclusively an oral process, it is now of course a mixture of oral and written processes. We should be careful not to underestimate how significant a role writing plays in the process of children being socialized into their culture to begin with and, indeed, the continuing process of socialization throughout the life course.

While today's technology has transmitted much of the oral tradition into visual media such as television and cinema for example, the significant influence of the written word remains evident. This can be seen in a number of ways such as books (serious, academic and literary tomes, popular literature, children's books and so on), newspapers and magazines. We need only to step into any bookshop or newsagents to appreciate the vast wealth and variety of written texts available to us, and close inspection of what is available enables us to realize just how much of the printed word material available to us is an influence on our culture.

One of the reasons why the written word is so influential in shaping culture is that it is, as Derrida would argue, there for us to consult and consult again. It is not like the spoken word which is offered, heard, then disappears and is, for the most part, forgotten. Even relatively ephemeral items such as weekly magazines can have a relatively enduring effect because an article, for example, can be read, reread, stored for future use, passed on to a friend and so on and, of course, the fact that there are so many written materials available means that it is likely that many of them will seek to 'speak to the moment' in order to gain people's attention. This means that many publications will deliberately seek to exploit current fads and fashions in order to be seen as 'in touch' with contemporary themes and issues.

Weekly or monthly magazines can also be very influential despite their relatively ephemeral nature because of the recurring themes and patterns that become associated with particular publications. That is, while a particular issue of a magazine may have little within its covers that is specifically influential in terms of wider culture, the development of the magazine's own culture (assumptions, unwritten rules, emphases and so on) will of course play a part in influencing the behaviour, attitudes and assumptions of at least a proportion of its readership. A good example of this would be fashion magazines which do not simply report current fashions, but can be seen actually to play a part in shaping what is seen as fashionable and what is not.

A more recent development in the use of the written word is the emergence of the Internet as an increasingly popular form of mass communication. Indeed, it could be argued that the emergence of the Internet is such a popular and widespread source of information and medium of communication that it constitutes another social revolution which may well parallel the revolution brought about by the invention of the printing press. In the same way that, according to Man (2002), printing contributed so much to the development of modernity, we are now left wondering whether the Internet will contribute as much to postmodernity, with its emphasis on fragmentation and the breakdown of grand narratives. Time will tell. We are also now seeing what some people are referring to as a further Internet revolution, namely the emergence of what tends to be referred to as Web 2.0. This term is used to describe Internet developments that have made it much more interactive than was originally the case in the early days of web use. For example, many websites now are not simply static, one-way providers of communication. Rather they are dynamic and interactive – dynamic in the sense that they are constantly changing, with new material being added all the time (for example, newsfeeds), and interactive in the sense that visitors to the site can make 'input' as well as receive 'output' (discussion forums, responses to blog postings and so on). *Well-being Zone* (www.well-beingzone.com) and *Social Work Focus* (www.socialworkfocus.com) are good examples of such a use of communication technology.

Of course, it is not only popular culture that is influenced or shaped by the written word to a large extent. If we consider aspects of so called high culture – literature, drama, opera, ballet and so on – these are often based on texts written centuries ago and preserved as classics of culture and civilization. Similarly, such central notions to political thought as democracy and freedom owe much to philosophical texts dating back to the days of Ancient Greece. In short, contemporary culture would be very different indeed if not for the influences of both longstanding classic texts and more modern cultural writings.

The history of writing

Crystal (1987) points out that the earliest examples of the use of written symbols date back to 3500 BC. These were large numbers of clay tablets found in what today would be referred to as Iraq and Iran in the vicinity of the Rivers Tigris and Euphrates. The use of these symbols indicates a systematic use of symbolic representations to combine into a written form of communication.

We can distinguish between phonological and non-phonological systems of writing, with early systems being mainly of the latter type. A non-phonological writing system is one which relies on graphemes, or pictograms as they are often called. This refers to the use of symbols which resemble the object they are intended to represent. A simple modern example would be a matchstick drawing of a person. Closely related to the use of pictograms is the development of ideographic writing. An ideogram is similar to a pictogram in so far as it represents a particular object or idea, but is different, in so far as an ideogram tends to be an abstract representation – that is, there is not necessarily a direct representational link between the symbol and its object.

Phonological systems of writing can be seen as a further development of this whereby abstract symbols do not represent objects or ideas directly, but rather sounds which can be combined to form words. Thus, English with its 26-letter alphabet is an example of a phonological writing system. This is because the symbols (letters) do not directly represent the objects or ideas to which they refer. Rather, these symbols are combined in spelling to provide the words which, in turn, refer to particular objects or ideas.

An example of a writing system that combines both phonological and non-phonological elements would be that of ancient Egyptian hieroglyphics. The term hieroglyphic comes from the Greek word for 'sacred carving'. The term hieroglyph is used to refer to three different types of symbol. First, there are ideograms which represent actual objects or ideas. Second, there are phonograms which are consonant symbols which can be combined with ideograms to provide new words. Third, there are determinative symbols, which Crystal (1987) defines as:

> signs that have no phonetic value but are placed next to other symbols to tell the reader what kind of meaning a word has. Words that could otherwise appear to be identical could thus be differentiated. An analogy might again be drawn with a word game in English that could distinguish the two senses of the word, *table* by adding a chair (for the item of furniture) and an eye (for the typographical arrangement). (p. 199)

The ability to use these three different types of symbols in a number of combinations provided the basis for a very powerful writing system which enabled a wide range of ideas to be represented in writing.

It is perhaps a sad reflection of the global dominance of the English language that it is relatively common for people to forget about the existence of other forms of writing system and to assume that the English language basis is the only one. Of course, such a view is easily shown to be inadequate by reference to, for example, Chinese character systems of writing or the use of the Arabic alphabet. The fascinatingly rich diversity of writing systems and, indeed, of language forms more broadly, can easily be lost in the process of globalization that places the English language at the forefront of so many social, economic and political developments.

The point has already been made that writing is one of the main foundation stones of education. This is in no small part due to the history of the development of universities. The traditional universities in the UK have their roots in the church and its early practice of using clerics to write down important matters. We can therefore see that today's system of higher education owes much to the historical work carried out in churches and the early universities based on writing.

It should also be remembered that writing is a feature of a wide variety of societies and cultures. While not all cultures have a tradition of writing or regularly used writing, we can easily recognize that the vast majority do. Again, it is important not to rely on the dominance of English as a global language to blind us to the fact that there exist so many different cultures with different writing traditions and literary heritages.

While links between language and power can easily be drawn, links between power and writing in particular are also important. A significant feature of the history of writing is that it has developed to become a very powerful medium. At its simplest level, putting something in writing can be seen to give it considerable force. It is no coincidence that important matters, such as legal contracts and formal records, are committed to writing. Writing intertwines with the concept of power in a number of ways, and so I shall return to this topic below under the heading of 'Writing and power/knowledge'.

Forms of writing

Writing can take many forms, ranging from the internationally renowned texts of authors such as William Shakespeare through to the humble shopping list. My intention here is not to provide a comprehensive account of the various forms of writing, but rather to explore a number of important issues. I shall comment on a number of forms of writing and draw out some of the implications for today's society. The first form or genre of writing that I wish to examine is that of literary prose. This can be divided into two main types: highbrow culture and lowbrow culture. The former refers to literary works which are regarded as classics, high points of literary achievement which can be seen to have had a significant influence on society and culture in general and the education system in particular.

Voice of experience 3.2

❝I learned a lot about people from my professional training; in particular, I found social psychology really interesting and useful. But I must say I have also learned a great deal that has helped in me in my work by reading quality novels and drama that have so much to say about the human condition.**❞**
Beth, a counsellor

Bearing in mind Bourdieu's notion of cultural capital, we can see that there is much to be gained from being able to quote from such sources. For example, being able to quote from Shakespeare, Bernard Shaw or some other such literary giant is something that attracts considerable prestige. Such works are characteristically assumed to be of value because they convey and capture aspects of the human condition. They are said to have a resonance with readers in so far as they connect with aspects of the reader's experience which are seen as fundamental features of what it means to be human. To what extent these works capture fundamental aspects of humanity and to what extent they reflect dominant cultural ideas remains an open question.

ACTIVITY 3.2

Are there any ways in which cultural capital – and especially differences in cultural capital – might affect your work? If you are not sure discuss the question with colleagues and see what issues arise.

Lowbrow literary works comprise a vast range of popular novels and related works often of a romantic nature. Books of this genre can generate enormous sums of money, and therefore have a significant economic and social role to play. While such texts would perhaps make no such high claims as being able to connect with fundamental features of human existence, they do, none the less, seek a resonance in the reader in relation to common experiences, hopes and fears.

The traditional approach to literary prose is to attach considerable value to highbrow culture works while attaching little or no value to lowbrow culture texts. However, in recent years, the development of cultural and media studies has begun to enable people to recognize that there is much of value in the more popularized lowbrow cultural works. This is because such works can be seen to reflect (and shape) important aspects of culture.

Poetry is another form of writing which exists in both highbrow and lowbrow forms. What is particularly interesting about poetry is that much of its power and appeal derives from the fact that, as a written form of language, it is very different from the spoken word. For example, many poems achieve their desired effect through the use of what would otherwise be seen as non-grammatical forms of language. In effect, we could see poetry as a form of playing with grammar in such ways as to produce particular effects, mainly of an emotionally expressive kind.

As with any other literary genre, poetry comes in many forms and varieties. What they tend to have in common is the expression or encapsulation of emotion. This includes emotions associated with humour as some forms of poetry take a humorous approach.

Another significant form of writing is what can broadly be referred to as academic writing. This includes, but is not limited to, the natural sciences, social sciences, philosophy and the humanities and so on. It is through such academic writings that bodies of knowledge can be seen to have developed. These are not only bodies of knowledge in the everyday sense of the term but also discourses of knowledge; that is, the language that is used within such writings creates a set of power relations, a point to which I shall return below. The use of technical language or jargon plays an important role in creating in groups and out groups. While there are clear benefits to people being able to rely on shorthand forms of language, there are also problems associated with this. One such problem is that academics from different disciplines may find it difficult to understand one another because of their respective styles of language use. For example, the subject matter of social psychology and sociology overlaps significantly in many respects, but the forms of language used by psychologists and sociologists respectively can be such that communication becomes very difficult at times. This is not simply a matter of language, but reflects broader historical trends. For example, to some extent, psychology has its roots in the biological sciences. It is therefore not unusual to come across a psychological text which refers to human beings as organisms and even uses the term *it* to refer to an individual ('The human organism and its environment'). By contrast, sociology has little connection with the biological sciences and is more attuned to academic legacies associated with political and philosophical thought (although sociology is these days increasingly paying attention to the significance of the body – see Turner, 2000a).

PRACTICE FOCUS 3.3

Ranjana was delighted to be offered a place on the course at her local university and, when she received the preliminary reading list, she set about working her way through it with gusto. However, she was very concerned when she realized just how difficult so much of the writing was to understand. She began to become very disheartened and questioned whether she was intelligent enough to get through the course. It was therefore a major relief to her when, on the first day of the course, one of the tutors stated explicitly that a lot of academic material is written in an unclear and unhelpful way and that students should try not to get too discouraged by this. She knew she would still have to wrestle with some pretty impenetrable stuff, but at least she knew that this was not a sign that she was lacking in intelligence.

Writing from a postmodernist perspective, Hollinger (1994) argues the case for what he calls 'dedifferentiation'. By this he means that academic and professional disciplines have developed their own terminology to the extent that artificial or arbitrary boundaries have been created. His argument is that a better understanding of humanity and the social world will require the breaking down of such artificial boundaries. If such a dedifferentiation is to be achieved, then clearly the question of language, particularly in its written forms, is one that will have to be addressed.

While I would not expect academic writing to be replaced by day-to-day colloquial use of language, I do, none the less, believe that there is considerable scope for making the insights of theory and research more accessible to a non-specialist readership (Thompson, 2010). Over a period of many years, I have had to encourage large numbers of students who felt disheartened and alienated by the forms of language they encountered in the academic texts they were required to read as part of their professional education and training. I have had to teach students some of the codes which enable them to make sense of formal academic writing.

One genre of writing that combines two of the above forms is that of literary criticism (or 'lit crit', as it is often known). There is a significant and steadily growing body of written work comprising what are, in themselves, academic texts but which relate to literary texts. Drawing out themes and issues from literary works has been an occupation of a number of writers and thinkers in the humanities for some considerable amount of time now. There are various schools of literary criticism, some of which overlap considerably with the social sciences. For example, there is both a marxist approach to literary criticism which focuses on the material economic base as exemplified in literary work and a post-structuralist approach which, as the name implies, seeks to move away from the notion of an underlying structure which gives shape to social experience.

Literary criticism can therefore be seen as an academic discipline which analyses literary works and relates them to wider issues of personal and social experience. It takes an existing body of written work and provides a secondary body of writing by analysing, comparing and commenting on the primary sources with which it concerns itself. As such, it makes a significant contribution to the world of writing partly by providing a major body of written work in its own right and partly by providing commentaries and analyses on other works which often act as a gateway to the primary literary base. For example, many people will, before reading the works of a major literary figure such as Chekhov or Tolstoy, first read a text of literary criticism which introduces the main themes and issues of the author's work and the social and historical context in which it was developed and written.

Of course, given the widespread availability and use of newspapers and magazines, any consideration of forms of writing must take account of these. Newspapers and magazines are part of the mass media. That is, alongside television and radio they have a very influential and widespread role in disseminating information, views and ideologies to the general public and/or specialist sectors within the populace. Of course, it is well known that different newspapers reflect different readerships, in the sense that particular newspapers can be identified with specific social groupings. For example, the appointments pages of *The Times* will be advertising very different posts from those listed in the situations vacant pages of the local newspaper. Variations among newspapers can therefore be seen to reflect variations within the social sphere more broadly. Such variation is manifested in various ways, including not only the content of the newspaper and the style of writing but also the typeface that is used and – traditionally – the size of the newspaper itself (broadsheet or tabloid).

Even a short visit to a newsagent's shop will reveal the plethora of magazine titles currently available, and these do not include the various other titles which are not generally available in non-specialist stores. That is, many magazines are available only from specialist outlets or by subscription.

The power of magazines to influence people has long been recognized, but has been particularly to the fore in recent years, especially in relation to the influence on young people of images of emaciated models. Much concern has been raised about increasing levels of eating disorders such as anorexia nervosa. While it is difficult to make definitive statements, it is known that the influence of magazines is potentially at least a very strong one and, of course, such magazines do not operate in a social or cultural vacuum. The 'message' of such magazines is often reinforced by other media such as television. In many respects, newspapers and magazines reflect Marshall McLuhan's famous argument that 'the medium is the message' – that is, it is not simply the content or style of language within the newspaper or magazine that contributes to meaning making, it is the very fact that it is a newspaper or magazine that also plays a part (McLuhan, 1964). For example, while there is much evidence to show that newspapers are not unbiased in their reporting of news (McQuail, 2000), the presentation of information in newspaper form does give it considerable authority.

The forms of written material considered so far have all been available on a large scale – that is, they have been published in one form or another. However, this should not lead us to neglect other non-published forms of writing. As an example of this, I shall look at the question of correspondence. Letters have been a significant form of communication for many centuries. While the vast majority are of a relatively private nature, some have been considered to be sufficiently important to have been published in anthology form. For example, de Beauvoir (1984) is a collection of letters between her and Jean-Paul Sartre chronicling aspects of their relationship and the philosophical and political work that they were both engaged in over a period of years.

Although letters are often used as an informal means of communication – for example, between friends or relatives – the very act of committing words to letter form can in itself be regarded as a form of raising the level of formality. This is especially the case when a letter is in a typed or word-processed form.

Given the massive volume of letters that need to be distributed in many businesses and public services, it is not surprising that many organizations rely heavily on the use of standard letters. While this can be a very efficient form of communication, it can also be problematic when a standard letter is sent in a non-standard situation. That is, the use of standardized forms of writing can be very effective in coping with situations with little or no variation from an expected norm. However, in those situations which do not fit neatly into such a standard format, the use of a standard letter can cause offence, lead to misunderstanding or even to a complete breakdown of communication. I shall concentrate more on the practical skills of communication in Part II of the book. However, we can note here that being able to distinguish between those situations where a standard letter is appropriate and those where it is not is an important and valuable skill.

PRACTICE FOCUS 3.4

Roy and Lucy were foster carers who looked after a boy with learning disabilities one weekend per month as part of a respite care scheme. One day they received a standard letter from the boy's school, giving details of a review meeting to be held later that month. However, it was not clear from the letter whether this was simply a notification of the meeting for their information or whether they were actually being invited to the meeting. They therefore rang the boy's parents and asked for their view of whether they were expected to attend. They too had received a standard letter which left them none the wiser as to what its purpose was. Neither set of carers was impressed with the school's ability to communicate effectively in writing.

Another skill which is also becoming increasingly important in this electronic age is the ability to distinguish between when a letter is the appropriate form of communication and when an email message will suffice. With an increasing reliance on electronic communication, the use of letters is understandably declining. However, there are some circumstances where a letter is clearly more appropriate than an email message. The use of email is discussed in Chapter 7 and also features again in Chapter 8 in relation to the question of managing communication systems.

On the subject of letter writing, Aitchison (1997) makes the following important comment:

> Clear, concise writing cannot be done in a hurry, as the French writer Pascal realized when he once wrote to a friend: 'I have made this letter longer than usual, only because I have not had time to make it shorter.' (p. 82)

The fact that expressing oneself clearly and effectively in writing is a skilful activity applies just as much to letter writing as to any other form of use of the written word.

As already mentioned, we are witnessing a growing use of email as a form of communication. In addition, the Internet is increasingly being used as a source of information for a variety of purposes. Although the Internet makes use of graphics and sounds, it none the less relies primarily on the written word. What we can refer to, then, as computer-mediated writing is therefore a not unimportant form of written communication, and one that is becoming increasingly prevalent as the technology becomes both more advanced and more readily available. We are witnessing a culture change in which electronic forms of communication are now rapidly establishing themselves as everyday aspects of working life – becoming the rule rather than the exception. See, for example, the discussion of the significant social changes brought about by mobile phone technology in Ling and Donner (2009). Even here, with a device designed initially for speech-based communication, we are seeing a major focus on the use of the written word through the prevalence of text messages – and, interestingly, the development of new forms of written language through the use of abbreviations – as well as email and Internet access on a mobile phone. What began life as a portable version of the humble telephone has now evolved into a mobile multi-media communications device.

However, despite these developments in communication technology in recent years, I feel that Clutterbuck (2007) is correct when he argues that:

> It is ironic that the explosion in communications (the technology of communication) has led to so little improvement in communication (the sharing of understanding and meaning and the building of relationships). (p. 234)

The development of new communication technologies does not replace the need for communication skills – on the contrary, it introduces a new set of skills that need to be learned if the technology is to be a genuine benefit in promoting effective communication, rather than a further barrier.

The development of new technologies of communication also raises other significant social issues, not least the potential exclusion of particular groups. For example, there is the danger that many older people who were not brought up in the digital age and do not have access to modern technological equipment are likely to lose out in a number of ways, as are many people whose lives are blighted by poverty. 'Digital disenfranchisement' is therefore a significant social challenge that we now face.

PRACTICE FOCUS 3.5

Margaret was initially very pleased to have an email address allocated to her, as she felt that this would save her a lot of time in communicating with people electronically rather than by the more time-consuming methods of phone calls, memos and letters. However, while the facility did save her a great deal of time, what she soon found out was that it also used up a lot of her time. This was because she started to receive a large number of unsolicited email messages: adverts, jokes, circulars which had nothing to do with her and various other irritations. She therefore realized that, if she was to get the best out of email as a timesaving tool, she was going to have to come up with some way of filtering out the inappropriate messages.

One important implication of the development of computer-mediated writing is the further dominance of the English language on a global level. Given that the Internet has its roots in United States military strategy (the use of a network of computers, rather than one large computer which would be vulnerable to enemy attack), it is not surprising that the English language is the main language of the Internet. However, the other side of the coin is that the existence of the Internet allows for the use of texts from other languages. Users of minority languages can now make their writings available in a relatively inexpensive form, and this is an opportunity that has already been seized upon by many. In the 'global village' of the Internet, it is likely that English will continue to predominate, but that does not mean that there is no room for the thousands of other languages used in the world to play a part also.

Although I have covered a wide range of forms of written communication here, it is important to note that I have not by any means covered them all. Consider, for example, the use of written language in advertisements. While radio and television advertisements have become well established, these have not replaced other written forms of advertisement – for example, in newspapers and magazines. Similarly, written language is used on advertisements, such as hoardings, and indeed even television advertisements rely on some degree of use of the written word. And now, of course, we are increasingly seeing the Internet as a platform for (written) advertising.

Clearly, then, when we consider the use of written language, we are encountering a wide diversity of forms. Each has its own characteristics and its own effects. Each has to be considered within its own context. This is a subject matter of considerable complexity and intricacy and I have only begun to tackle this difficult territory in what I have covered so far. The study of diverse writing forms and their implications for individuals, communities, cultures and whole societies could well form the basis of a life's work. It is no simple or straightforward matter.

ACTIVITY 3.3

How comfortable do you feel with using different forms of written language (letter, forms, reports and so on)? What could you do to improve your skills in this area?

Writing and power/knowledge

The term 'power/knowledge' is one that is closely associated with the work of Michel Foucault. Although it is closely linked to the common-sense notion that knowledge is power, Foucault's theory is not quite so simple as that, as Bell (1993) explains:

'Power/knowledge' refers to the processes by which power and knowledge interact. The processes may be complex and contradictory ... processes

whereby, through the operations of power, knowledges are formed. …
Foucault does not argue that power and knowledge are the same thing.
Rather, they are entwined. (p. 44)

Of course, knowledge does not come exclusively from writing but it would be
very naive not to recognize that writing forms a significant foundation of our
knowledge base. Consider, for example, the major disadvantages encountered
by people who are unable to read.

Consider also, for example, the large number of books and magazine articles
which offer 'advice and guidance' on a wide range of topics. These 'guidelines'
are often prescriptive instructions, rather than guidelines geared towards encouraging critical reflection. They can therefore be seen to carry considerable power
in terms of their ability to influence people's actions and understandings.

Power is a concept which is commonly oversimplified and assumed to be
always a negative matter (see Thompson, 2007, for a discussion of these issues).
Foucault, however, points out that it can also be enabling and positive, a source
of resistance and challenge as well as domination. Here again, power and
writing are closely intertwined. This is because, on the one hand, established
writings are used as a source of authority to influence the beliefs, actions and
attitudes of particular groups of people or the population as a whole. Such
attempts to influence can be either overt or covert. An example of an overt
attempt to influence would be religious texts which are explicitly moralistic
in their tone. Examples of covert influences would include various forms of
literature, novels, plays and so on, which have an at least implicit 'message'.
Foucault would argue that such influences are only to be expected. This is
because he presents a model of power as being 'diffused'. That is, he sees
power as not being restricted to people in certain structural positions within
a hierarchy, but rather as a feature of human relations more broadly. Where
there are people together, there are relations of power. These relations of power
become embodied within texts and their use.

Voice of experience 3.3

❝I must admit I was quite naive when I came into this type of work. I
thought that power was something the doctors and the hospital bosses had
and we didn't, simple as that. But it didn't take me long to realize that power
is much more complex than that. Pretty much everything we do has a power
dimension to it, one way or another – between us and the patients; us and
the doctors; the doctors and the patients; us and other professionals – it's
mind boggling really.**❞** *Liam, a psychiatric nurse*

An important concept in Foucault's work is that of discipline. He is not using
it in its everyday sense of sanctioning someone for wrongdoing. Rather, he is

using it to describe the process by which society keeps its citizens 'in line'. A key term for Foucault is that of discourse – frameworks of language and meaning through which social powers are exercised. While the term discourse is generally associated with the notion of conversation, and is therefore more suggestive of verbal forms of language, a discourse can of course exist in a print medium. In fact, it can be argued that the weight of influence associated with written materials gives them extra power.

PRACTICE FOCUS 3.6

Martin was a very committed manager but he often found it difficult to get his message across. This was largely because he was seen as a mild-mannered, rather than assertive, person. However, one day he attended a training course on communication skills and he took the opportunity to talk to the trainer during the coffee break in order to get her advice on how he might be more successful in getting his team members to take more notice of him. Her advice proved to be very significant, as she suggested that he should commit very important matters to writing and make it clear that he was doing so because of the importance of what he was trying to get across. This proved to be a very worthwhile move on his part as the extra weight of written communication gave his team a very clear message that he 'meant business'.

Another important aspect of the relationship between writing and power/knowledge is the prescriptive approach to grammar as discussed in Chapter 2. That is, those people who argue that grammar should be seen as a set of rules which prescribe how language should be used are in effect exercising power. They are seeking to influence the use of language and, as Foucault would emphasize, language use must always be seen in the context of power relations. For example, by arguing that particular forms of language associated with a regional dialect are 'incorrect' or 'unacceptable', a prescriptive grammarian is attaching a low level of status to such forms of language use, thereby attributing greater power to people who do not speak such regional dialects.

Given that language in general, and written language in particular, has such a close association with power, it can be seen that prescriptive grammar is a form of control of the language, even though proponents of this view may not recognize it as such. This is an example of what Foucault would refer to as 'discipline' – that is a subtle form of regulating society through language and discourse.

Conclusion

This chapter has shown that written language is not simply a secondary form or derivative version of speech. Writing as a form of communication has its own patterns, characteristics and nuances. It is an entity worthy of study in its own right, rather than, as many people would see it, a watered-down form of spoken language. In some respects, writing has much in common with the spoken word but, as we have seen, in other respects it is quite significantly different. While the development of email as an increasingly popular form of communication can be seen to narrow the gap between writing and speech to a certain extent (although it exists in written form, it follows many of the conventions of spoken language), writing and speech continue to occupy separate but related worlds. We run the risk of distorting and oversimplifying a very complex set of issues if we fail to recognize both the similarities and differences between the written word and speech.

There can be no doubt that writing is an extremely important form of communication. As we have seen, it has a long and significant history and takes many forms. Even in today's high-tech world of information and communication technology (ICT), writing continues to occupy a central role. Its importance yesterday and today cannot therefore be doubted, and it seems highly unlikely that it will occupy anything less than a vitally important role in the future.

POINTS TO PONDER

- Why is written communication such an important part of working life across the people professions?
- How might written communication 'go wrong' or fail to achieve its objectives?
- What needs to happen to maximize the effectiveness of written communication?

CHAPTER 4

Speech and conversation

Introduction

Just as the previous chapter showed that writing is an important form of communication, this chapter explores the various ways in which the spoken word can also be seen as a vitally important aspect of communication. In order to develop our understanding of the use of the spoken word, I shall examine three sets of issues. First, I shall look at speech, the actual use of the spoken word in communicating. I shall examine a range of important issues which will help us to develop an understanding of both the complexity and the importance of the spoken word. Next, I shall present a brief overview of what is known as 'paralanguage', the various factors (tone of voice, for example) which have a bearing on how spoken language is used. Finally, I shall explore the important topic of body language or nonverbal communication.

We are, of course, dealing with a subject of enormous complexity. The use of the spoken word, combined with paralanguage and body language, produces a set of complex dynamics which operate at a variety of levels. These levels do not always correspond. For example, it is possible (and not uncommon) for what is actually said to be contradicted by the way in which it is said – that is, the speech form is contradicted by the paralanguage. An example of this would be a person who says, 'I am very sorry' but whose paralanguage, or possibly body language too, indicates that there is no regret or apology actually being expressed. These complex and intricate dynamics of interpersonal communication are the subject matter of this chapter. Most of us learn these skills at a basic level at least as part of growing up, and so it is sometimes not appreciated how complex or important they are because we have become so accustomed to using them with relatively little difficulty for the bulk of the time.

A theme that has become established in this book is that of meaning making. When people interact with other people, each party is involved in a process of interpreting the situation, making sense of it and acting accordingly. It is for this reason that Shotter (1993) argues that the basis of social life is 'conversational'. By this he means that a great deal of the meaning that we make of our lives comes from our interactions with other people – our conversations. This shows just how important speech and conversation are as a basis of communication. Our interactions are not simply functional, in the sense that they allow us to pass messages back and forth between individuals and across and between groups. They go beyond this to make a significant contribution to the processes by which we make sense of the world and our place within it.

The context

Before getting too involved in the intricacies of speech and conversation, we should first recognize just how important is the context in which such speech and conversation take place. The context of an interaction sets the scene and shapes the meanings that will be attributed to what is said. For example, if I ask: 'How are you?' while sitting at a hospital bedside, then this question has a very different meaning from when it is used in general conversation – for example, when bumping into an acquaintance in the street. In the former case, it is likely to be a genuine request for information about the other party's state of health, whereas in the second case, it is more likely to be a ritualized form of greeting. This is an example of what are known as contextualization cues – the small but significant indicators of the social situation we are involved in:

> Sociolinguists who study interaction argue people draw on a range of contextualization cues in deciding what kind of language event something is and how they should behave (Gumperz, 1982). According to Gumperz, contextualization cues guide people's expectations about how conversational and other exchanges should develop, appropriate modes of speaking, the interpersonal relations involved, and the speaking rights of those involved. (Wetherell, 2001a, p. 18)

In order to make sense of an utterance, then, we have to begin by asking the question: What is the context in which this utterance is taking place? To use the technical term, what is the 'language event' that is taking place here?

In Chapter 1, reference was made to Bourdieu's concept of 'habitus' – the storehouse of cultural facts and assumptions which have an important influence on an individual's behaviour. Without wishing to repeat the points made in Chapter 1, we should none the less note that habitus is an important aspect of the context in which speech and conversation take place. Utterances are not made in a cultural vacuum. Each participant in a conversation will bring with him or her a set of cultural assumptions about what is happening, what the status of the interaction is and what meanings should be attributed to it. Where participants in a conversation have different cultural backgrounds, there is therefore considerable scope for misunderstanding. This point and, indeed, the whole topic of the context in which speech and conversation take place, will be examined in more depth in Chapter 5.

PRACTICE FOCUS 4.1

When the party of Russian visitors arrived, there was a great deal of excitement about this first step in a process of developing an international exchange programme. All involved were looking forward to meeting their guests. However, while the visit did prove to be a very positive and enjoyable one, what they had not bargained for was the number of occasions when there were misunderstandings between the British and Russian participants in the scheme. These misunderstandings were due not so much to language difficulties (most of the visitors spoke excellent English and they also had the services of a very competent interpreter), but more to cultural differences – the various taken-for-granted assumptions and unwritten rules of social interaction which were clearly very different between the two groups. This was a good example of how communication is much more than just language, even though language use is clearly a major component of communication.

The point has already been made that communication involves conveying not only information but also a relationship. It has also been argued that relationships involve power. In considering speech and conversation, we therefore have to take account of relationships and the power dimension in particular. A conversation between two or more people is not simply a mechanical passing of information, but rather involves a complex web of dynamics. In one chapter, I cannot hope to cover all the important issues relating to this complex subject matter, but I can at least begin to lay the foundations for a better understanding.

Speaking and listening

Just as we noted in Chapter 3 that there are different types of writing (or different 'genres'), we can also note that speech can be divided into genres as well. Examples of speech genres would include:

- formal interviews (in relation to job applications, for example);
- highly ritualized greetings (discussions about the weather);
- transactions (ordering a round of drinks in a pub);
- tutorials at a college or university;
- arguments;
- chat-up lines; and
- general social chit chat.

Clearly, there is enormous diversity when it comes to speech genres. What is particularly interesting about this diversity is that the vast majority of people become very adept at handling themselves in a wide variety of genres, recognizing which behaviours and which forms of language are appropriate in the particular circumstances. This shows how highly skilled we are in handling conversational encounters.

We have already come across the concept of language games, and it is one that is worth revisiting here in relation to speech and conversation. As Billig (2001) explains:

> Philosophers, Wittgenstein argued, are prone to muddle if they do not understand the customary practices of language, or what he called 'language games'. Given that language is socially shared, there must be public criteria for the use of words. We learn how to use words such as 'table' and 'chair' by observing how these words are used: in this way, we learn to play the appropriate language games, in which such words are used. One of Wittgenstein's great insights was to claim that precisely the same happens with the use of psychological words, such as 'remember', 'feel' or 'see'. These words are used in various 'language games' and their sense must be understood in terms of the practices of their usage. Wittgenstein warned against assuming that such psychological words stand for internal processes, which provide their criteria of usage. (p. 211)

Becoming competent in the art of using speech in conversation therefore involves learning the rules of these language games and being able to determine which words or forms of language are appropriate in particular sets of circumstances. We have only to watch and listen carefully as people are in conversation (real-life conversations or dramatic representations on television or at the cinema, for example) to realize just how skilful an activity human conversation is.

Schirato and Yell (2000) adopt a similar line of argument when they discuss the notion of 'cultural literacy', which they define as: 'a knowledge of meaning systems and an ability to negotiate those systems within different cultural contexts' (p. 1). This is an important definition as it indicates that the skilled conversationalist needs to be able to understand not only which words are appropriate but also which meaning systems and cultures apply. For example, few fluent speakers of the English language would struggle to understand the meaning of the word 'interview'. However, to a human resource recruitment consultant, the term interview would clearly apply to a face-to-face meeting involving a job applicant and one or more representatives of a potential employer. To a social worker, the term interview would refer to a formal or informal meeting with a client. To a police officer, the term is likely to apply to an 'interrogation' which is so formal that it is likely to be tape recorded. Clearly, then, the term interview means different things to different people in different contexts. However, the term is used with relatively little confusion or ambiguity, such is the level of skill and competency of experienced users of a language that they are able to distinguish between the different usages of the term with little or no difficulty. The main point to emphasize here, then, is that speech and conversation involve a considerable level of skill and competency, although it is unlikely that people will realize just how much cultural literacy they are drawing upon in their day-to-day conversations and verbal encounters.

One important aspect of the use of speech is what is known as 'phatic' communication. This refers to the type of conversation which has a very low content level in terms of information being directly conveyed, but which is none the less very significant in terms of forming or sustaining relationships. A classic example of phatic communication would be discussions about the weather, where neither party is particularly interested in the weather, but is just using a relatively harmless conversation to lubricate the wheels of social interaction. While the direct information content of such communication may be negligible, the meaning is none the less very significant – for example, when two people who know each other come face to face, if one greets the other, but the other does not return the greeting, the significance of this can be immense, perhaps even leading to the breakdown of the relationship altogether.

PRACTICE FOCUS 4.2

When Brian began his professional training he was very keen to do well. He put a lot of time and effort into studying and was anxious to put his learning into practice. However, he was quite taken aback when his personal tutor took him to one side one day and told him she had concerns about his communication skills. This came as a great surprise as he had always thought of himself as being quite articulate and quite an effective communicator. His tutor, however, had to try and get across to him that, while his communication skills were quite advanced in some ways, what he didn't do was to engage in small talk. His tendency not to use phatic communication gave people the impression that he was rather aloof and uncaring – and this gave the wrong message. His tutor therefore advised him to work on developing more experience of using his skills to engage people through everyday pleasantries in order to avoid this misleading impression that he was distant or aloof.

Phatic communication is highly ritualized, in the sense that there are established patterns to be followed. This again shows that communication is not simply about conveying information.

This example shows the importance of feedback. That is, holding a conversation with someone involves not only presenting information to them, but also receiving information from them and adjusting one's own contribution to the conversation accordingly. For example, if I give a cheerful greeting to someone but their response indicates that they are far from cheerful, perhaps having suffered a significant loss or other misfortune, I would quickly adjust my tone of voice and the actual speech used to backtrack on the cheerfulness and adopt a more empathic point of view. In return, the other party may recognize that I have made this adjustment and show gratitude and appreciation for the fact that I have done so, perhaps thanking me for my concern. This is a good example of feedback in action, where the contribution of one participant influences the other or others and vice versa. Fiske (1990) shows the important role of feedback in the following passage:

> Feedack, then, has this one main function. It helps the communicator adjust his or her message to the needs and responses of the receiver. It also has a number of subsidiary functions. Perhaps the most important of these is that it helps the receiver to feel involved in the communication. Being aware that the communicator is taking account of our response makes us more likely to accept the message: being unable to express our response can lead to a build-up of frustration that can cause so much noise that the message may become totally lost. Though feedback inserts a return loop from destination to source, it does not destroy the linearity of the model. It is there to make the process of transmitting messages more efficient. (p. 22)

This use of feedback indicates one of the main differences between speech and writing. When I write something, I may eventually get feedback in response to what I have said but, in many cases, there will be no feedback at all and, where it does occur, there is likely to be a significant time lag. This makes writing a very different enterprise from speech where the case can be very significant with numerous feedback adjustments being made in the space of only a few minutes. Heritage (2001) refers to this characteristic of speech as 'reflexivity' as he comments: 'changes in an understanding of an event's context will evoke some shift or elaboration of a person's grasp of the focal event and vice versa' (p. 51).

ACTIVITY 4.1

Making good use of feedback is an important part of self-awareness (noting how people are responding to what we are saying or doing). Watch people interacting with each other, either 'live' or on television or in a film and see if you can spot examples of the effective use of feedback. Are there any lessons you can learn from this that will help you develop your own self-awareness and feedback skills?

An important aspect of feedback is empathy. This refers to an individual's ability to 'read' another person's emotional state and to act accordingly. This is similar to sympathy but subtly different. This is because to express sympathy implies that we share the feelings we are recognizing in the other person. For example, to send a message of sympathy to someone who is grieving at a loss is not only an act of being supportive to that person, but also an acknowledgement that we feel some of degree of loss too. Empathy, by contrast, is where we are able to appreciate a person's emotional response to a situation, but without necessarily experiencing those feelings ourselves. For example, I can recognize that someone is angry and thus respond to them in a way that acknowledges that anger and attempts to deal with it constructively without feeling any anger myself. That is, I do not have to share someone's feelings to be able to empathize with them and respond in a helpful way which promotes effective communication.

Voice of experience 4.1

"Having a disabled son has helped me in my work. I have been able to see huge differences between the different people working with him and how he has responded to them. Some have great empathy skills – and those are the ones he finds it easy to relate to – while others have been pretty clueless in that department – and those are the ones he just won't take to.**"** *Barbara, a care manager in a learning disability team*

To provide appropriate feedback as part of interpersonal encounters, then, we do not need to sympathize with the other party (that is, have the same feelings that they are having) but we do need to be able to empathize if we are to be successful in our communications – particularly those in which emotions are running high. I shall revisit this theme of the emotional dimension of communication in Chapter 6 when I discuss what has come to be known as 'emotional intelligence'.

One of the implications of feedback or reflexivity is that all parties involved in a conversation share a degree of responsibility for constructing the meaning within that verbal encounter. Scollon and Scollon (2001) argue that language is ambiguous by its very nature and they link this to the notion of the joint construction of meaning in and through conversation:

When we say that language is always ambiguous, what we mean is that we can never fully control the meanings of the things we say and write. The meanings we exchange by speaking and by writing are not given in the words and sentences alone but are also constructed partly out of what our listeners and our readers interpret them to mean. To put this quite another way, meaning in language is jointly constructed by the participants in communication. (p. 7)

Conversation involves a complex process of negotiation of meaning. For example, a supervisor may wish to reprimand an employee for his or her poor quality of work. However, the employee may seek to renegotiate the meaning of the conversation by, for example, thanking the supervisor for his or her 'advice'. In saying this, the employee is resisting the supervisor's definition of the conversation as one based on reprimand and reframing it as one in which advice is being given. The supervisor may then 'up the stakes' in terms of negotiation by reaffirming the original view of the conversation as one involving a reprimand. However, in doing so, he or she is risking the situation becoming more tense and conflict-ridden than might otherwise have been the case and may therefore be reluctant to do so. If, however, the supervisor does assert the original view, then the employee is faced with the choice of either accepting that version of events and acknowledging the reprimand or, for his or her part, upping the stakes further by continuing to renegotiate the situation as one which the supervisor is likely to be reluctant to accept.

One way of understanding this joint construction of meaning is to recognize that meaning is 'emergent' through the process of interaction. Some theorists would go a step beyond this to argue that not only is meaning emergent in interaction, but so also is our identity. As discussed in Chapter 1, the postmodernist view of identity is of a subjectivity that is developed in and through communication. As Coupland and Jaworski (2001) explain:

> Communication is, then, a ritualised process that allows its participants to construct and project desirable versions of their identities, enacted in a succession of performances targeted at specific audiences. Because social actors in conversation are inter-dependent, the behaviour of one participant defines and constructs social relations and the identities of other members of the group. Thus, social meaning is emergent in interactions and the identities of social actors are multiple and dynamic (changeable in the course of interaction). (p. 135)

The significance of emergent meaning and identity through social interaction is something that is studied through discourse analysis. This is a technique which involves the close and detailed scrutiny of particular 'texts' (that is, any written or spoken 'block' of language). This is an approach which can give significant insights into social interaction and communication (see Wetherell et al., 2001a and 2001b).

Another important aspect of speech and conversation is the important role of diversity. I have argued elsewhere (Thompson, 2011) that equality and social justice are dependent on recognizing that we live and work in a diverse society, and that such diversity is an asset to be valued rather than a problem to be solved. However, this presents some degree of complication when it comes to communication. This is because communication can be seen to work best when people are similar, or at least on a similar wavelength. We have to recognize, then, that there is a tension between communication and diversity, although we should not be defeatist and assume that this means that the valuing of diversity is something that has to be abandoned in favour of effective communication.

PRACTICE FOCUS 4.3

Mary was a very skilful communicator who enjoyed her job because it involved liaising with a wide variety of people across the whole organization. She spent much of her time forming and developing links with key people. However, she was surprised when, at her annual appraisal, her line manager criticized her for failing to address issues of diversity. That is, Mary was criticized for spending a lot of time with people she perceived to be like herself, and perhaps neglecting people whose background was different from her own. At first, she was quite shocked to hear these comments and thought her line manager had got it wrong. However, following discussion and thinking the issues through, she came to realize that her line manager was probably right, although Mary had never deliberately set out to avoid certain people. She had understandably been drawn to the people she felt more comfortable with. One of her targets set during the appraisal was therefore to develop better working relationships with those people who were of a different background to herself.

Scollon and Scollon (2001) draw attention to the role of shared assumptions in facilitating communication:

> it should be clear that communication works better the more participants share assumptions and knowledge about the world. Where two people have very similar histories, backgrounds, and experiences, their communication works fairly easily because the inferences each makes about what the other means will be based on common experience and knowledge. Two people from the same village and the same family are likely to make fewer mistakes in drawing inferences about what the other means than two people from different cities on different sides of the earth. (p. 21)

In a similar vein, Tannen (2001) writes of what she calls the 'double bind of communication'. As she comments: 'communication is a double bind in the sense that anything we say to honour our similarity violates our difference, and anything we say to honour our difference, violates our sameness' (pp. 153–4). We have to be careful here not to oversimplify the situation. In some ways we are all the same (for example, we bleed if cut). In other ways, we are all different – we are all unique individuals. A major component of the social skills base that we developed in growing up is the ability to deal with similarities and differences. However, it has been recognized that an overemphasis on similarity for the sake of solidarity can be expensive when it comes to valuing diversity (Thompson, 2011) – that is, it is a common part of socialization to learn to value people who have much in common with ourselves, but to mistrust or even devalue people who are significantly different. This form of socialization has the effect of blocking the path to cultural enrichment and the benefits of diversity. While communication between people who have much in common may well be more simple and straightforward, I would argue that the effort required to communicate effectively with people who do not share the same background is well repaid in the benefits to be attained.

It would clearly be a mistake to neglect the power relations involved in speech and conversation. One particular aspect of power relations can be seen in the notion of positioning (Davies and Harré, 2001). It is commonly the case that participants in conversation seek to 'position' each other – that is, they seek to allocate a particular role or social position to one or more parties in the conversation. In the example given above of the supervisor and employee negotiating the status of their interaction, we can see that the supervisor was trying to position the employee as the guilty party while the employee was resisting being positioned in that way. Positioning is thus a form of power play that operates within interpersonal interactions. Influencing skills can therefore be seen to include the ability to position other people effectively. Similarly, in a more negative vein, exploitation can take place through the process of positioning – that is, the exploiter positions a person in a way which is detrimental or disadvantageous to him or her. The person doing the positioning gains at the expense of the person being positioned.

However, power should not be seen in a purely negative light. As Foucault has pointed out, power also has its positive side. For example, Tannen (2001) argues that power can be used to establish solidarity. She argues that what may be seen by some as an attempt to dominate a conversation may actually be intended as a strategy for establishing rapport and thus, solidarity. Indeed, this is one possible source of communication breakdown. For example, if I say to someone, 'sit down', this may be a power play and an attempt to establish dominance. However, it could also be an attempt to help the person concerned to feel comfortable and at ease in my presence. Of course, much will depend on the context and such factors as tone of voice, a topic to which I shall return below.

Another important concept in relation to the power dimension of speech and conversation is that of 'heteroglossia'. This is an idea which derives from the work of Bakhtin (1986). He used this term to refer to the 'dynamic multiplicity of voices' (Maybin, 2001, p. 67). Language as it is used in speech and conversation involves various intersecting elements, such as genre, registers and even idiolects. Within this complex interplay, there are competing voices struggling to be heard in the mêlée of heteroglossia. This has much in common with Foucault's notion of power as something which is not simply located in structural positions (for example, the boss has power while the workers do not), but rather as a feature of the complex interactions between people in their day-to-day exchanges and the discourses on which these are based. According to Foucault, while some discourses may be dominant in their influence and their ability to shape what is defined as reality, in effect social life is characterized by a multiplicity of discourses. This multiplicity has much in common with what Bakhtin refers to as heteroglossia – the social struggle brought about by the dynamic interactions between competing multiple voices. Coupland and Jaworski (2001) give an example of this when they refer to Graddol's (1996) study of the label on a bottle of wine. The label will show a number of different 'voices' or genres. This will include a description of the type of wine and perhaps its qualities, a bar code and a health warning.

Power relations in terms of speech and conversation also manifest themselves in terms of social differences – for example, class differences. As Guirdham (1999) points out:

> Systematic studies show that middle-class speakers tend to talk more, use more varied vocabulary, and more varied grammatical constructions than do working-class speakers. There is evidence that class differences in communication also exist on the non-verbal level – appearing already in preschool age children; middle-class children are less affected than working-class children by whether an instruction is spoken in a 'positive', neutral or negative tone of voice. (p. 80)

She then goes on to argue that we should none the less avoid making the mistake of assuming that one form of language is correct while the other is incorrect, or that one form of language is superior to another (as noted in Chapter 2). The question of social differences in the use of language has been a major one for some considerable time, generating a great deal of discussion and no little heat. One aspect of this has been the distinction between elaborated and restricted code. Elaborated code refers to forms of language which are rich, complex and multilayered compared with the simpler, narrower usages involved in restricted code. Restricted code relies on a smaller vocabulary and simpler form of syntax. The work of Bernstein in this area has shown that it is a mistake to assume that restricted code is inferior to elaborated code, although this is an easy mistake for people to make (Bernstein, 1971; 1973). As Guirdham (1999) points out, there is an important parallel between the distinction between elaborated and restricted code and the distinction referred to earlier between high context and low context communication. Each form of communication fulfils a different function and operates according to a different set of rules. This is a long way from the simplistic and prejudicial notion that there is one 'proper' form of language. The reality is far more complex than this. As Fiske (1990) helpfully explains:

> Even the words Bernstein has chosen – elaborated and restricted – have positive and negative social values. But if we are to make the most of Bernstein's work, we must discard these value judgements. Elaborated codes are not *better* than restricted codes, they are *different* and perform different functions. We are all of us individuals, we are all community or group members. We need restricted and elaborated codes equally. *Coronation Street*, and popular art of this sort, actually does more to keep our scattered diverse society together by providing a shared experience than does a highbrow, culturally valued play by Samuel Beckett. The terms 'restricted' and 'elaborated' must be seen as descriptive and analytical: allowing value judgements to become attached to them will merely obscure the issue. (p. 73)

PRACTICE FOCUS 4.4

Tim and Rhian were delighted when Rhian's promotion enabled them to move to a much more upmarket area. They were very happy when they moved into their new house. However, their joy was to be shortlived as they soon found themselves to be the victims of prejudice about language. In their previous area, Tim and Rhian were accepted in the community as they spoke in much the same way as other people did. They had not bargained for the fact that many people in their new area would look down on them because of their speech patterns. They were very disappointed that people could be so narrow minded.

The very process of listening is also an aspect of speech and conversation to which we should pay attention. This is because listening is, as we shall see in Chapter 6, a very skilful activity and an important pivot on which effective communication rests. We cannot expect to be successful in our attempts to communicate if we are not able to listen effectively. McKay et al. (1995) identify 13 'blocks to listening', as follows:

1. *Comparing* If you are busy comparing yourself with the other person, then it is unlikely you will be listening fully. It is easy for us to be distracted by considering whether we 'measure up' to the person we should be listening to.
2. *Mind reading* This involves 'trying to figure out what the other person is *really* thinking and feeling' (p. 8). It involves trying to second guess what the person is trying to communicate instead of actually listening to what is being said.

3. *Rehearsing*　By this what McKay et al. mean is the tendency to be thinking about what you are going to say in reply rather than actually paying attention. The ironic thing here is that the less you listen to the other person, the more likely you are to respond inappropriately. Rehearsing is therefore likely to be counterproductive on many occasions.

4. *Filtering*　As the name implies, this refers to filtering out certain aspects of what is being said – only listening to those bits that you want to. A common example of this is when people do not 'hear' a criticism of them. Conversely, people with low self-esteem will often not listen to positive messages about themselves and will somehow filter out anything complimentary and only take on board neutral or negative messages.

5. *Judging*　This refers to disregarding someone because you disapprove of them for some reason – for example, not listening to someone because you regard them as unintelligent or a troublemaker or whatever. Although McKay et al. do not mention it, this could also apply to relying on discriminatory stereotypes – for example, a man not listening to a woman because he is dismissing the validity of her opinion, or a white person not listening to a black person because the latter's views are not valued.

6. *Dreaming*　It is not uncommon, when in conversation, to drift away from what is being said and engage in our own private thoughts or daydreams. This may be because the other person has said something that has triggered off a thought or memory of your own, or it may be because your daydreams are more interesting than the boring conversation you are engaged in.

7. *Identifying*　This involves translating what the other person says into your own feelings and experiences and feeding it back to them, rather than listening to them talk about *their* experiences. For example, someone starts to tell you about their experience of being lost and, before they get very far into the story, you cut across them and start telling them a story about an experience of getting lost that you have had. It is as if their experience is only important to the extent that it relates to yours – and this is the message this type of behaviour is likely to give: 'your experiences are not important, but mine are'.

8. *Advising*　This happens when someone gives advice about how to solve problems, rather than listens to the feelings about those problems that are being expressed. It is a common mistake made by many people in the people professions who are geared up to problem solving and may therefore fall into the trap of adopting the more

comfortable role of adviser than the perhaps more demanding role of listening carefully and empathically as someone expresses their feelings.

Voice of experience 4.2
❝This is a lesson I learned in my private life and was able to apply to my work. One day my sister was very distressed because she suspected her boyfriend had been two-timing her. I was very concerned about her and wanted to help so I started giving her advice about how she could set about finding out whether it was true or not. Of course, she bit my head off and told me she wanted me to listen to her and understand, not to try and take over.❞ *Ken, a drugs education worker*

9. *Sparring*   This can take two main forms. First we have the tendency to argue and debate rather than listen. The person who engages in this type of behaviour is more interested in proving a point than actually communicating with another human being. It is often done in the form of a 'put-down' or sarcastic remark. Second is 'discounting' – discounting what the other person has said, as for example, when a compliment is given and the person receiving it plays it down to the point where the person who gave the compliment feels that his or her appreciation has not been taken on board.
10. *Being right*   Unshakeable convictions combine with an unwillingness to take on board any criticism to produce the problem of 'being right'. The result is that, however convinced the person is that they are right, they are not actually listening to what is being said as they are preoccupied with defending their own perceived invulnerability.
11. *Derailing*   Two common ways of 'derailing' a conversation are (i) to change the subject suddenly; and (ii) to make a joke of the situation or what is being said. In either case, the same message is being conveyed: 'I am not interested in what you have to say'.
12. *Placating*   Sometimes we can be so concerned with 'being nice' and not upsetting people that we are concentrating on how to keep them happy rather than listening to them. Once again, there is a considerable irony here in the sense that this approach could very well upset someone if they realize that you are playing placating games rather than having the respect to pay attention to what is being said.

ACTIVITY 4.2

Look carefully at the twelve obstacles to listening outlined above, then make some notes about how, for each one of these, you can try to make sure that you can avoid the pitfall concerned.

It should be clear from this list that there are various ways in which communication can suffer or break down altogether because one or more parties allow such blocks to listening to stand in the way of making a proper connection. It should also be clear that these are important considerations to take into account in the world of professional practice. We will seriously undermine our effectiveness as communicators – and therefore as professional workers – if we allow ourselves to lose sight of these issues and thereby fail to address them.

Paralanguage

The term paralanguage is used to refer to the various elements which accompany and amend the spoken word – for example, tone of voice. Paralanguage is very important, as it can add extra meaning to what is actually being said or can even contradict or undermine it. For example, someone trying to reassure others may fail to do so if their tone of voice and so on are far from reassuring. We have to recognize, then, that paralanguage is not simply a surface gloss, an added extra. It is, in fact, a vital and fundamental part of effective interpersonal communication. This can be illustrated by the popular saying: It's not what you say, it's the way that you say it. For example, 'hello' can be a simple greeting. However, if I say it with rising intonation, it can become a question implying 'is there anybody there?' If I say it with a tone that first falls and then rises, it can imply puzzlement – what's going on here? Another example would be the use of the term, 'why'. With one tone of voice it can be a simple enquiry, while with another, it can be a very threatening comment. What these examples show is that, if we are to have an adequate understanding of speech and conversation, we need to have at least a basic grasp of what paralanguage is and how it works.

The topic of paralanguage is an extremely complex one and, once again, I am going to have to limit myself to a basic overview of some of the key issues, rather than a comprehensive or exhaustive analysis. Paralanguage can be divided up into the following main areas:

- *Speed*   The speed at which we speak can add extra meaning. For example, fast speech can indicate a degree of excitement, while slow speech can indicate boredom or even depression.

- *Tone*   Spoken language can be seen as a form of music in which tonality plays an important part. This is a multidimensional aspect of language use but, at its simplest, it can be seen in terms of a continuum between gentle tone at one extreme to harsh tone at the other.
- *Loudness*   While some people may speak characteristically more loudly or more softly than others, changes in the loudness at which persons speak can be highly significant. Uncharacteristically loud speech can indicate a number of emotions, such as aggression or anxiety. Quiet speech could indicate timidity or could actually be a deliberate strategy on the part of the speaker to calm down the other party.
- *Pitch and intonation*   The study of speech rhythms is known as 'prosody'. Pitch refers to how high or low a particular word or utterance is made. Intonation refers to the musicality of an utterance – that is, the way pitch rises and falls while speaking.

These four elements have been briefly outlined in isolation from one another but, in reality, in the complex world of actual speech and conversation, the four elements interact quite considerably. What adds to the complexity is that different dialects of the same language may use these factors in different ways. For example, in most parts of the UK, rising intonation at the end of an utterance indicates that it is a question. However, in some regional accents, this is not necessarily the case, with a rising intonation being used for a straightforward statement that is not a question. In addition, the complexity is deepened by the fact that many people speaking a particular language which is not their first language, may well bring the paralanguage features of their first language to the language they have learned. For example, an Urdu speaker may speak English using paralanguage features that are more characteristic of Urdu. Once again, this is not to make a value judgement and to say that such usage is incorrect, but rather to indicate that different speech communities can and do use paralanguage in different ways.

The use of paralanguage is something that is also very relevant to the subject matter of Chapter 6 where I explore the practicalities of interpersonal interactions. Being able to use the most appropriate forms of paralanguage in the circumstances can be an important part of getting our message across and ensuring that, as far as possible, we engage with the other participants in a way that provides a solid foundation for effective interpersonal interactions. We should not be surprised if inconsistencies between what we say and how we say it result in unnecessary tensions which act as barriers to communication, rather than provide a firm foundation on which to build.

Nonverbal communication

The term 'nonverbal communication', or 'body language' as it is also commonly known, refers to the bodily movements which accompany speech and which add meaning to the interaction. The term 'kinesics' is used to refer to the study of movements in general, and so the study of nonverbal communication can be seen as a subdivision of kinesics. As with paralanguage, nonverbal communication can be subdivided into a number of main components.

- *Facial expression*   The most obvious use of facial expression is smiling. However, this term also refers to other significant gestures such as raising an eyebrow. This is often one of the most noticeable aspects of nonverbal communication, as it is very common practice for people to look at each other's faces when communicating – as the phrase 'face-to-face communication' indicates.
- *Eye contact*   This is, of course, a very powerful means of communication. It can be used for a wide variety of purposes ranging from establishing solidarity and concern through to being threatening and intimidating. Again, eye contact is very important, as unusual patterns in this aspect of body language can leave people feeling very uneasy.
- *Posture*   The posture we adopt in sitting or standing can say a lot about our frame of mind or our emotional state. Some forms of posture

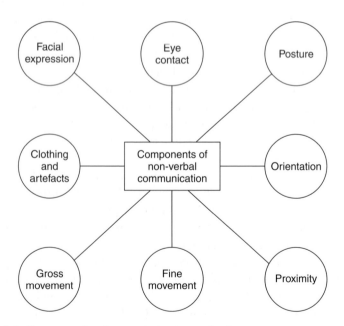

Figure 4.1 Components of nonverbal communication

are ritualized – for example, standing to attention in a military parade, but generally it is not quite so choreographed. In some situations, posture can be very revealing. For example, a person who is feeling dejected is likely to show this in his or her posture.

- *Orientation*   Whether we face towards someone or away from them can speak volumes about our attitude towards them, how we value them (or not) and perhaps even our intentions towards them. For example, turning away from someone (in disgust, perhaps) can be a very powerful gesture indeed.

- *Proximity*   How closely or otherwise we sit or stand in relation to someone can be very meaningful indeed. For example, many illicit lovers have been caught out by the fact that their proximity indicated to others a greater degree of intimacy than they would like to have made apparent.

- *Fine movement*   This refers to small movements of parts of the body which can be very significant – for example, a nod of the head, a wave of the hand or a furrowing of the brow. These can often be very subtle, but none the less very significant in the message they convey and the impression they create.

- *Gross movement*   This refers to more large-scale movement of the body or parts of the body. Walking or running away from someone would be clear examples of this. These are often associated with more extreme situations, but do none the less occur quite frequently. For example, at a social gathering, someone may walk the long way round to where they want to go in order to avoid a particular individual that they do not wish to interact with.

- *Clothing and artefacts*   In the majority of situations, the clothing we wear will say something about how we perceive that situation. For example, wearing formal clothing at a court appearance or job interview indicates respect and that we are taking the proceedings seriously. The use of artefacts can also be significant: the wearing of a ring can indicate marriage or engagement, and fidgeting with a pen or other such object can indicate boredom.

The point was made earlier that paralanguage adds significantly to the complexity of speech in conversation. Of course, nonverbal communication adds a further layer of complexity.

Fiske (1990) makes the important point that nonverbal communication is 'indexical' – this means that it can be seen to say something about our identity, our sense of who we are. This is because body language is partly cultural and partly personal. That is, my use of body language will owe much to the culture in which I have been brought up and in which I now live. Indeed, different

---

PRACTICE FOCUS 4.5

Sara was an experienced practitioner who was keen on working with students and helping them develop their knowledge and skills. But, she knew from the moment she met Tim that she was not going to enjoy working with him as much as she had with previous students. His intense eye contact was very unsettling for her and it made her feel very uneasy. She tried to understand this level of eye contact in terms of his eagerness to pay attention and learn. None the less, she found herself feeling very tense in his company. (Thompson, 2009b)

---

cultures have different rules about the use of nonverbal communication. For example, in some cultures, nodding one's head indicates *no* rather than *yes*. Someone who is knowledgeable in the use of nonverbal communication may be able to identify aspects of my cultural background from the way in which I use body language. However, it is not simply a matter of culture. There will also be aspects which are personal mannerisms, parallel with the idea of an idiolect (see also the discussion of Bourdieu's notion of 'habitus' in Thompson, 2010). For example, there may be many people who indicate their intentions by drumming their fingers on the table, but they may not do it in just quite the way I do it. It can be an interesting exercise to develop learning and awareness of these important issues to observe people's use of body language and determine which aspects reflect cultural background (that is, are shared with other members of that person's culture) and which are specific to that individual – are individual mannerisms or characteristics.

ACTIVITY 4.3

What mannerisms or characteristic forms of nonverbal communication do you use? (If you cannot identify these for yourself, talk to somebody you know well about it and see what they say.) Once you are clear what your characteristic nonverbal communications are, think carefully about whether they are a help or a hindrance when it comes to communicating. Also think carefully about how you can make best use of the positive aspects and try to ensure that the negative aspects feature less in how you come across to people.

It is important to emphasize that nonverbal communication is culture specific – that is, that different cultures have different ways of utilizing nonverbal communication. For example, Scollon and Scollon (2001) use an illustration given by Erickson and Schultz (1982) of a group of African-American employees whose body language was misinterpreted to their detriment:

Erickson and Schultz … analyzed criticisms of African-American employees in American companies. Even though their production schedules met or exceeded those of employees from European-based ethnic groups, their employers described them as 'lazy' workers. Erickson and Schultz established that this judgement was based upon the very subjective impression their employers had formed on the basis of their posture. These African-American employees who were working on a production line used a relaxed stance and moved with casual, swinging motions as compared with members of ethnic groups who stood with a more rigid posture between actions and then when they moved did so with highly focused, direct and energetic movements. (p. 202)

This is a good example of how myths and uncritical assumptions about language and communication can lead to highly problematic consequences, not least in terms of discrimination and oppression. Of course, many other examples of cultural differences in nonverbal communication could be given. Consider, for example, the view that Italians are passionate people. How much of this derives from their characteristic use of body language? Indeed, cultural stereotyping can be seen to owe much to the way in which we attach meaning to particular forms of body language.

Voice of experience 4.3

❝I take the anti-racism part of my work very seriously, but it can be hard work at times. The young people's heads are so full of stereotypes, and they pick up so quickly on any subtle differences they see in people's physical presentation. I have to keep challenging, gently and constructively, but firmly. It doesn't take much for them to latch on to cultural differences and try to use them against people. I have my work cut out when it comes to teaching them about valuing diversity.**❞** *Albie, a youth worker*

It is unfortunate that nonverbal communication is often treated in an uncritical and oversimplified way. For example, it is not uncommon for statements to be made to the effect that 90 per cent of communication is nonverbal. As Scollon and Scollon (2001) point out, this is an absurd notion, as we have no reliable way of quantifying communication. It is therefore meaningless to state that 90 per cent of communication is nonverbal – a much more sophisticated understanding is called for. However, while it is indeed absurd to attach percentages to aspects of communication, we can, none the less, recognize that nonverbal communication is more powerful than verbal communication. By this, I mean that, where a statement is made verbally which is contradicted by the accompanying body language, it is generally the body language which is given credence. For example, if someone says, 'Yes, I'm fine', but their body language indicates that they are far from fine, then clearly it is the body language that we will pay attention to. It is for this reason that people who wish to practise lies and deception have to be able to control their body language if they wish to be effective and, indeed, recognizing nonverbal communication which is inconsistent with the verbal message is a common way of discovering that somebody is not telling the truth.

Of course, learning how to use our own body language and to read other people's nonverbal communications is part and parcel of growing up. From a very early age, we learn how to pick up on other people's signals and to give signals ourselves. In this respect, there seems little mileage in teaching people how to use body language when it is part of our everyday interactions. However, when it comes to using nonverbal communication in the people professions (the helping professions of social work and social care; nursing and other health care roles; counselling and psychotherapy; youth and community work; probation and youth justice work; advice work and pastoral care; mediation; and so on, plus the world of management, supervision, leadership and human resources), there is much to be gained from learning how to use body language at an advanced level. Indeed, much of the success of professional practice can be seen to owe a great deal to the ability of practitioners to be able to use nonverbal communication at an advanced level. For example, a counsellor who is able to calm and soothe an agitated person and a manager who is able to motivate and stimulate a group of staff are both likely to be drawing heavily on their advanced levels of ability in nonverbal communication.

PRACTICE FOCUS 4.6

Pam knew that the team meeting was going to be a stormy one after the previous week's events where there had been considerable tension that came very close to overflowing. She was also fully aware that it was her responsibility to make sure that the meeting was a constructive and positive one. In order to do so, she knew she would have to draw on what she had learned about the effective use of body language when she undertook her professional training. After a difficult but successful meeting she was delighted that her advanced use of nonverbal communication had played a key part in establishing her leadership role in the meeting and had thus helped her to handle a very difficult situation. She had managed to use body language to supplement and reinforce her message that she was in control. She was very glad that she had taken on board the important messages about the need to continue to develop our understanding and use of body language if we are to maximize our effectiveness in interpersonal encounters.

Conclusion

Of course, a significant component of our day-to-day lives is based on social interaction with others. When we consider that a significant proportion of that interaction takes place through speech and conversation, then we can begin to realize just how important these are as the basis of communication. When we also recognize that so many occupations rely on effective verbal communication for their success, then we can begin to realize that the skills involved in the effective use of speech, paralanguage and body language are paramount. Without a high level of competency in the use of the spoken word, it is highly unlikely that anyone will be able to achieve a significant degree of success in any occupation which involves working with people, their problems and their challenges.

This applies across the board regardless of the specific professional setting or context. Indeed, wherever people come together to do business – whether literally or metaphorically – much will depend on the ability of the participants to communicate effectively, both verbally and nonverbally. This chapter has set the scene by examining some of the key aspects of the knowledge base, although it must be recognized that this is only a small proportion of the huge knowledge base available to us. This chapter therefore paves the way for Chapter 6, where we shall explore some of the practical implications of communicating with people through interpersonal interactions in general and Chapters 7, 8 and 9 where we focus on specific aspects of such interactions.

One important thing that this chapter should have alerted us to is the danger of 'resting on our laurels'. The vast majority of people manage to achieve a high level of skill in the arts of speech and conversation. Indeed, many of the people who read this book will be highly skilled communicators when it comes to speech and conversation. However, none of us will be perfect in this regard. We will all have our weak points as well as our strengths, our debits as well as our credits. What is needed, then, is an attitude of mind informed by a commitment to continuous professional development. These are such complex, subtle and far-reaching issues that no one person can realistically hope to learn all that there is to learn or leave no room whatsoever for improvement. The remaining chapters should play a part in identifying areas for further development so that we can continue to learn over time about the fascinating world of communication – and, in particular, how to ensure that it is *effective* communication.

One important set of skills which is very much part of all this are those associated with 'reading the context' of communication – recognizing and dealing with the rich tapestry of contextual factors that have a bearing on communication and the use of language. It is to these very contextual factors, or a selection of them at least, that Chapter 5 is devoted.

POINTS TO PONDER

- What do you see as the key learning points from this chapter?
- What difference might your new understanding make to your practice?
- Has this chapter identified any additional learning needs for you in relation to this subject matter? If so, what are these and how might you try and address these needs?

Context and meaning

Introduction

One of the recurring themes in what has been covered so far in this book has been the importance of meaning, what Fiske (1990) refers to as the 'dynamic interaction between reader and message' (p. 145). The theme of meaning continues to be an important one in this chapter also. This is because a major focus of the chapter is that of the context of communication and, of course, meaning owes much to the context. As Fiske (1990) comments:

> Reading is not akin to using a can opener to reveal the meaning in the message. Meanings are produced in the interactions between text and audience. Meaning production is a dynamic act in which both elements contribute equally. (p. 164)

In this passage, Fiske is using the term text to refer to any body of language whether written or spoken. In this sense, text is being used to refer to anything which can be 'read' in a metaphorical as well as literal sense. Burr (2003) explains this usage as follows:

> anything that can be 'read' for meaning can be thought of as being a manifestation of one or more discourses and can be referred to as a 'text'. Buildings may 'speak' of civic pride, like the town halls and factories of the industrial revolution or of a yearning for the past as in the current trend for 'vernacular' building. Clothes and uniforms may suggest class position, status, gender, age or subculture and as such can be called texts. Given that there is virtually no aspect of human life that is exempt from meaning, everything around us can be considered as 'textual', and 'life as text' could be said to be the underlying metaphor here. (pp. 66–7)

Meaning, then, emerges from interactions and is therefore closely linked to the idea of the context in which communication takes place. This chapter cannot realistically cover all aspects of the context of communication. Even a whole book would fail to cover adequately the range and depth of this vast topic. I shall therefore be restricting myself to a number of what I see as key aspects. Building on my earlier work (Thompson, 2006a; 2011) I shall concentrate on three separate but interrelated levels: personal, cultural and structural. This threefold approach is similar to that taken by Rubinstein (2001) in which he divides social life into three main dimensions: agency, culture and structure.

Rubinstein argues that many attempts to develop sociological understanding have been flawed because they have adopted what he describes as an 'additive' approach to culture and structure. That is, they have presented these two domains (the cultural domain of shared meanings and the structural domain of power relations and life chances) as two separate areas without taking account of their interpenetration – the dialectical relationship through which they influence and shape one another. Rubinstein therefore proposes a 'synthetic' approach – one which takes account of the process through which:

> these two components of action can be conceived to reveal how they shape or 'mutually constitute' one another. Highlighting this process should facilitate research on how it happens – that is, how ordinary actors synthesize culture and structure in their everyday lives. (2001, p. x)

Space does not permit a detailed analysis of these theoretical issues, but the point I wish to emphasize is that we should not make the mistake of seeing the three levels of the personal, cultural and structural as entirely separate domains in a static 'snapshot' of social action, but rather as a dynamic process of interaction between and across the three levels. They form a complex, dynamic web of interactions which play such an important role in setting the context for human interactions and thus for communication and language.

In relation to the personal level, I shall comment on the significance of identity and also on the role played by emotion. In relation to the cultural level, I shall examine some key issues relating to the social construction of communication and the processes of meaning making. The structural level is concerned with social divisions – that is, the way society is organized into its component parts, classified under such headings as class, race and gender and the ways in which power and life chances ('the array of costs and benefits', as Rubinstein, 2001, p. ix, calls them) are distributed in line with such divisions. For present purposes, I shall concentrate in particular on gender. Finally, I shall address the thorny but significant question of 'political correctness'. These are all key elements of the context in which communication takes place and therefore play an important part in shaping the meanings that are attributed to the messages we seek to convey and to those we receive.

Underpinning these discussions will be, once again, the theme of power for, as Kress (2001) puts it, 'power is at play in all linguistic (inter)action' (p. 35). Similarly, Woodward (1997) argues that:

> All signifying practices that produce meaning involve relations of power, including the power to define who is included and who is excluded. Culture

shapes identity through giving meaning to experience, making it possible to opt for one mode of subjectivity ... amongst others available. However, we are constrained, not only by the range of possibilities which culture offers – that is, by the variety of symbolic representations – but also by social relations. (p. 15)

By 'signifying practices' Woodward means those aspects of social interaction through which meaning is conveyed or generated. This is consistent with the discipline of cultural studies which places emphasis on the intersection of language, meaning and power (Barker and Galasinski, 2001).

Identity and emotion

The point has previously been made that language is recognized as the most salient aspect of ethnicity and, of course, ethnicity is a significant aspect of identity. We have also noted that identity can be seen to be constructed through social interactions (and therefore fluid and changing), rather than being a fixed entity. Once we begin to see identity as being linked to social interaction, we are of course also involving communication and language. Communication and language therefore play a key role in constructing and maintaining a sense of identity. If we did not communicate with others, how would we sustain a coherent sense of who we are?

The other side of the coin involves recognizing that identity also influences communication and language, in the sense that the identities of the participants within a social interaction will play an important part in setting the context for whatever communication takes place. For example, in considering the participants within a conversation, we need to address such questions as:

- Who are they?
- How do they see themselves?
- How do they see each other?
- Are there any discrepancies between how they perceive themselves and how they are perceived by the other party or parties in the interaction?

Such discrepancies can, of course, lead to significant communication breakdowns. For example, if a person perceives him- or herself as a leader within a particular group, but this is not a perception shared by the other members of the group, then we can realistically expect significant communication difficulties to occur within the interactions – not to mention significant conflicts.

Although identity is generally seen as a very personal matter – it is, after all, what makes us unique individuals – we should also recognize that there are close links between identity and the wider levels of the cultural and structural

---

PRACTICE FOCUS 5.1

The meeting was convened to look at how the various professionals involved could work together to develop the new project. Sue knew that her role as chair would be difficult because of the differing backgrounds of the participants. However, she had not realized just how different people's perspectives on the project would be and how much work she would have to do to lay the foundations for so many different people to work in partnership. It became clear to her that people brought with them their own 'baggage' in terms of their respective professional identities and that this had a significant impact on how they perceived the project, how they perceived each other's roles and respective contributions and therefore how they communicated with one another.

---

dimensions of social life. Of course, it is easy to recognize that an individual's identity owes much to the cultural context in which he or she was brought up and in which he or she now operates. Similarly, structural factors can also be seen to have a significant bearing on identity formation. Consider, for example, the influence of class and gender on our sense of who we are as we grow up.

Class influences can be seen to apply at two levels: objective and subjective. By objective, I mean class-related factors, such as income and socioeconomic standing more broadly. A person's class position will therefore have a significant influence on his or her life as a result of the constraints and opportunities afforded by belonging to a particular socioeconomic group. For example, poverty will make certain opportunities unavailable, while those not living in poverty are likely to have a much wider range of opportunities. By subjective I mean the factors that relate to how we interpret or make sense of our experience. That is, while members of the same family may objectively share the same class position, each may interpret it differently. For example, one family member may regard the family's low socioeconomic position as an indication that there is little point in aspiring to a more affluent lifestyle and will therefore resign him- or herself to remaining in that class, while another member of the same family may look upon his or her class position as a source of motivation and thus draw upon it as a basis for seeking to make progress through education or other such opportunities for social mobility. Similarly, one member of a family may feel a degree of shame or stigma as a result of low socioeconomic position while another member of the same family feels intensely proud of their solid working-class roots.

Similarly, gender can be seen to be experienced at two levels – objective and subjective. Due to the 'gendered' nature of the society in which we live, we will tend to be treated differentially in certain ways as men or women, whether we like it or not. That is, people will commonly make assumptions

ACTIVITY 5.1

What do you see as your own class position? How might this affect the way you communicate with people (i) from the same class background; and (ii) a different one? What lessons might we learn from this when it comes to trying to achieve optimal levels of effective communication?

about us along the lines of gender stereotypes (the cultural level of shared meanings) and there will be differences in terms of access to power and opportunities depending on our sex (the structural level). At a subjective level, our gender, and the expectations and social patterns that accompany it, will be something that we can either:

- *fully embrace* – adhering as closely as possible to cultural messages about femininity or masculinity;
- *fully reject* – deliberately moving away from such cultural expectations as far as possible (what is often referred to as 'gender-bending'); or
- *accommodate ourselves to* – somewhere along a very broad continuum between those two extremes.

That is, how we *experience* our gender will also be a factor in influencing our identity as it develops over time.

I have chosen class and gender as examples of structural factors, but of course much the same could be said of other structural aspects, such as race and ethnicity.

Voice of experience 5.1

"Identity is a topic you can't really get away from when you work with teenagers. Experimenting with who you are is all part of what it is all about, I suppose. It makes what I do challenging at times, but interesting too.**"**
James, a foster carer

A further important part of the personal level which is also, at least indirectly, related to identity is that of emotion. It is important to recognize that the relationship between language and communication on the one hand, and emotion on the other, is extremely complex. This can be seen to apply in at least three ways:

- *Language 'causes' emotion* Consider, for example, how often emotions arise as a result of something that has been said. For example, if a person becomes angry, this may be because of something that another party has done, but it is just as likely to be as a result of something that another party has said. Another example would be poetry and the way in which a poem can evoke a wide range of emotional responses.

- *Language conveys emotion* We have developed very subtle and effective means of conveying emotion through language. The vocabulary of emotion is a very rich and wide-ranging one, being capable of quite nuanced expression.
- *Language can be shaped by emotion* The language forms a person will use will generally owe a great deal to the emotional state of that person and, similarly, the response he or she receives is likely to be shaped in part at least by that emotion.

Emotion can also be seen to be closely linked to gender and therefore to identity. It is generally widely recognized that men and women tend to deal with emotions differently, although this is a subject that is often oversimplified. However, despite these oversimplifications, there are significant patterns that can be identified in relation to emotion and gender. Seidler (1998) makes apt comment in this regard. His comments are extensive but they are worth reproducing in full:

> But men often grow up to think that it is only necessary to give time and attention to a relationship when it is breaking down or when there is some 'problem'. Since they think of themselves as independent and self-sufficient, it can be difficult for them to recognize the emotional needs their partners have. Rather than listen to what they have to say, men often assume that it is their task to offer 'solutions', since often this reflects the ways that men learn to deal with their own emotional lives. Men can feel that women are being *irrational* and *ungrateful* in refusing the help they are willing to give. It can be difficult for them to recognize that their partners want something different, sometimes just the chance to be listened to without offering solutions. So it is that men and women can be talking across each other, since they have often learnt to relate to language in different ways. But when it is men's power and control that is being challenged men often resort to an emotional withholding, refusing to share more of what is going on for them until the woman 'sees reason', or else responding violently. (p. 197)

How we 'do emotion work' will feature as a significant aspect of both our own identity and the social interactions on which this is based. Indeed, we can see that emotions are a very significant aspect of the context in which communication takes place. It is easy to see how emotions such as anger, sadness, joy, disgust and shame can influence how we seek to communicate with other people and how we interpret and respond to their communications. Space does not permit a detailed analysis of the role of emotion in contextualizing communication, but it should be clear that any serious detailed study of the context of communication will need to take account of emotion (see the discussion of emotional intelligence in Chapter 6).

PRACTICE FOCUS 5.2

Phil had only been with the team for about six months when significant conflicts arose and it became clear that all was not well. He had a number of dissatisfactions, mainly of a minor nature but, when added together, they amounted to quite a lot. However, Phil did not raise his concerns directly with anyone, a fact that led to considerable tension and resentment, resulting in a very strained atmosphere. Phil's line manager had to take him on one side to try to find out what was wrong, at which point a flood of dissatisfactions came forth. Phil therefore had to be given a very clear message that he had to raise concerns as and when they arose, rather than allow them to build up and spoil the team atmosphere. He acknowledged that he had always found it difficult to express his feelings but he accepted the need to do so for the sake of harmonious working relationships.

Culture and meaning

Culture is the second of the three levels of social reality that I have indicated to be particularly important. What makes culture so important and so interesting is that it is socially constructed. By this I mean that a culture is a set of shared meanings, assumptions and understandings which have developed historically in a given community (a geographical community or a community of interest – for example, a professional community). Cultures are not genetically transmitted from one generation to the next. They exist only through the fact that they are communicated – that is, the shared meanings which constitute a culture are manifested in day-to-day actions and interactions within that culture. In acting in accordance with a cultural norm, I am not only allowing the culture to influence my behaviour, I am also making the abstract cultural norm a concrete reality through my actions. It is in this sense that culture exists and is reproduced through communication and social interactions.

This is closely related to the idea of a discourse – that is, a set of meanings and practices which not only reflect reality, but also actually constitute that reality:

> Foucault uses the term 'discourse' to refer to the way in which language and other forms of communication act as the vehicle of social processes (see Foucault, 1977; 1979). For example, medical discourse not only reflects the power of the medical profession but actively contributes to constructing, re-enacting and thus perpetuating such power. (Thompson, 2006a, p. 32)

Scollon and Scollon (2001) also emphasize the importance of meaning in terms of culture and discourse. 'The meanings are interpreted within a cultural envelope created by the discourse system from which a person speaks' (p. 241).

The concept of habitus introduced earlier is also a very relevant one here. In discussing the cultural storehouse of habitus, Bourdieu (1991) argues that an important element of this habitus is the 'set of rules' which govern who can speak when, whether or not they will be paid any attention and whether the points they make will be seen as being of value or even legitimate. In other words, Bourdieu sees unwritten rules about linguistic and communicative behaviour as being part and parcel of a habitus. Although Rosengren (2000) does not use the term 'habitus', he is on very similar territory when he talks of a culture as a reservoir of meaning:

> human societal culture is a great reservoir of meaning, which is constantly being drawn upon when human beings communicate and interact – within generations and between generations. This reservoir of meaning defines an important difference between animal and human communication. A defining feature of human culture is that it is a product of the human brain. But conceptualized in terms of communication, it is as if it should exist also *between* human brains. Culture lives when meaningfully communicated. (pp. 58–9)

Culture, then, is clearly a very powerful factor when it comes to communication, as it provides this reservoir of meaning from which we make sense of our day-to-day communicative interactions. However, Kendall and Wickham (2001) go a step further when they write of culture in terms of a set of ways in which people order the world and, interestingly, a set of ways in which the world orders people. What they mean by this is that, while our day-to-day actions and interactions contribute towards maintaining and reproducing cultural norms and assumptions and so on, our actions and interactions are also largely constrained and/or shaped by the cultural context in which they occur. If culture helps us to make sense of the world we live in, then clearly it is a very powerful influence in shaping our thinking and behaviour. Culture therefore plays an important role in maintaining social order. As such, it is a fundamental part of social life. When we consider that language can be seen as the basis of culture (Guirdham, 1999), then we can see that language also plays a role in contributing to the social order. Indeed, this is highly consistent with Foucault's notion of discourse and its role in regulating society. We therefore have to recognize that when we see culture as a set of shared meanings, assumptions and norms, we are thereby attributing an extremely important role to culture in terms of both the macro level of the social order and the micro level of day-to-day communicative interactions.

PRACTICE FOCUS 5.3

Stephanie had been very pleased to be offered the job, as she had been very impressed by the organization in general and the team of staff in particular when she had been interviewed. Accepting the post meant moving 120 miles from home but she felt that this was worth the upheaval for such a good job. While she was not to be disappointed by the job, she found moving to a new area very demanding. This was because the local culture was just so different from what she had been used to. She had to get used to a lot of new local words and a lot of new customs as well. Even though she was still in the same country, it did not seem like it, such was the change of culture she had to adjust to.

In keeping with Rubinstein's (2001) notion of a synthetic rather than additive approach to these issues, it is worth revisiting the subject of emotion which we earlier discussed under the heading of the personal level. We can now reconsider emotion under the heading of the cultural level, as emotion is clearly also a matter of culture. Gergen (1999) describes emotion as a 'cultural construction':

> That is, we may understand emotion not as a feature of our biological make-up, a constitutional urge that drives our actions, but as a component of cultural life. The work of cultural anthropologists helps us to appreciate this possibility and its many implications. (p. 109)

He goes on to provide three examples of what he means by this:

1. There are enormous cultural variations in how emotions are expressed – cultures do not necessarily have the same 'rules' for emotional expression.
2. It is difficult to establish cross-cultural translations of key concepts – does a smile mean exactly the same in one culture as it does in another?
3. Emotions are culturally constituted – they can be seen as 'cultural performances', defined within specific cultural parameters rather than (or as well as) internal states.

This is a very different approach to the study of emotion from traditional, psychologically based accounts. However, it is an approach that is now receiving increasing attention (see, for example, Fischer, 2000; Williams, 2001). It is also an approach that has significant implications for professional practice, in so far as attempts to respond appropriately to emotional issues that do not take account of the cultural aspects may turn out to be very inappropriate.

In what ways do you feel emotions affect your efforts to communicate effectively? Discuss this idea with colleagues and see what, together, you can learn about the significance of emotion in shaping interactions between people.

Structure and social divisions

Society, of course, is not a level playing field. We can see that it is based on what are known as social divisions, such as class, race, gender, age, disability, sexuality and so on. A person's life chances (and therefore his or her power) will owe much to where he or she is located in terms of this hierarchy of social divisions. For example, as we noted earlier, class has a major influence in terms of income and financial security and therefore distributes life chances to people on a very unequal basis according to their position within the class structure. The study of social structure and social divisions is a huge topic in its own right, and so we have to be selective in order to tackle structural issues in relation to communication and language. For this reason, I am going to focus here specifically on the social division of gender – that is, the processes through which life chances are allocated on a differential basis to men and women.

The relationship between gender and language is once again a complex one. However, what is clear is that there is a large and growing body of evidence which strongly suggests that not only do men and women tend to use language differently, they are also treated differently in language. Let us consider both of these aspects in turn.

The argument that men and women tend to use language differently dates back to the the work of Tannen (1990). She used her own empirical research to argue that women tend to use language on a more co-operative basis – that is, they are concerned with what she refers to as 'connectedness'. Men, by contrast, tend to focus on using language as a means of gaining status or establishing territory. In other words, women's use of language tends to concentrate on co-operation while men's use of language is more geared towards competition. Uchida (1998) reports on similar findings:

> Relying on studies of children's interactions through play in same-sex peer groups, Maltz and Borker contended that American girls and boys differ in the following aspects in the way they use language: Girls learn to create and maintain relationships of closeness and equality, to criticize others in acceptable ways, and to interpret accurately the speech of other girls (1982: 205), whereas boys learn to assert one's position of dominance, to attract and maintain an audience, and to assert oneself when others have the floor

(1982: 207). This shows a pattern similar to that suggested by Gilligan's (1982) work on sex differences in moral development. Indeed, more recent analyses of children's and adolescents' talk with same-sex friends also show sex differences consistent with these patterns. (pp. 281–2)

What we have to remember is that research is rarely, if ever, definitive and such studies also have to be seen in the context of ethnic differences. That is, while these studies may show systematic patterns of different language usage between men and women in particular cultures, we cannot assume that this is therefore a universal pattern. However, there does seem to be sufficient evidence to support the point that men and women tend to use language in different ways in certain cultures at least. The idea that men and women are treated differently in language is also an important point. While feminist scholarship has drawn our attention to the 'invisibility' of women (that is, the tendency for women's contributions to be undervalued or even to go unnoticed altogether), Cameron (1998a) writes of women's silence rather than invisibility. She points out that, in those linguistic registers which are most highly valued in society (religious, political, legal, scientific and poetic) women's voices are rarely, if ever, heard. It can be argued that the situation arises partly because women are often excluded from arenas of power, and therefore have little opportunity to contribute to such discourses and partly by the point that even where women are present, their voices will often go unheard.

PRACTICE FOCUS 5.4

Lin had to do a project as part of her college course. She decided that she would study the role of the mass media in modern society. She had not intended to focus on gender issues. However, the lack of women's voices in the media was something that came to her attention very early on in her preparations for her project. She was amazed that this was so striking, and yet she had never noticed it before. She raised the topic with her tutor who explained to her that it is not uncommon for people to fail to realize just how male dominated the media are. In fact, the tutor argued, it is partly because the media are so male dominated that we have learned to take for granted the relative absence of women's voices in the public sphere.

In recent years, much attention has been given to what has come to be known as sexist language. As we shall note below, this is a topic that has tended to become grossly oversimplified. However, the argument that language usage has significant gender implications is a powerful and realistic one; for example, I have often used the following exercise on training courses with very positive effect in terms of raising people's awareness of the significance of language and gender. First, I ask the group to identify words which are used in a positive way to refer to men who seek as much sexual experience as possible. The group will then very quickly produce a list of these, usually starting with such words as 'stud'. I then ask them to identify negative terms that would refer to a man who seeks as much sexual experience as possible – that is, terms which would be used to disapprove of such behaviour. At this point, the group begin to struggle and generally find it difficult to identify such terms. I then ask the group to switch genders. That is, I ask them to identify positive terms which can be used to refer to a woman who seeks the maximum sexual experience. Again, the group is likely to find this very difficult and may not be able to come up with any at all. Finally, I ask the group to identify any negative or disapproving words for women who seek as much sexual experience as possible and, of course, the group very quickly comes up with a long list of often offensive terms.

The point of this exercise is to show that the English language is not neutral in terms of how it treats gender. The existence of certain terms within our vocabulary and the absence of certain others is highly significant in showing that the language is 'loaded' in terms of the assumptions about gender which it carries. The exercise also helps to get across the point of the extent to which language use is a cultural matter – that is, so much of the language that we use reflects the assumptions and 'unwritten rules' of the culture in which we have been brought up.

Voice of experience 5.2

❝I was in my forties before people started referring to me as a woman. You get so used to grown women being called 'girls' that most people don't even notice the significance of it. And when you object to it, people start accusing you of 'political correctness' – whatever that is supposed to mean!**❞** *Donna, a disability adviser*

An even more telling and more worrying example of this is to be found in the work of Cameron (1998a). She writes about the ways in which newspapers report rape and quotes the following two examples:

The first comes from a 'quality' newspaper, *The Daily Telegraph*, the second from a popular tabloid, *The Sun*. I reproduce them both to show that we are not dealing with the idiosyncrasies of a single journalist or newspaper but with an institutionalized set of conventions.

A man who suffered head injuries when attacked by two men who broke into his home in Beckenham, Kent, early yesterday, was pinned down on the bed by intruders who took it in turns to rape his wife. (*Daily Telegraph*)

A terrified 19-stone husband was forced to lie next to his wife as two men raped her yesterday. (*Sun*)

My interpretation of what is happening in these reports is that the act of rape is being represented as a crime against a man rather than a woman. Rape was originally synonymous with theft: to rape a woman was to rob her father or husband of her value by rendering her unchaste – hence the fact that a man who raped a virgin might be compelled to marry her as a punishment. (pp. 11–12)

While this is perhaps an extreme example in some respects, it is none the less a very real one. In addition, we can find numerous day-to-day examples which also support the view that language presents reality as 'a man's world'. As we have already noted, language constructs reality and that reality is generally constructed as a male one. Consider, for example, the work of Rosengren (2000), an author who writes very insightfully about communication, but even he falls into the trap of (perhaps unwittingly) using language as a means of reinforcing male dominance when he comments that 'language is *man's* most important tool of communication' (p. 30, emphasis added).

PRACTICE FOCUS 5.5

Jenny had not long taken up her first post on the managerial ladder when she was asked to attend a conference on 'Management in the Twenty-First Century'. She travelled down to the conference not really knowing what to expect but looking forward to learning more about management. Over the three days of the conference she did indeed learn a lot. However, what struck her most forcibly was the number of men there. She was used to working in settings where women were in the majority, but she started to realize now that the world of management power is predominantly a man's world. She was not naive enough to expect a gender balance at a management conference but the sheer weight of male numbers did bring home to her quite forcibly just how male-dominated the world of management is. She also noticed how the language used also reflected the preponderance of men and wondered how she would cope in such a masculine world. (from Thompson, 2011)

The fact of male bias in language is further demonstrated by the following passage from Glastonbury (1992) when he makes the very telling comment that:

we need go no further than the word processor on which this paper was written. The thesaurus has a quaint line in ethnic and gender 'neutrality'.

'Black' is described amongst other things as 'evil, nefarious, wicked'; 'white' as 'pure, spotless, undefiled'. 'Man' is 'humanity, chap, guy'; 'woman' is 'handmaiden, housekeeper, maid'. (p. 21, cited in Bates, 1995, p. 71)

As Glastonbury's comments show, it is not only in relation to gender that language manifests a bias. Such bias can be seen to reflect power relations more broadly, including class, race, ethnicity and other such structural factors, rather than gender alone.

We are here clearly dealing with some very complex issues. In some respects, what we are seeing is a battle over meaning. In the latter part of the twentieth century, feminist scholars and activists began to challenge the male dominance implicit in the use of language, reflecting Volosinov's view that meanings are always the result of ideological struggles (Schirato and Yell, 2000, p. 26). As we shall note below in relation to the subject of political correctness, these struggles have not always been successful. However, it is none the less important to note the problems associated with the sexism inherent in language, for as Doyle (1998) argues, sexist language can be seen as a poor form of communication:

> If our language leads to misunderstandings or offends people we are trying to reach, it fails to do what we want it to do; it ceases to be an effective tool for communication. Language that is sexist has this effect. (p. 149)

ACTIVITY 5.3

How might *your* gender affect the way you communicate (i) with people of the same gender; and (ii) people of the opposite gender? Consider this in relation to yourself, but also watch out for significant differences in terms of how men and women communicate within and across gender boundaries. Try to identify what these gender patterns might mean for your own communication efforts.

Political correctness

Wise (1995) argues that political correctness has become 'a catch-all and derisory term used to discredit all positive action against oppression' (p. 106). That is, political correctness has come to be used as a device which has the effect of distracting attention from important issues, resulting in their being trivialized. As attempts have been made to challenge the discrimination and inequality inherent in many forms of language use, it has unfortunately become the case that many such attempts have become counterproductive. For example, Penketh (2000) writes of the 'sometimes ludicrous excesses' of politically correct attempts to amend language use, such as the banning of asking for a black coffee (we shall examine when it is likely to be appropriate and when not to use the term *black* in Chapter 6). As a result of the oversimplifications of political correctness, genuine efforts to challenge the use of language to perpetuate discrimination and inequality have been undermined or even ridiculed (see Thompson, 2007).

Despite these problems, we should none the less recognize the significant power of language. While the excesses of political correctness fall at one destructive extreme of a continuum, at the opposite destructive extreme is the view that language is not important, that we can use it as we see fit without worrying about discrimination or oppression. In between these two unhelpful extremes, lies a promising and positive way forward built on the notion of 'linguistic sensitivity'. By this term, I mean the ability to recognize the power of language and in what circumstances such power can be abused or misused in reinforcing or establishing patterns of inequality and discrimination. Soydan and Williams (1998) argue that the choice of terminology is necessarily a political matter:

> The construction of language and the selection of terminology is necessarily political. Common language in use reflects a world view and in itself can reproduce relations of dominance and subordination (Noel 1994). Language is a key medium through which dominating groups reinforce their superiority and prescribe the inferior status of minority groups. There has, for example, been considerable debate on the use of labels such as 'black' people, 'coloured' people, 'people of colour' in reference to ethnic minority groups and it is clear that the acceptability of labels depends on the speaker and who owns the terminology and the agenda for communication. For example, black people in Britain have claimed the word 'black' as a political term to demarcate a collective position and rejected the term 'coloured' as the language used by the dominating group to describe them. (p. 17)

An example of the political significance of choice of terminology can be found in the history of Australia. Kress (2001) describes the contentious issue of whether those people who arrived from Britain in Australia after 1788 should be referred to as settlers or invaders. Clearly, the first term implies that the arrival of the British was an innocuous event which did not have detrimental consequences for the already existing inhabitants, while the latter term implies that their arrival was an unwelcome one which caused significant problems. Whether we choose the former term or the latter will clearly depend on our political views about that particular historical event. Nelson (1997) gives a similar example when he argues that the choice of names for countries and other locations can be highly significant in political terms. In his discussion of map making and the history of place names, he gives several examples of struggles to assert power through the use of a particular form of terminology:

A nation's identity is wrapped up in its place-names which mark the presence and history of a people. Not every national boundary is like the Red Sea, geographically fixed. Hundreds are disputed, each one triggering cartographic duels between mapmakers. Japanese maps show old Japanese names for some of the Kurile Islands, now occupied and claimed by Russia, whose maps, of course, show Russian names.

Is it Ivory Coast or Côte d'Ivoire? Burma or Myanmar? Governments disagree and international maps are inconsistent. 'Happy the land that has a name truly related to its history, euphonious and easy in use, unambiguous, and giving offence to none,' writes C. M. Matthews, whose *Place Names of the English-Speaking World* is a standard reference in the field. (pp. 4–5)

Language is therefore clearly a political matter, although, of course, that in itself does not justify a political correctness approach.

One of the main failings of the oversimplified political correctness approach to these issues is that it has not taken account of the need to change meanings rather than simply words. Its proponents have failed to take on board the subtlety and sophistication of language and communication and have thus relied on the naive assumption that promoting forms of language more consistent with equality and diversity is simply a matter of banning certain words and using certain others in their place. As Cameron (1998b) puts it:

The crucial aspect of language is meaning: the point of non-sexist language is not to change the forms of words for the sake of it but to change the repertoire of meanings a language conveys. It's about redefining rather than merely renaming the world – a point which many current guideline writers seem to grasp imperfectly if at all. (p. 161)

In the same paper she argues that it is important to explain to people the rationale as to why their particular use of language needs to change. Unless it is explained to speakers what is problematic about a particular usage, it is unlikely that they will appreciate the need for change, but very likely that they will dismiss the whole enterprise as 'political correctness nonsense'. This is why Chapter 6 will include discussion of strategies that can be used to help promote forms of language which do not reinforce discrimination and oppression.

An example of the lack of understanding of the subtleties and complexities of linguistic sensitivity was to be found in *The Independent* newspaper on 6 June 2000 when the case of a job centre manager banning a job advertisement was reported. He deemed the advertisement inappropriate because he felt that the terms 'hardworking' and 'enthusiastic' were discriminatory against people with disabilities. The then Secretary of State for Education and Employment, David Blunkett, intervened personally and asked the Employment Service to 'ensure that this sort of nonsense does not happen again'.

So far, I have made reference to discriminatory language use primarily in relation to gender and to a lesser extent, race. However, we should note that language can be used to construct or reinforce discrimination against any social group. For example, Coupland and Jaworski (2001) make an important point when they argue that:

> In our own studies of how discourse constructs identities for people of different ages, we argued that 'Tracking the social construction and reproduction of old age through talk seems an effective research orientation for demonstrating that "elderliness" is a collective subjectivity as much as a biological or biographical end-point' (Coupland et al. 1991, p. 207). (p. 141)

That is, old age is socially constructed (largely through language use) and is not simply a biological life stage (Sue Thompson, 2005). The term 'the elderly' refers to a large heterogeneous group of people covering an age span of 50 or more years. It is therefore a very misleading item of terminology. It is also part of a much broader ageist discourse which constructs older people as 'past it' or 'a burden on society'. It does not take a detailed analysis of the language that is used to refer to older people to realize that it is predominantly very discriminatory, based predominantly on negative stereotypes. This is a subject to which we shall return in Chapter 6 where we explore the practicalities of interpersonal interactions.

Voice of experience 5.3

❝It really annoys me when people use patronizing language when they are talking about older people. They just don't seem to realize how inappropriate it is to use that sort of language. I'm sure they would hate to be called an 'old dear' when they get to that age.**❞** *Ruby, the manager of a nursing home for older people*

What is needed, then, is not a simplistic political correctness approach which develops a taboo list of words. Rather, we need a more sophisticated approach based on linguistic sensitivity, the ability to identify which forms of language use are potentially or actually problematic in terms of reinforcing discrimination and oppression. I would argue that what we need in effect is a new cultural politics:

> Cultural politics concerns the writing of new stories with 'new languages' (or to be more exact, new configurations of old languages or new usages of old words) that embody values with which we concur and that we wish to be taken as true in the sense of a social agreement or commendation. Cultural politics centres on the struggle to define the world and make those definitions stick. Consequently, cultural politics concerns the multi-faceted

processes by which particular descriptions of the world are taken as true. This includes forms of cultural and institutional power so that cultural politics concerns both languages and policy. (Barker and Galasinski, 2001, p. 61)

PRACTICE FOCUS 5.6

Mike returned from a course on equality issues with a list of words that were deemed to be inappropriate and which should be avoided. At the next team meeting he was asked to feed back to the team about the course. He photocopied the list of terms to avoid and circulated these copies at the meeting. However, two of his colleagues were unhappy about being told what they could and could not say and therefore pressed Mike to explain why these particular words were held to be inappropriate. Mike was able to explain some of them, but not all. This situation caused a lot of bad feeling, as some members of the team felt it was patronizing to be told to avoid certain words without an explanation as to what was problematic about them being forthcoming. Mike wished that these issues had been raised at the training course and he was kicking himself now for uncritically accepting what was put forward by the trainer.

Conclusion

This chapter has argued that the context of communication is vitally important. In it I have demonstrated that there are a number of important issues relating to, at the personal level, identity and emotion. I have further pointed out that, at the cultural level, there are significant issues relating to the social construction and meaning making that is a day-to-day part of our social reality. As I see it, culture is not simply a backdrop to communication, but rather a central factor in shaping what happens in communicative interactions. I have also argued that it is important to understand how the structural level affects communication. In particular, I have examined how gender is an especially significant aspect of social structure and social divisions when it comes to communication in general and the use of language more specifically. This led into a discussion of political correctness where I was critical of oversimplified approaches. In its place we need a much more sophisticated approach based on the important notion of linguistic sensitivity. It is partly, but not exclusively, the task of Chapter 6 to make some progress in that regard, although we have to acknowledge that, realistically, this will not be enough to make the changes that are needed. However, it should be remembered that this is an introductory textbook and makes no claims to offer definitive solutions.

This chapter has reinforced many of the messages put forward in Chapters

1 and 2, particularly in terms of challenging simplistic models of communication which present it as a relatively simple process of passing messages between people and seeking to minimize the 'noise' that can act as a barrier to effectiveness. What we have seen is that communication goes to the heart of the social order. It is intricately intertwined with the various webs of cultural patterns, assumptions and meanings that characterize society, as well as the complex network of structural patterns which govern the distribution of power and life chances. Communication is very much an individual matter but, as we have seen, it is also very much a cultural and structural matter too.

POINTS TO PONDER

- What are the most important lessons to be learned from this chapter?
- In what ways might the cultural context influence how communication takes place and whether it is effective?
- What main implications does the cultural context have for your practice?

Practice

Introduction to Part II

Part I laid the foundations for our discussions in Part II. The explorations of theory in the first five chapters have provided a solid foundation for making sense of the complexities of using communication in practice contexts. A theme running through Part I has been the significance of communication – to spell it out explicitly: without effective communication we will not have effective practice.

We can take this a step further by arguing that effective communication is also an important part of promoting our own well-being. As Wiesmann (2003) argues:

> Our ability to create and sustain our social world depends in large measure on how well we communicate. People's social skills are crucial to their well-being – individually and collectively. The importance of understanding skilled behavior in all its complexities cannot be overstated. (cited in Hargie, 2006a, p. 1)

This, then, is our starting point. In exploring the practical aspects of effective communication to complement the theoretical aspects covered so far, we need to be aware just how important the issues are – how much there is to be gained by maximizing our knowledge and skills and how big a price there is to pay for getting it wrong.

Of course, discussing practice aspects of effective communication, as we shall be doing in the six chapters that form Part II, will be of little value in its own right. It will only be of benefit if it is part of a broader process of developing critically reflective practice (Thompson and Thompson, 2008). You should therefore not expect Part II simply to give you instructions on how to go about developing your communication skills. The situations you are likely to encounter in practice will often be very complex and demanding. Simple, formula approaches to such situations are likely to be far from adequate, and there is even a very real danger that they will be counterproductive – that is, doing more harm than good.

As we go through each of the chapters, you will be given the opportunity to reflect on how the ideas you encounter can cast light on the practice world – but you will need to do that reflecting yourself, to use the insights you gain to feed your own understanding and help you develop your own approach. It is not a matter of being taught *the* way to communicate effectively. Rather, it involves the more complex process of using the understanding gained as a foundation for developing your own (critically reflective) approach.

One final point to note is that it is important not to think in terms of 'getting the theory stuff out of the way' so that you can concentrate on the 'brass tacks' of real practice. 'Real' practice has to be based on understanding, so Part II should be seen as an extension of Part I, rather than a replacement for it. You may therefore find it helpful to refer back to the key issues discussed in Part I from time to time to ensure that you consolidate your learning across the whole book.

CHAPTER 6

Interpersonal encounters

Introduction

This chapter is not simply a set of prescriptions about how people should behave in interpersonal interactions, what language they should use or avoid, or what style of communication they should adopt. For one thing, the subject matter is far too complex for me to offer simple prescriptions for practice that would be of any real benefit and, for another, I feel it is far more beneficial for people to develop a raised level of awareness of the issues involved in inter-personal encounters. This raised level of awareness can then act as the basis of continuous learning in this area, rather than simply be a short sharp lesson in what to do and what not to do. My aim, then, is to facilitate learning at a much deeper level rather than simply issue a list of dos and don'ts. This is con-sistent with the concept of reflective practice (Thompson, 2000a) which is based on the notion that we do not become competent practitioners simply by 'applying theory to practice' but, rather, through a more complex and subtle process of integrating theory and practice or of *theorizing* practice – that is, drawing on a professional knowledge base to make sense of the practice situ-ations we find ourselves immersed in (Thompson, 2010). It is not a case of learning *either* from experience *or* from formal theory and research, but rather learning from the integration of the two – what does my experience tell me? What does the professional knowledge base tell me? What can I learn by com-bining the two?

Language is not the only factor in the success, or otherwise, of interper-sonal encounters. However, as we shall see below, it is clearly a very impor-tant one indeed. Czerniawska (1997) makes apt comment when she argues that:

> The benefits which can be realised from using language more effectively come from recognising the role it plays in communicating with customers and consciously making the most of the opportunities this provides. Most companies fail to exploit the resource simply because they do not see it as one: language is invisible to them and you cannot get a return on an asset you do not know you have. (p. 104)

This applies not only in the world of commercial companies, but also more broadly in public service work and, indeed, in any form of work which involves people coming together.

Many people will be familiar with neurolinguistic programming (or NLP for short) as an approach to understanding communication and interpersonal interactions. However, I shall not be drawing explicitly from that knowledge base in this chapter. This is because, as Knight (1995) indicates, much of what is involved in NLP is not new. In my view, the strength of NLP is that it brings together a number of elements into a relatively coherent whole. However, its weakness is that it overestimates a biological element within the multidisciplinary nature of communication and interaction. This is something I find quite problematic as a theoretical underpinning to practice. It is for this reason that I shall not be paying major attention to NLP as an explicit theory base, although some of the ideas presented within an NLP framework will feature in this chapter.

The remainder of the chapter is divided into four main sections. In the first, 'Setting the scene', we explore a number of contextual factors which could be seen to have a bearing on interpersonal encounters. The following section, headed 'Maximizing effectiveness', explores a number of issues which can be helpful in avoiding difficulties and seeking to ensure that communication achieves optimal levels in terms of successful outcomes. Next comes a section headed 'Avoiding discrimination', which builds on some of the ideas presented in Chapter 5 in relation to the dangers of adopting an oversimplified political correctness approach. The emphasis is on developing linguistic sensitivity without falling into the trap of a political correctness approach which can be destructive and counterproductive. Finally, we look at a small number of other issues which can play a part in determining the outcome of interpersonal encounters.

Setting the scene

There is much about interpersonal interactions which cannot be predicted or anticipated. There will be all sorts of unexpected twists, surprise developments and other such potential spanners in the works, such is the nature of personal and social interactions. However, despite the relative commonness of such unexpected developments, what we have to recognize is that so much of interpersonal communication can be predicted in advance. That is, there is much we can do to plan for making the most of our interpersonal encounters.

A major part of this planning revolves around answering the question: What is the context? For four words, this is a surprisingly big question, as the response can be a very long one indeed, involving not least the following six elements:

1. *Social*   The coming together of two or more people in a social interaction clearly has psychological implications for the people involved, given what we know about the complex workings of human psychology. However, what we also need to realize is that, even in small-scale micro-level interactions, wider social factors have a significant part to play. The coming together of people from different class groups, different genders, different racial or ethnic groups and so on, can play a major part in shaping the basis of the interactions between them. Even where people are within the same social groupings – in terms of gender, for example – the influence of social factors may still be very strong. For example, two men talking together may find it difficult to discuss matters of an emotional nature because of the way they have been brought up to see emotion as a topic of conversation that is generally seen as unsuited to masculinity (see Bates and Thompson, 2002, for a discussion of these issues). Being aware of the social background of the participants in an interpersonal encounter will not guarantee that no misunderstandings will occur, but the more prepared we are in terms of understanding such issues, the less likely is a communication breakdown.

2. *Physical*   This involves asking such questions as: Is this the right place (and right time)? The physical setting of an encounter can often prove to be a major obstacle to the success of that interaction. Sometimes we have no control over the physical setting, but there are often occasions when we can make significant changes which can be of major benefit. Important questions to ask, therefore, are: Is this the optimal physical setting for the interpersonal interaction concerned? If not, is there anything I can do to improve the situation?

Voice of experience 6.1

"My first placement was a bit of a disappointment, but my second one more than made up for it. My practice teacher was excellent and I learned so much from him. In particular, I learned a lot of practical techniques. One was about choosing the setting very carefully. Some people seem to have no rationale for doing home visits or inviting people to the office – it seems to happen at random, but I learned on that placement that the venue the discussion takes place in can make a big difference, so I always choose carefully – and that has stood me in good stead.**"** *Sandy, a youth justice worker*

3. *Relationship*   Clearly, the relationship between the participants will have a significant bearing on the process and outcome of any interactions. Sometimes difficulties can arise because participants view the relationship between them in rather different ways. For

example, A may regard B as a potential love interest, while B may regard A as someone who will never be anything more than a friend or even acquaintance. Sometimes, then, the basis of a relationship has to be clarified in order to improve the likelihood of a positive outcome. This can be particularly important in terms of professional relationships. For example, sometimes it may be necessary to explain the difference between being a friendly professional and being a friend in order to establish an appropriate professional footing. Without such clarity, considerable confusion, misunderstanding and ill-feeling can be generated.

4. *Mood/state of mind*   Sometimes it is just not the right time or place for a particular social interaction, not because of the physical setting but, rather, because of the psychological setting. At such times, we have to make a decision. We can either seek to change the mood – for example, if somebody is being very lighthearted and we are trying to put across a very serious message (that they may face disciplinary action, for example), we may wish to seek to change the mood by making it clear that the individual's state of mind is not appropriate to what we have to say or the message we are trying to put across. Alternatively, we may decide that, in the circumstances, it is not appropriate to try and change the mood and will seek an alternative opportunity for raising the issue we wish to discuss. For example, if a person is in a state of mild shock as a result of receiving bad news, it would be unwise to try and discuss other issues with them at that point, as they are unlikely to take such matters on board.

5. *Speech genre*   Thinking about the type of speech encounter we are about to have can be very useful as a basis for planning. For example, if we know that we are likely to face an argument with someone, then we can help to prepare for this by doing our homework thoroughly, marshalling our arguments and gathering our evidence before them. This can be a significant boost to confidence and can therefore be a major help in seeking to ensure a successful interpersonal encounter. Speech genres can also be important in other ways. For example, if the genre you are about to engage in is a meeting, it can be useful to be clear in advance about the status or level of formality of the meeting. For example, your planning for a meeting may be very different if you know that it is a very formal meeting as compared with a much more informal get-together of colleagues.

6. *Purpose*   This is a major feature of the context of social interaction. Sometimes people come together in interpersonal interactions purely for the pleasure and satisfaction they gain from spending time with other people. However, in very many cases, particularly in a

professional context, there is (or at least should be) a very clear purpose to the encounter. It can be very helpful indeed to be clear about why you are interacting with one or more individuals, what you hope to gain from the encounter and similarly, what they hope to gain from the encounter. A lack of clarity about purpose can lead to immense confusion and a great deal of time being wasted as well as often raising considerable ill-feeling among participants. Such a lack of clarity may also fail to reveal the fact that participants may be working to different agendas – that is, people may be speaking at cross purposes without realizing that they are doing so. In a work setting, it is often useful to 'set out one's stall'. This involves making it clear to other people why you are interacting with them; what the basis of your professional role is in that particular situation (see Thompson, 2009a, for a discussion of the idea of 'setting out your stall').

ACTIVITY 6.1

Think of a piece of work you have been involved with and consider how each of the six areas outlined above shaped the context of your interactions. How might you want to use your knowledge of these areas to improve the effectiveness of your communication?

PRACTICE FOCUS 6.1

Ben normally worked alone. However, for one particularly demanding piece of work, he was asked to join forces with Suki, a much more experienced colleague. They discussed the situation together and planned how they would tackle it. The first step was to be a meeting with the clients. It was agreed that, as Suki was the more experienced of the two, she would take the lead role. When the meeting began Ben was amazed at how skilfully and effectively Suki explained the purpose of the meeting, the reasons for their working together and so on. He was very impressed by the way she 'set out the stall' – and it was very clear to see that the clients were equally impressed. Ben decided that this was a skill that he would need to develop, as it was certainly very effective in establishing a platform for communication.

Overall, the aim of preparation and planning is to minimize the effect of 'noise'. We noted in Chapter 1 that noise is the term used to refer to anything which can get in the way of effective communication, any barrier to success. This can be literally noise (trying to have a conversation on a mobile telephone

while there is considerable noisy traffic around), or can be used metaphorically to refer to other disturbances in the process of communication. Of course,
planning will not guarantee the absence of unwanted noise, but it will certainly increase the percentages of being successful in doing so.

Maximizing effectiveness

Learning how to take part in interpersonal encounters is very much a part of
growing up and becoming part of one's culture – learning the unwritten rules
of how to relate to one another. We therefore start from a position of strength,
in the sense that the vast majority of people are already able to demonstrate
competence in the basics of interpersonal communication. My aim here, then,
is not to begin at the beginning, but rather to look at how we can achieve, and
build further upon, an advanced level of knowledge and skill with a view to
maximizing our effectiveness. We begin by looking at the use of rituals in conversation in the form of 'phatic communication'.

As we have noted, the term phatic communication is used to refer to the
sort of conversation which has little or no direct meaning in terms of its
content, but which acts as a significant lubricant of social interaction.
Greetings, chats about the weather, and other such examples of small talk are
what phatic communication is all about. One important part of maximizing
effectiveness in interpersonal communication is to get the balance right in
terms of phatic communication and a more focused discussion. Consider the
two extreme scenarios. On one side, consider the example of someone who
meets up with a professional colleague for a particular purpose, but spends
nearly all the time together engaged in chit chat. This is likely to be not only
a considerable waste of time, effort and energy, but it could also be a significant source of irritation for the other party, and therefore not a good idea in
terms of trying to establish or maintain effective working relationships. At the
other extreme, we could have someone who is so focused on the particular
aims of the business interaction that no time at all is given to the pleasantries
of social interaction. This can create a very tense or even hostile atmosphere,
which makes interpersonal encounters difficult. People can feel very ill at ease
if the other party in an interaction behaves in this entirely 'businesslike' way,
with no attention given to the human dimension of an interaction. This can
be not only unhelpful, in making people feel ill at ease, but may also be perceived as being disrespectful, if not insulting. What is important, then, is to
be able to maintain an appropriate balance between phatic communication
and a focus on the actual business for which the interaction is taking place –
using phatic communication as a means to an end, rather than an end in itself.

A common very successful tactic in seeking to achieve this balance is what
can be referred to as the CBC approach (chat – business – chat). This involves

beginning with some pleasantries (chat), quickly moving into the main focus of the interaction (business) and then ending with further pleasantries (chat). This is not guaranteed to work, but it is a well-established technique which has shown itself to be very effective in the majority of cases.

One important point that I was lucky enough to be able to learn in the early stages of my career is the idea that 'all action is interaction'. What this means is that, within an interpersonal interaction, what I do depends partly on what the other person in the interaction is doing, and what he or she does depends partly on what I do. That is, there is a dynamic set up between us. This is an important principle of effective interpersonal encounters. For example, if I want somebody to remain calm, then I should make sure that I do not do anything which inflames the situation. At base, this sounds very simple and straightforward. However, within the complex and intricate web of interactions, it can actually become a much more complicated state of affairs. Often, interactions take place at a very high pace and we may not be aware of much of what is going on between us. For example, after a particular encounter, it may be only much later that I become aware that I was getting angry during the interaction, although the other participant may have been aware of that right from the start. Sometimes, we can get so engrossed in the content of an interaction that we lose sight of the process and fail to recognize what impact the other person's behaviour is having on us and what impact our behaviour is having on the other person or persons. It can therefore be invaluable to develop a higher level of awareness of what processes are operating in interpersonal interactions, as some of the comments below will illustrate.

PRACTICE FOCUS 6.2

Jeff enjoyed being busy and having a lot of fingers in a lot of pies. However, when one colleague left and another went on long-term sick leave, he found himself in a position of significant work overload. Fortunately, this only lasted for two months and then he was able to relax a little. However, once the bad patch was over, he was able to look back and review what had been happening during the period of overload. One thing he recognized was that the busier he got, the more he tended to lose the plot and not keep track of what was happening. That is, being overloaded meant that he failed to notice important processes that were going on in his dealings with other people and he came to realize that it was largely a matter of good luck that he had got through without making any serious mistakes or alienating any important people.

There are two main ways in which we can develop this higher level of awareness. First, we can adopt a more conscious or reflective approach to our interactions

– that is, we can concentrate very hard on developing our knowledge and skills as we go about our interactions. This may be difficult and laboured at first, but should get easier over time. To complement this process, we can also develop our level of awareness by becoming more observant of interactions between other people. This can happen in a real life situation – for example, by watching colleagues, friends and so on, interacting and/or through watching interactions on films and television. The more we observe and concentrate, the more aware we can become, and the more we can learn. However, at this point, I should give a health warning. You run the risk of losing friends and gaining a reputation for being a very strange person if you overdo the interactional observation or you do it in such a crude and unsophisticated way as to attract attention to yourself and make other people feel uncomfortable. My advice in encouraging you to become more observant and aware of interactions is not intended as a recipe for making you into a social outcast.

An important concept in terms of maximizing effectiveness is that of 'active listening'. Unless we have a hearing impairment of some kind, we are, of course, able to hear, but this does not necessarily mean that we are able to listen. People can often become so wrapped up in their own concerns that they are not actually listening to the other person. This can be disastrous in terms of interpersonal encounters, leading to a breakdown in communication and considerable ill-feeling – why should I bother to listen to you if you can't be bothered listening to me? Listening is therefore an essential part of successful interpersonal communication (Moss, 2008). We have to be careful that we are not so intent on getting our message across to the other person that we are not taking on board what message they are trying to give us. Active listening takes this idea a step further. What it involves is not only listening attentively, but making sure that the other party is aware that we are listening – for example, through nodding or what is known as reflecting back. Reflecting back can be achieved through, for example, the careful and selective use of questions. Person A: 'I was so annoyed when I found out that he had torn up the letter'. Person B: 'He tore up the letter?' Person A: 'Yes, I was so annoyed'. This example illustrates how the careful use of reflecting back can get across the message that we are indeed listening and that we are taking on board what is being said to us. This can be very reassuring and can make for a very firm basis for an interpersonal interaction.

Linked to this is the idea of acknowledging feelings. That is, if someone is clearly showing signs of being affected by one or more emotions, it may be helpful for us to acknowledge the fact. If the emotion is crystal clear, then it is usually safe to acknowledge it openly. For example, if somebody is overtly demonstrating anger, then you can make a comment to the effect of 'I'm not surprised that this situation makes you angry'. However, if the emotion is not quite so clear cut, it is generally safer to ask rather than to state. For example,

'Do you find it upsetting to talk about the fact that he tore up your letter?' The effective use of acknowledging feelings is a highly skilled process. I would therefore urge caution in how you use this technique. You may find it helpful to witness how more experienced colleagues use this approach or, once again, try to observe its use in daily interactions. The advice to 'acknowledge feelings' is certainly not a simple rule to be followed mechanically.

PRACTICE FOCUS 6.3

Wendy attended a course on handling aggression and was very pleased that she had come away from the day with a lot of good ideas about how to defuse tensions and avoid conflicts spilling over into aggression or violence. In particular, she valued the idea of acknowledging people's feelings, especially anger. In fact, it was not long after the course before she had the opportunity to put her learning into practice. She was confronted by a very angry man and she feared that he was going to become violent if the situation was not handled carefully. She therefore used what she had learned by carefully acknowledging that she understood why the situation had made him so angry. This did not calm him entirely, but it was clearly a step in the right direction.

We have already come across the important concept of face. This refers to how participants in social interactions achieve and maintain status and (self-)respect. It is a major influence on social interactions. This is because participants will generally strive to maintain their own face without wishing to undermine the face of others (unless they are deliberately trying to do so – for example, in terms of an aggressive encounter or an attempt to make someone feel uncomfortable or deskilled). Matters relating to face can also be a significant source of humour, intentionally or otherwise – for example, referring to someone who takes him- or herself too seriously as His Lordship or Her Highness.

An important implication of the concept of face is that we must be very careful to ensure that we do not act in such a way as to make it difficult for other parties to maintain face. This involves being sensitive to other people's esteem needs and their self-respect. That is, we should not act or speak in such a way as to undermine another person. However, this is more easily said than done when it comes to communicating with people who are part of a social group that tends to be discriminated against. For example, in communicating with older people, it is very easy to slide into the stereotypical assumptions which can lead to people feeling patronized. It is therefore important to avoid the use of terms such as 'old dear'. At its simplest level, the basic rule is to treat people with respect but, in particular, to recognize that certain groups who are traditionally treated less respectfully present an additional challenge. For example, the influence of our upbringing and the stereotypes on which it is so often based can lead us to assume that a disabled person is actually more disabled than they really are or even to assume that they also have a mental impairment (see the discussion in Chapter 9). Becoming skilled at 'face work' is therefore an essential part of effective interpersonal communication.

An important concept that is related to the notion of face is that of assertiveness. Contrary to popular belief, to be assertive does not mean to be pushy or to be 'stroppy'. The reality is far more complex than this. Basically, the theory of assertiveness is based on the idea that there are three communication styles: aggressive, submissive and assertive. An aggressive style is one which puts one's own needs first at the expense of the other party. A submissive communication style is the opposite of this, putting the other party's needs first and neglecting our own. An assertive style is an attempt to balance the two to produce interactions which are helpful to both parties. This is a complex subject matter but, at its simplest, it involves seeking approaches to communication which avoid the destructive extremes of aggression and submission and enable us to have constructive and positive relationships with others based on assertiveness (see the further reading section for guidance on literature relating to this topic). Being effective at assertiveness is based not only on what we do, but also on what we say – and not only on what we say but on the way that we say it. That is, our use of language (and body language) is a major part of establishing relationships based on mutual respect for one another's needs and interests.

Body language, or nonverbal communication, is not only an important part of assertiveness, but also a significant part of successful interpersonal encounters in general. While we learn how to use our own body language and to read the nonverbal communications of others at an early age in our development, we should not become complacent about this. This is for two reasons. First, there may be an aspect of our nonverbal communication that we are not aware of. For example, consider how many times you have come across teachers, lecturers or other public speakers who have mannerisms which are highly distracting and counterproductive, but of which they seem to be generally unaware. Second, although we all learn the basics of nonverbal communication as part of the process of growing up, there is much to be gained by learning to use these skills at a more advanced level. As Honey (1990) comments: 'a heightened awareness of non-verbal behaviour has the potential to help us to be even more effective in our face to face encounters' (p. 156).

In both cases, we can make progress through developing a higher level of awareness of what is happening when we use body language.

> ### ACTIVITY 6.2
>
> What problems might arise if we were to ignore the 'messages' conveyed by nonverbal communication? Discuss this with one or more colleagues and see what lessons you feel can be learned from this.

The theme of nonverbal communication is also relevant in terms of ensuring the appropriate degree of consistency across the speech, paralanguage and body language that we use. The point was made in Chapter 4 that, where there is a discrepancy between either speech and paralanguage, or between speech and nonverbal communication, this can cause confusion and mistrust. It is important to note that it is the speech element which tends to be perceived as the weakest. That is, if I say 'I am not annoyed' but I do so in an annoyed tone of voice, then it is clear what message I will actually be giving, just as an aspect of body language which contradicts what a person's voice is actually saying is likely to overrule the spoken element of the communication. Consequently, if we wish to maximize the effectiveness of our interpersonal communication, we need to ensure that as far as is reasonably possible, our speech, paralanguage and non-verbal communication are consistent. Often an inconsistency will arise due to a lack of clarity in our own thinking or feeling about subject matter – that is, we cannot realistically expect clear communication to be the outcome of unclear thinking.

Another important aspect of communicative effectiveness is what has come to be known as emotional intelligence. This is a relatively new term which describes one's ability to be able to deal with emotional issues – one's own feelings and those of others. As with NLP, much of what goes under the heading of emotional intelligence can be described as old ideas in new clothes. However, some of these ideas are none the less important ones. Interestingly, emotional intelligence shares with NLP an overemphasis on biological factors (see, for example, Goleman, 1996). Much of what is described in emotional intelligence terms as biological factors can easily be explained in terms of social, cultural and psychological factors – there is no need to rely on 'biological reductionism' (that is, the tendency to overemphasize the role of biology in social life).

According to the emotional intelligence literature, there are two main strengths associated with the emotionally intelligent person. First, there is the ability to recognize and deal with our own feelings to be 'in touch with' our emotions. This is not about self-indulgence or the emotional equivalent of navel gazing, but rather a much more positive and constructive emphasis on self-awareness. Our emotional responses affect not only our own behaviour, but also how we are perceived and dealt with by other people. At a very simple level, if I am calm, I am more likely to influence the people around me to be calm, whereas if I am agitated, I am more likely to influence other people to be agitated too. This is clearly a vitally important part of interpersonal interactions. Developing emotional intelligence therefore involves developing a much higher level of self-awareness. There are various ways in which this can be achieved (see Thompson, 2009b, Chapter 1). A good starting point in this regard is to think about (or discuss with a trusted colleague or friend) how we recognize our own feelings. For example, if I am angry, what aspects of my behaviour indicate to other people (and myself) that I am angry? At one level, this may sound simple and obvious but at another level, it is actually quite surprising how often we are not aware of the emotions that are influencing us at a given time.

Voice of experience 6.2

"After my father died I tried to get back to normal as soon as I could. I thought this meant that I wasn't giving off any signs that I was grieving (I found the sense of normality quite reassuring at a really difficult time, so I did not want anyone making a fuss). So, I was quite surprised when I bumped into an ex-colleague of mine and straight away she asked me what was wrong, saying that she could tell that I wasn't my usual self. I had had no idea that I was giving off any emotional signals, but obviously I was.**"** *Nina, a community nurse*

The other side of the emotional intelligence coin is the ability to recognize and deal with emotions in other people. It is not uncommon for some people metaphorically to run a mile when they encounter strong feelings in another person. It is as if we feel the need to shelter ourselves from emotion, or certain emotions at least. An emotionally intelligent person is therefore someone who is able to recognize feelings in other people and the impact they are having on that person's behaviour and contribution to a social interaction. An emotionally intelligent person is also able to respond appropriately to such emotions and will not avoid them, distort them or play any other game which involves failing to deal effectively with the emotional dimension of interpersonal interactions. The study of what these days goes under the broad heading of emotional intelligence can therefore be seen to have significant implications for maximizing our communicative effectiveness in interpersonal encounters.

Another significant principle underpinning effective interpersonal communication is what I would refer to as, 'You reap what you sow'. By this, I mean that what we put into an interaction will often influence quite significantly what we get out of it. A very simple example of this would be: if I am not friendly towards another person, I should not be disappointed when he or she is not friendly towards me. A further good example of this is provided by Thomson (1996). He draws a distinction between a complaint and a request

> **PRACTICE FOCUS 6.4**
>
> Ben and Suki had been working on the same project for some time, with Suki trying to help the less experienced Ben to develop his knowledge and skills. One thing she noticed was that Ben often became engrossed in his own feelings and concerns and did not really take on board other people's feelings. This sometimes led to difficulties because Ben's approach seemed to leave other people thinking he was not interested in them, since he did not appear to connect with their feelings at all. Suki wondered how she could try and get this point across to Ben, to try and help him be more alert to the messages he was getting from other people about their feelings. The irony was that she needed to find a way of doing this without hurting *his* feelings.

for help. He describes the example of a person who is unhappy with the level of service they have received. If, in raising this issue, they use the language of complaint – for example, they state explicitly 'I wish to complain' – then they should not be surprised when they receive a defensive response. It is, after all, understandable that what could be perceived as an attack would result in at least a defence if not a counterattack. If, however, the issue is raised as a request for help, then it is much more likely that the person concerned will receive a positive, helpful response rather than a defensive one. This is not to say that people should never complain, but rather that they should be careful and, indeed, strategic in how they phrase their complaint. If the person wishes to do battle, then the language of complaint is quite appropriate. However, if the person quietly wishes for their issues to be resolved, then clearly a request for help is likely to be more productive – you reap what you sow.

This approach has much in common with solution-focused therapy, as discussed in Chapter 2. That is, if you use the language of problems, people will think in terms of problems, but if you use the language of solutions, people are much more likely to think in terms of solutions (Myers, 2008). In this way, you play a part in constructing a more positive framework as a basis for your interaction (de Shazer, 1988). Although this approach has its roots in therapeutic work, I have found that it can be extended to a much broader range of interpersonal interactions. It is not simply a therapeutic technique, but rather a useful strategy for influencing the shape, tone and direction of an interaction.

The distinction between open and closed questions is also an important issue in terms of the theme of you reap what you sow. A closed question is one which tends to produce a simple yes or no response (Are you happy to be here?). By contrast, an open question is one which allows for a wide variety of responses (How do you feel about being here?). I have come across students who have been taught that open questions are good questions but closed questions are bad ones when it comes to facilitating interpersonal communication. However, this is an oversimplification of a much more complex reality. Open questions are particularly useful in the early stages of an interaction in order to encourage dialogue and discussion. However, closed questions can be very useful, particularly towards the end of an interaction, for concluding, focusing down and so on. What is needed, then, is not prejudice in favour of open questions at the expense of closed questions, but rather the ability to recognize which is more appropriate in which circumstances. The skill of being able to use open and closed questions appropriately is therefore a highly valued one in terms of interpersonal encounters.

From this brief discussion of maximizing effectiveness, it should be clear that there are various ways in which our effectiveness in interpersonal interactions can be maximized or, at least, enhanced. However, there are two important points to emphasize here by way of conclusion. First, it is important to recognize that the points discussed here have been selective. They are by no means the complete list of possible strategies or issues to consider in terms of seeking to make the most of the interpersonal encounters we undertake in our work or, indeed, in our lives in general. Second, it has to be recognized that reading about these issues will not be enough on its own (especially one section of one chapter of an introductory book). While reading about these issues and developing our awareness and understanding certainly has a significant role to play, if we are indeed to maximize our effectiveness, we need to go beyond this. Simply reading about matters will not make us better practitioners as if by magic. What we need to do is to continue to study, debate and learn about these issues while also raising our awareness as we practise through a reflective approach and making use of training opportunities as and when they arise.

Avoiding discrimination

I have argued in this book and elsewhere that the relationship between communication and language on the one hand and power and discrimination on the other is an important one. I have also argued that what is needed in order to make progress in respect of these issues is a greater degree of linguistic sensitivity, rather than a simplistic political correctness approach. Such linguistic sensitivity will not develop overnight, but it is to be hoped that the discussions here will help to raise awareness and will be helpful in offering some practical strategies that can be used as a starting point. However, please note that they are precisely a starting point and should not be seen as prescriptive rules to be followed unthinkingly. As in all matters relating to people and their problems, a reflective approach is called for – that is, one which is based on careful consideration of what we are doing and why we are doing it, analysis of our work so that we can evaluate it and learn from it, and so on.

While it would be naive not to recognize that much discrimination is deliberate and overt, with an intent to do harm to other people, it would also be unwise to fail to recognize that a significant proportion of discrimination arises not as a result of malice, but rather through ill-informed or insensitive action – that is, much discrimination can be seen to be unwitting, based on ignorance and a lack of awareness of the complexities of the issues involved. In view of this, it is important to recognize that unwitting discrimination can be both caused by ineffective communication and a contributor to it. For example, if, in my interactions with another person I base my actions on a discriminatory stereotype, then I am not only perpetrating discrimination, but also communicating ineffectively, as stereotypes have the effect of distorting communication. While many people seem to prefer to avoid the complex and thorny issue of the relationship between discrimination and language/communication, it is clearly a mistake to do so, as a failure to address these issues can be so significant in terms of contributing to discrimination and undermining effective communication.

One important point to be aware of is the significance of power in interpersonal interactions. Consider, for example, the important points made by Schirato and Yell (2000):

> Power is manifested in general by asymmetry in the meaning choices available to the powerful and the less powerful. Those who exercise power in a speech interaction tend to:
>
> - control turn-taking in dialogue;
> - interrupt;
> - control what is under negotiation (through speech function);
> - control the topic being discussed;
> - control the degree of directness or indirectness (indirectness, euphemism and 'watching your words' are associated with the less powerful; and
> - control the use of address terms (use of titles rather than first names shows status).
>
> This is neatly summed up in Fairclough's statement that 'power in discourse is to do with powerful participants controlling and constraining the contributions of non-powerful participants' (1989: 46). (p. 142)

It is important that we should not oversimplify what Schirato and Yell are saying here. For example, in using the terms powerful and less powerful, they are not implying that this applies in absolute terms. As we have already noted, power is a much more complex subject than this. In terms of interpersonal interactions, we all have some degree of power, even if that power is only to turn away and not listen. However, in reality, interpersonal interactions are based on very complex power dynamics, and the greater the level of awareness we have of these dynamics, the better in terms of (i) understanding what is going on; and (ii) being in a position to influence it (see Thompson, 2007).

I share with Cameron (1998b) the view that providing simple guidelines on what to say and what not to say is not appropriate when it comes to trying to avoid discrimination. In my experience, this simplistic approach is not only ineffective, but also can lead to considerable ill-feeling and resentment. It also encourages a dogmatic orthodoxy which has unfortunately plagued many attempts to promote equality and value diversity. I therefore wish to make it entirely clear that the comments that follow are intended as guidelines to facilitate a reflective approach to this matter, rather than rules to be followed mechanically. I certainly do not wish to be part of an approach which reduces the complexities of linguistic sensitivity to a simple list of, on the one hand, taboo words that should be avoided and, on the other, 'right on' phrases or fashionable buzzwords that should be used.

If we are serious about avoiding discrimination in our interpersonal interactions, I believe it is very important that we avoid language that:

- *Excludes*   Some forms of language imply that certain activities (particularly those associated with positions of power) are reserved for particular people. For example, the term 'chairman' implies that this is a position reserved for men whereas the alternatives 'chair', 'chairperson' or 'convenor' do not. Some people argue that 'everyone knows that chairman can refer to a woman'. However, this argument misses the point. It fails to recognize that the usage of such a term reinforces the idea that positions of power belong primarily to men. Some people will argue that a chair is an object that you sit on, and not a person. However, this is not a satisfactory argument, as the term chair is used in universities to refer to people who hold the rank of professor.
- *Depersonalizes*   This refers to the use of language in such a way as to rob people of their individuality or even of their humanity. Examples of this would be 'the elderly' rather than elderly people or older people, or even the more respectful term, 'elders'. Another example would be the tendency to refer to an individual with a learning disability in the plural. For example, someone meeting an affectionate individual who has Down's syndrome may say: 'They are very affectionate, aren't they?' as if the person concerned is simply an example of a category, rather than a unique human being in his or her own right.
- *Stigmatizes*   Some forms of language have negative or derogatory connotations, and so we have to be very careful about how these are used if we are to use them at all. Terms like 'dirty Arab' are clearly

problematic ('You've got gravy all over your sleeve, you dirty Arab'). The use of the term 'black' is less clear cut. Sometimes it is used in a purely descriptive sense – for example, 'black shoes', 'blackboard', 'black coffee', and has no negative connotations. However, it is often used in a stigmatizing way – for example, 'black mark', 'black day', and so on. Similarly, a white lie is an acceptable one, while a black lie is not. There are two unhelpful extremes here, with a healthy balance in between. At one extreme, we have people who believe that virtually any use of the word black is actually or potentially racist and therefore avoid such relatively harmless usages as blackboard, black coffee and so on – an approach which has led to considerable ridicule of attempts to challenge racism, as well as considerable confusion about these issues (Thompson, 2009c). At the other equally unhelpful extreme, we have people who insist that there is no problem in the usage of the word black at all, and will use it very insensitively in a way which contributes to racist assumptions that black people are inferior to white.

• *Reinforces stereotypes*   Discriminatory stereotypes are not only destructive and unhelpful in general, but also have the effect of distorting communication. However, it is unfortunately the case that stereotypes are commonly reinforced by the language used by many people. For example, the term Irish is often used to refer to an action or a person who is deemed to be stupid or slow on the uptake ('That was stupid; that was an Irish way of doing it'). Of course, stereotypes will only persist if we perpetuate them through the language that we use.

• *Legitimizes discrimination*   The term 'legitimize' means to present something as if it is acceptable or legitimate. Some forms of language imply that unfair discrimination is acceptable – for example, the term 'domestic' can be used in some contexts to imply that violence against one's partner is less of an issue than violence against anyone else. This means that the uncritical use of the term 'domestic' can contribute to situations where the victims of violence in the home receive less protection than others because 'it's just a domestic'. The problem, then, arises from the *uncritical* use of the term, rather than in the term itself, a point missed by the proponents of political correctness.

Some people might have expected the list to include reference to the need to avoid language that is offensive. However, I have not included this, as I regard it as something that should be taken as read. I am also conscious that there is a danger that an emphasis on language which may be perceived as offensive can distract attention from the wider issue as discussed here. For

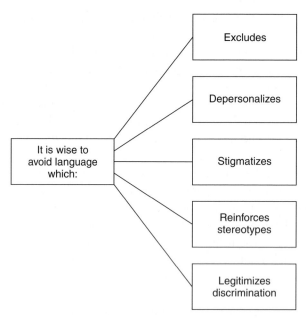

Figure 6.1 Problematic forms of language

Sandra had got to the point where she had been told off for saying 'politically incorrect' things so many times that she was completely confused by the issue and therefore decided just to keep her mouth shut as far as possible and try to avoid further criticism. Unfortunately, this contributed to what was already a very tense and defensive culture. When she was invited to attend a course on equality and diversity she made excuses as to why she couldn't attend. However, her line manager insisted in the end and she went along very reluctantly and very warily. Fortunately, she was very pleasantly surprised by the course, as the trainer spoke openly about the dangers of political correctness orthodoxy and argued the case for a much more flexible approach based on linguistic sensitivity. She was therefore much clearer about why language is important and why it is necessary to be aware of the dangers of reinforcing discrimination. She understood that she should not be so defensive and, if challenged about what she said, to be open to learning about why it was seen as unacceptable or inappropriate. However, she was also pleased to hear it said that people often complain about particular forms of language use when there is, in fact, nothing to be concerned about.

example, I have known some women to comment to the effect that they do not find the use of the term 'man' to refer to all of humanity as offensive, but, again, this misses the point that it is not about such language being offensive, but rather reinforcing existing unequal power relations and assumptions about the respective roles of men and women in terms of who has power and life chances and who does not.

In relation to the five areas of language to be avoided, there are three further points that I wish to emphasize. First is the question of humour. Often people object to attempts to develop linguistic sensitivity by arguing: 'It was just a joke'. While I would certainly not wish to ban or even discourage humour, I think the point has to be made that the fact that a discriminatory remark is made in a humorous context does not alter the fact that it is discriminatory and therefore unfair or offensive to a particular individual or group of people. Challenging the discriminatory use of language in humour should therefore not be equated with being a spoilsport with no sense of humour. It is perfectly possible, and indeed quite common, for there to be considerable humour in a situation without the need to be unfair or oppressive towards particular individuals or groups of people.

ACTIVITY 6.3

How might you distinguish between forms of humour that are perfectly harmless and unproblematic and those that are discriminatory and thus oppressive? How might you gently and constructively challenge people who are using the latter type of humour?

Second, and just as important, if not more so, is the need to avoid complacency. I have run large numbers of training courses relating to equality and diversity on which the topic of linguistic sensitivity is commonly discussed. It is not unusual for some people to object to some of the comments I make on the grounds that they regard them as being 'over the top'. For example, I have had people say to me that 'everybody knows' that the use of black in a derogatory or negative sense is not intended as a way of being racist towards black people. However, I was very fortunate on one particular course to have two black participants present who objected strongly to the complacency of their white colleagues' contributions to the discussion. Their argument was that, if you are part of the majority group and you are therefore not stigmatized through use of particular forms of language, you may well find it difficult to understand the need to change such language. However, if on a daily basis an important part of your identity is presented as something which is bad, poor or to be ashamed of, then the need for linguistic sensitivity becomes very apparent indeed. We should therefore be very careful to distinguish between 'political correctness', which would have us banning the use of perfectly harmless words, and a genuine commitment to *linguistic sensitivity* which alerts us to the problems that can be caused by an ill-informed or insensitive use of language. We therefore have to be very alert to the dangers of being complacent about these matters. What seems a minor irritation in terms of changing a particular form of language to one group of people, may be a very significant issue indeed to other people whose lives may be seriously affected by the discriminatory assumptions that are reinforced, or even carried, by such uses of language.

Third is the importance of taking into account the developmental level of the other party or parties in a particular interaction and communicating with them accordingly. The obvious example of this would be in working with children, a point to which we shall return in Chapter 7. However, we should also remember that the significance of a person' developmental level does not apply simply to children. At the other end of the developmental scale of the life course we can have situations where interpersonal interactions are undermined by inappropriate uses of language. For example, in conversation with older people it is not uncommon for problems to develop because of uncritical assumptions being made. For one thing, we should not fall into the trap of taking on board the ageist myth that older people are necessarily deaf. Again, this seems an obvious thing to say but it is surprising how many people automatically begin to shout when they speak to somebody above pensionable age. Returning briefly to the theme of discrimination, it is sadly the case that ageist assumptions lead to older people being spoken to in patronizing and disrespectful ways – for example, the use of childlike or 'infantilizing' language.

PRACTICE FOCUS 6.6

Len had mixed feelings when his elderly mother was admitted to a residential home. On the one hand, he felt sad that she had had to give up her own home, particularly as she had lived there for over 50 years and it held so many memories for her of her life in general and her sorely missed late husband in particular. On the other hand, he was quite relieved that she would now get well fed and have the supervision she needed, as he had been concerned about how often she was falling over. However, he soon became worried about how his mother was being cared for. In terms of her physical care and well-being, he had no concerns whatsoever, but what he did find objectionable was the language that some of the care staff used in talking to her. He felt that they were often over familiar and treated her like a child. Matters came to a head when she spilled a cup of tea and one of the care staff told her she was 'a naughty girl'. It was at this point that Len felt the need to make a formal complaint about the lack of respect shown to his mother.

An important point for me to emphasize is that I am not advocating a defensive approach to the use of language where people become 'tongue tied' because they are so frightened to speak and make a mistake. Linguistic sensitivity will not be helped by such a defensive, anxious approach to these issues. What is much more constructive is for (i) people to be prepared to learn from their mistakes if they speak naturally and fluently, as they would normally do, but subsequently discover that there may be a problematic aspect to their use of language; and (ii) to raise awareness generally of the significance of language, so that these issues can be discussed, debated and progressed. Without such open debate, people will not learn and will therefore either continue to use unhelpful language or will become so anxious and defensive that effective communication is seriously hampered. My view on the practicalities of this complex and thorny subject is that, if we become aware of the problematic nature of a particular form of language, then we should seek, as far as possible, to avoid using such language. If, however, someone objects to a particular form of language and it is not apparent to us what is objectionable about it, then I feel it is important to enquire what the basis of the objection is, so that further learning can take place and/or myths about why particular terms should be unacceptable can be challenged.

Voice of experience 6.3

"It was like a breath of fresh air when Jo joined the team. I was not entirely happy about some of the language being used at times – it was a bit off, to say the least – but I didn't want to say anything and spoil the nice atmosphere in the team. But Jo came in, made it quite clear of her disapproval when inappropriate language was used, but did it sensitively and constructively and soon had the backing of the team when she was able to get across to them why certain terms were problematic. It was an object lesson in effective communication. It made me feel a bit deskilled in some ways, but that was a small consideration, bearing in mind what a positive difference her input had made.**"** *Brian, a team manager*

Conclusion

As so much of our existence is lived through the medium of communication in general and language in particular, it is clearly of central importance that we make the most of our interpersonal encounters if we are to make the most of our lives. The importance of these issues cannot therefore be overemphasized. However, what should also be emphasized is the immensity of these issues. By now, there should be no doubt in any reader's mind that the world of interpersonal encounters is a very complex and intricate one. The knowledge and skills required for effective interactions are both extensive and of great importance.

However, the good news is that we are not starting from scratch – we learn the basics of communication and interpersonal encounters as part of growing up within our own particular culture. The task, then, is not to begin at the beginning, but rather to build on the strong foundations that we already have as a result of our upbringing. It is to be hoped that this chapter, through raising awareness of many of the issues involved, can play at least a small part in helping to move towards achieving those advanced levels of practice.

By way of conclusion, an important point to make is that effective interpersonal encounters can be seen to owe much to the process of 'managing language'. Czerniawska (1997) makes the point that: 'managing language is a very important part of managing a business' (p. 125). To this, we can add that managing language is not just an important part of managing a business, but also of any enterprise which involves working with people, their problems and their challenges, whatever the setting or work context. Whether you are a social worker working in a deprived community, a nurse working in a high-tech hospital or a manager working with directors of multi-million pound enterprises, it remains the case that so much of the success of your work will depend on the effectiveness of your interpersonal interactions and, in turn, so much of their success will depend on your communication skills in general and your use of personal interaction skills in particular.

POINTS TO PONDER

- What do you see as the key learning points to have emerged from this chapter?
- What do you see as your main strengths in interpersonal interactions? How can you build on them?
- What do you see as your main areas for development? How can you build these up?

CHAPTER 7

Communicating with children and young people

Introduction

The knowledge base outlined in the previous chapters can be seen to apply to communication across the board, but what we shall note in this chapter is that there are additional factors that need to be taken into account when communicating with children and young people. This is the first of three chapters that explore such additional factors that need to be taken into consideration (Chapter 8 focuses on communicating with groups while Chapter 9 relates to communicating in situations where there are communication difficulties).

The chapter is divided into five main sections. We begin with a discussion of the significance of the stage of development the child or young person is at. This paves the way for a consideration of the context in which communication takes place and the particular significance of this for working with children and young people. Next there is a section on 'connecting' with children, followed by one on 'connecting' with young people. Finally, we focus on developing our skills to try and ensure that we are communicating to the best of our ability when it comes to trying to engage with children and young people.

Understanding development

We are, of course, not born as fully formed adults with a mature understanding of the world. The reality is that childhood is a process of development, an ongoing learning experience, with different children having different levels of understanding depending on where they are up to in that learning process. Age can be an indicator of stage of development, but is rarely enough on its own. This is because, while age can give us a starting point for anticipating level of development, there will be many other factors that also have a significant bearing – for example, the role of parents, opportunities for stimulation within their environment, quality and quantity of interactions with other children and indeed with adults. Sadly, there will also be for many children significant obstacles to development in the form of abuse and possible subsequent trauma. I shall return to this point below.

The importance of the developmental level cannot be overemphasized. This is because, if we base our communicative efforts on a misreading of the level of development (and therefore level of understanding), we can fail not only to communicate what we intended to, but also run the risk of communicating an inappropriate message. For example, by talking to a child in ways they cannot understand, the result can be confusion, lowering of confidence, a sense of alienation and thus significant barriers to forming an effective working relationship.

Clearly, we would not communicate with a five-year old in the same way as we would communicate with a fifteen-year old. This does not mean that I expect effective communicators to be experts in human development, but I would argue that it is necessary to have at least a basic understanding of development issues if we are to make the most of our interpersonal interactions with children and young people. While the idea that we should adjust our communicative style according to the age or developmental level of the other person may seem obvious, I have been surprised over the years to realize just how many people seem to have little or no understanding of how to communicate with children and young people. It is therefore important to be aware of such issues in our interactions.

In trying to appreciate the major role of developmental level in shaping our communications, it is essential that we are aware of the significance of strands of development. By this I mean that development is not a simple, one-dimensional process. There are different elements or 'strands' that can be identified:

- *Physical*   This refers to biological maturation, the growth of the body in line with expected milestones.
- *Cognitive*   The term 'cognitive' refers to processes of thinking, processing information, memory and so on.
- *Emotional*   Our ability to handle emotions and moods ('affect') develops over time.
- *Social*   The ability to relate appropriately to other people and to adapt to differing social situations is also an important part of development.
- *Moral*   Learning the difference between 'right' and 'wrong' and developing our own values or principles is also a developmental process.
- *Linguistic*   Language development is partly linked to cognitive and social development but is an important dimension of development in its own right.
- *Ontological*   Ontology is the study of being or of reality. Our growing sense of who we are, how we fit into the world and so on are ontological concerns. The term 'spiritual' development is also often used in this regard, although some people reserve this term (misleadingly, in my view) for the development of religious beliefs.

ACTIVITY 7.1

Think of a child you know and try to work out where they are up to in terms of their development relating to each of the above seven areas or 'strands'. Compare notes with one or more colleagues to see what you can learn about child development from this.

Because of these different strands, 'uneven' development is quite common. This refers to situations where a child or young person can be quite advanced in one or more aspects of development, but relatively undeveloped in others (see Practice Focus 7.1 below). This is something important to be aware of, as failing to recognize its significance can mean that we can misread a situation. This can work in one of two ways. First, based on a relatively advanced level of development in one area, we may overestimate the level of development in other areas (for example, a child who is quite socially skilled may none the less be struggling to deal with their emotions). Second, we may underestimate (and thereby potentially undermine) a child's capabilities in one area because we recognize that they are struggling in another area of development – for example, not recognizing that a child who lacks social skills is actually quite intelligent (cognitively well developed).

PRACTICE FOCUS 7.1

Before she took up a post in a new project working with abused children Roberta had worked for years in adult mental health and had seen the consequences in adulthood of child abuse. For the most part she was quickly able to adapt her knowledge and skills to her new area of practice. However, one thing she struggled with to begin with was communicating with the children involved in the project. She quickly realized that this was a more difficult and more skilful undertaking than she had anticipated. In particular, she realized that different children had different levels of understanding and skill, so she would need to adapt her approach to suit each individual child.

One situation proved to be quite an eye opener for her in terms of the need to understand the complexities of development. She was working with Lisa, a tall 12-year-old who had reached puberty and looked more like an 18-year-old. She found herself slipping into talking to her as if she were a young adult until, in one of their one-to-one sessions, Lisa picked up a doll and started to talk to it in a way more reminiscent of a six-year-old. The con-trast was quite stark and really registered with Roberta who learned from this experience that she would have to be much more careful – and professional – in choosing what level of communication to adopt with specific children.

A further important aspect of development is the question of attachment. This refers to the type and quality of bonding that a child has achieved with key adults, especially their parents or primary carers. This is a complex topic worthy of much fuller attention than I am able to give it here (see the 'Guide to further learning' at the end of the book), but the following brief comments should be sufficient to make the point that attachment issues are an important part of what we need to consider in communicating with children and young people. It is generally argued that there are four different types of attachment:

1. *Anxious/avoidant*   This is an insecure attachment characterized by avoidance of contact.
2. *Secure*   This is seen as the optimal attachment based on a strong bond with the mother or other significant carer.
3. *Anxious/ambivalent*   As the term implies, this is characterized by ambivalence about contact.
4. *Disorganized*   This type of attachment manifests itself in confusion and apprehension.

Part of our assessment therefore needs to be a focus on attachment, as this will influence the child's behaviour and emotional responses, and therefore our interactions with them. However, it also needs to be recognized that, as with the use of any theoretical perspective, a critical approach is called for, so that the theory does not become a form of unquestioned rigid dogma that does not develop over time (Thompson, 2010).

What we have discussed so far in relation to development has focused on general processes of development – that is, those that apply to all children and young people. However, there are also exceptional factors that need to feature in our understanding – in particular, the impact of abuse and trauma.

While abuse is thankfully not the norm, it would be naïve not to recognize that it is a significant issue in the lives of many children, especially those children who are receiving professional help because of family, behaviour or education problems. Abuse does not necessarily lead to trauma, nor is abuse the only source of trauma. However, there are sufficient interconnections between the two phenomena to justify discussing them together.

Voice of experience 7.1

"Most of the training we have had has been helpful but the day we did on trauma and abuse was especially helpful. It explained so much of the behaviour we had seen and gave us some very helpful ideas about how we might respond in future.**"** *Kim, a foster carer*

Abuse can affect communication in the following ways:

- An abused child may be reluctant to communicate (directly) as a result of a lack of trust instilled in them by one or more abusive relationships.
- Nonverbal communication may take on additional significance due to possible barriers to verbal communication (for example, a child may disclose abuse through play or drawing because they do not feel confident or comfortable enough to disclose verbally).
- Certain areas or topics may become taboo to the child because of associations with the abuse (for example, a child abused on a camping trip may be unwilling to discuss anything connected with camping or even holidays more broadly because the subject matter is too painful).

In addition, trauma can complicate matters because:

- It can distort perception;
- The intense fear generated can be a major barrier to communication; and
- Concentration can be adversely affected.

Added to this, abuse and trauma are closely associated with loss, in so far as there is a strong likelihood that they will produce a grief reaction, and potentially a very strong grief reaction. This can also combine with feelings of rejection. As Johnston, Roseby and Kuehnle (2009) comment:

> Loss – be it the loss of a loved one, loss of the marriage, loss of the intact family, loss of cherished hopes and dreams, or the threatened loss of one's children – evokes powerful feelings of anxiety, sadness, and fear of being abandoned and alone. Rejection, on the other hand, evokes feelings of inadequacy, of having failed, and of shame and humiliation. (p. 7)

They go on to argue that different children will have different capacities (and I would add different levels and forms of social support) for dealing with these feelings. It is therefore important that we 'tune in' to the impact of abuse and trauma (and therefore loss and rejection) on children's lives, as this will have a bearing on how we communicate with them (and how well we do so). For example, we may unwittingly reinforce their difficulties if we are insensitive to their experiences and their feelings.

There are, then, various ways in which a child or young person's level of development can be significant in shaping how we manage our efforts to communicate with them. What is needed is a balance: in order to communicate in developmentally appropriate ways. This involves not expecting too high a level of comprehension of the adult world, but without being patronising or 'talking down' to them. This may appear simple on paper, but can be quite

---

PRACTICE FOCUS 7.2

Roberta's anxieties about communicating with children quickly dissipated once she settled into her new post. Her colleagues were very helpful in giving her advice and pointing her in the direction of some important texts to read. What she quickly started to realize was that the children she worked with were all showing signs of grieving in one way or another. Although they 'communicated' their grief in varied and subtle ways, she was able to recognize it. This was because in her previous work in adult mental health she had been involved in helping people recognize (and deal with) the role of grief and trauma in their lives. She was therefore able to adapt her learning to working with abused children and to see how the grief and trauma in their lives played a key part in shaping their behaviour and their development. This, in turn, she came to realize, had a significant impact on how they communicated – how well they did so, in what ways they preferred to and what difficulties they encountered. This helped her to realize how skilful her colleagues were and how much more she had to learn in her new field of practice.

---

difficult in practice. It is in fact quite a skilful undertaking. We shall return to the question of skill development below.

Understanding the context

Clearly the developmental level of the child or young person throws up some important issues for us to consider and there can be no substitute for having a sound understanding of child development (see the 'Guide to further learning'). However, these are not the only factors to consider. Individual factors relating to the child need to be understood in the context of the wider setting in which the interactions take place. In this section we explore some important questions that need to inform our practice:

- *What is the wider sociopolitical context?* Is the child or young person living in poverty? Are there class-related factors that influence communication? Is racism an issue to consider? Are experiences of racial discrimination affecting the situation? Are we able to ensure that our interactions are 'ethnically sensitive' – that is, appropriately attuned to the cultural needs and practices of the child or young person concerned? These and other big-picture-related questions are important ones to ask if we are not to run the risk of missing some potentially significant aspects of the situation. No one exists in a social vacuum, and so everyone will be influenced by wider social factors.

This includes the children and young people that we are seeking to interact with and ourselves, of course. There can be problems when aspects of this broader social context do not fit comfortably together and are not well handled – for example, when a professional uses middle-class forms of language in speaking to a working-class child. This can produce alienation and distance, and therefore barriers to communication.

- *What is the specific interaction context?*   Does the child or young person understand why you are there? Are they clear why you are speaking to them? Do they understand what the purpose is? Is it a general 'get to know you' type of interaction or one with more specific goals relating to your professional role and their specific needs or problems? Again these are important questions to ask, as the answers to them will shape not only your expectations of the situation and what direction it should go in, but also what the child or young person expects to happen. These expectations will, in turn, influence the behaviour of both parties and will therefore have potentially quite significant consequences for the nature, quality and outcomes of the communication processes taking place. In order to maximize the effectiveness of our communication, we therefore need to be sensitive to the situational factors that can help or hinder us in our efforts. If we just plough on regardless without reflecting on these issues, we could find ourselves seriously disadvantaged, therefore providing the people we serve with a lower level of assistance than we are capable of.

- *How does the child see you?*   Are you a friend who can be trusted? Are you an 'official' who is to be given a wide berth? Are you seen as source of help and support or as a potential threat? Are you perceived as a 'soft touch' who can be relied upon to produce 'goodies' and outings and therefore someone to be manipulated? Or do you have a genuine 'connection', a rapport that can be built on to good effect? The answers to these questions are likely to be influential factors in determining the direction and effectiveness of your communication. It is very easy to lose sight of these matters and simply relax into an everyday conversational style that we feel comfortable with, but which may not be appropriate to the circumstances.

- *Is this the right time and place?*   Is the child distracted because their favourite TV programme is due to start? Are they tired and unsettled because they have just got back from school? Is this a place where they feel comfortable and safe? Are there no distractions at, or negative associations with, the place in which you are interacting? The importance of the setting needs to be emphasized, as it can play a key role in the effectiveness or otherwise of getting our message across and, just as importantly – if not more so – genuinely listening to the child or young person. This is partly a matter of planning (thinking ahead where possible) and partly being sensitive to the situation as it is occurring and responding accordingly. This is another example of the importance of critically reflective practice (Thompson and Thompson, 2008).

- *What is the emotional context of the situation?*   Are you and the child or young person both relaxed? If there are any tensions, where are they coming from? Do they need to be addressed? Are they anxious? Are you anxious? Being able to understanding feelings ('emotional intelligence', as it is often called these days) is a basic requisite for being able to communicate effectively in the difficult situations that members of the helping professions are so often called upon to deal with. When it comes to working with children and young people, this is especially important, as they may lack the social skills to manage their feelings that maturity brings to a certain extent. This puts a degree of responsibility on the adult to try to make sure that the emotions brought to the interaction and produced by it are carefully and safely managed.

These matters can sound relatively straightforward in principle, but can prove to be much more difficult in practice – again emphasizing the importance of developing the necessary skills.

'Connecting' with children

Communication was defined in Chapter 1 as 'social interaction through mes-sages'. It is not simply about transmitting and receiving messages in a straight-forward, technical sense. The 'social interaction' part is also crucial. Communicating with children involves a process of 'engagement' – that is, of making meaningful connections with the child concerned. It is only in this way that we can effectively get our message across and take on board what the child is saying to us – by creating a communicative 'bond'. This involves the following elements:

- Using appropriate forms of language in terms of vocabulary, sentence construction and so on (the appropriate 'register' – see Chapter 2), based on the child's level of development;
- Using appropriate body language (see below);
- Choosing the right time and place (as discussed above) and making sure the length of time together is appropriate (not so short that it fails to make an impact and not so long that it strains the child's ability to concentrate);
- Choosing appropriate topics, points of interest that will help engage the child;

- Blending 'phatic communication' (talk geared towards oiling the wheels of social interaction and rapport building: greetings, chatting/small talk and use of humour) with 'business talk' (discussing whatever needs to be discussed to help or support the child); and
- Emotionally 'holding' the child where needed (Weld, 2009).

These are all important ingredients, but I want to focus on two of them in particular: nonverbal communication and emotional holding. Nonverbal communication can be divided into two parts, general and specific. By general, I mean the everyday use of gesture, posture and so on to support and reinforce our verbal communications (see Chapter 4). This is always an important part of face-to-face interaction, but can be especially so in working with children whose understanding of language is likely to be less sophisticated than their adult counterparts. We learn the basics of effective nonverbal communication as part of our upbringing, but with further learning and practice, we can develop these basic skills into a more advanced repertoire. We can learn how to use our body more subtly as a basis for communication and 'connecting' with the child. A key part of this is observation: watching the child carefully (but unobtrusively); watching other people to note how they use body language. This gives us the 'raw materials' for learning, the foundation on which we can build over time.

More specifically, in terms of the use of nonverbal communication, is the judicious use of play (or what is often referred to as 'direct work'). This involves developing the knowledge and skills to engage with children in a focused way through the semi-structured use of play. By semi-structured I mean that it is not entirely free flowing and spontaneous, but nor is it rigidly predefined. Puppets and dolls are among the tools that can be used to provide a non-threatening basis for this type of communicative work. Various forms of artwork are also often put to good use in this regard (Rymaszewska and Philpot, 2006).

Voice of experience 7.2

❝I found direct work quite scary at first. I felt very uncomfortable with it until I started to see the very positive results it was starting to produce. That gave me the confidence to get involved in a more relaxed way and feel more at ease with what I was doing. It is very rewarding work, as it so often leads to some lovely progress in helping the child find a way forward.**❞** *Lydia, a child therapist*

One particular form of direct work is what is known as 'life-story work'. This involves working on a one-to-one basis with a child to help them establish a clear picture of the path their life has followed so far. It generally involves the use of drawing and photographs to provide a linking thread that establishes a narrative ('tells the story') in ways that help the child develop understanding, self-respect and a basis for moving forward more confidently, in a more empowered way. This approach is often used with children who have been abused, with a view to helping them 'recover' from the traumas involved. It can also be very effective in working with children who have had a lot of changes in their life – for example, children removed from their home who then have a number of placement breakdowns, producing a pattern of confusion, instability and insecurity. See the 'Guide to further learning' at the end of the book for information about relevant literature for this important topic.

'Emotional holding' is a term used to refer to the process of making the child feel emotionally safe and secure. It is the metaphorical equivalent of giving the child a reassuring hug (and may well include literally doing this at times, depending on the circumstances). Emotional holding involves forming an effective rapport to the point where the child gains a sense of security from knowing that there is a competent, reliable adult who can be trusted to support and protect them (Weld, 2009).

PRACTICE FOCUS 7.3

Margaret had worked with children for many years as a classroom assistant before starting her new post at the children's centre. She managed to 'connect' with the children for the most part and was able to do a good job and gain a great deal of job satisfaction. However, with some of the children, especially the ones who had experienced problems and upsets in their lives, she found it much harder to make those connections and build a rapport. It was as if something was stopping her getting through to them. This worried her as she wanted to do a good job for all the children she worked with and not just the majority. After a while, though, she noticed that Nita seemed to be able to engage with all the children and, if anything, she found it even easier with precisely the children Margaret struggled with. She found this intriguing so, to begin with, she watched Nita carefully to see what she could learn about her approach. After picking up quite a few clues form doing this, she decided to talk to Nita about the situation. Nita was very helpful and supportive and explained to Margaret what she had learned at university about 'emotional holding'. Margaret learned a great deal from this and, interestingly, she felt so reassured and supported by what Nita had said (and how engaging and interested she was in saying it), that she felt she was, in a way, being emotionally held by Nita – knowing that she had a competent and reliable person that she could trust to help her made her feel much more confident and empowered. She realized, then, that emotional holding was not just something that was helpful for children.

Emotional holding is closely linked to communication, as there is a two-way relationship between them. That is, emotional holding not only relies on effective communication, but also facilitates that communication – a child will not feel 'held' without good communication, but a 'held' child will be much easier to communicate with than one who does not feel secure and is therefore not prepared to 'open up'.

Before leaving the subject of connecting with children, it is important to note that there are significant links between communications difficulties and behaviour problems for children, in the sense that the two sets of issues frequently occur together. This idea is captured in the following comments from Cross (2004):

> There is mounting evidence for a link between communication difficulties and emotional and behavioural problems. Of those children who have communication difficulties, 50 to 75 per cent are likely to develop emotional and behavioural problems and psychiatric difficulties of all kinds. This means they are three to four times more likely to develop such difficulties than other children. Sixty to 95 per cent of children who have emotional and behavioural difficulties are also likely to have communication difficulties (Baker and Cantwell 1987; Camarata, Hughes and Ruhl 1988). This raises the question, why are the two so closely linked? (p. 41)

I cannot answer the question Cross raises, but I can make the important point that these links emphasize the importance of communication. Cross's comments strongly imply that, if we want to reduce the incidence and intensity of behaviour problems, then we need to take seriously the challenge of helping them develop their communication skills.

ACTIVITY 7.2

Why do you think communication difficulties are so closely linked to emotional and behavioural difficulties? Compare notes with one or more colleagues to see what you can learn from considering these issues.

'Connecting' with young people

Much, if not all, of what applies to communicating with children also applies to communicating with young people, with, of course, suitable amendments made to take account of differences in developmental level. My comments here, then, should be seen as additional to my comments about connecting with children, rather than as a replacement for them.

There is no consensus about when someone stops being a child and becomes a 'young person', and it is probably not meaningful or fruitful to try and pin down the transition to a particular age. The use of the terms 'young people' or 'young person' is perhaps a recognition that the transition from childhood to adulthood is generally a gradual one. Indeed, the term 'adolescent' literally means (in the process of) becoming an adult. Our concern in this chapter, then, is with how to relate to someone who is no longer entirely a child, but has yet to reach full adulthood.

An important point to re-emphasize is that development occurs along various strands, and so uneven development is not uncommon. That is, a young person may be very mature in some ways, yet still quite childlike in other respects. We have to be careful not to mistake one aspect of development for the whole picture and thereby distort that picture. Practice based on a distorted picture can be very dangerous practice, potentially doing more harm than good. Again, there is no substitute for having a good understanding of human development.

Adolescence is often characterized as a time of conflict. Ginott (1969) goes some way towards explaining this: 'As parents, our need is to be needed; as teenagers their need is not to need us. This conflict is real; we experience it daily as we help those we love become independent of us' (cited in Faber and Mazlish, 2006, frontispiece). There is, then, an inherent conflict, as the very nature of adolescence is rooted in conflict – in terms of the tensions between wanting to hold on to cherished and comfortable aspects of childhood, while also wanting to embrace the advantages and privileges of adulthood. However, we should not confuse conflict and a degree of tension and turmoil with stereotypical notions of teenage rebellion. The vast majority of young people pass through adolescence without entering into any significant rebelliousness.

We have to ask ourselves: Are teenagers really that different or is it that they are responding to how they are treated, based on stereotypical assumptions and associated expectations? In other words, if we buy into stereotypes about young people we can create a self-fulfilling prophecy, we can provoke unhelpful reactions. An important starting point, therefore, for communicating with young people is to ensure that we are not allowing misleading stereotypes to influence our expectations and thus our interactions with them.

Communication, of course, contributes to and depends upon relationships. It is therefore essential that we work towards developing relationships based on mutual respect. This can at times involve the skilful use of authority, but it is unfortunately the case that some people attempt this by variations on the theme of barking orders and then wondering why the get a largely noncompliant, if not actually hostile, response. It is not simply a matter of 'treating young people like adults', as that may mean that some of their remaining childlike needs are not met, and it may also involve setting them up to fail if we have adult expectations that they are not yet mature enough to meet – perhaps resulting in a lowering

PRACTICE FOCUS 7.4

Anna was surprised when she attended a course on anti-discriminatory practice to realize how broad based the subject was. She had assumed it would be mainly about dealing with racism, with perhaps some emphasis on sexism. She had not appreciated that it would apply to discrimination against any minority group. She was therefore very surprised to see that there was an exercise on the course about discrimination against children and young people. Despite her surprise, she found the exercise both interesting and useful. In particular, she was fascinated by the discussion of how stereotypes of young people can be so harmful and misleading. Even though she had worked with young people for quite some time, she had never given such matters a moment's thought, but the training exercise made her realize that these were important considerations that would need to be addressed. She therefore decided to put this topic on the agenda for a future team meeting so that her colleagues could have the opportunity of exploring the issues she had been learning about.

of confidence and self-esteem and the creation of unnecessary tensions. So, again, we return to the key theme of skill development. Communicating effectively with young people is a skilful business.

To gain respect we first have to show respect – even in the face of non-cooperation or even hostility. This puts pressure on the young person to reciprocate, to show respect in return and is therefore worth persevering with. In some cases it may take a long time to achieve the position of mutual respect, but communication is likely to be seriously compromised unless and until that point is reached. Showing respect does not mean tolerating unacceptable behaviour, nor does it mean adopting an attitude of 'anything goes'. The reality is much more complex than this. It is partly about the words we use and how we use them, partly about our nonverbal communication and partly about our whole attitude, about the whole way we present ourselves to young people. If they get no sense of genuineness from us, then we should not be surprised if their response is based on suspicion and mistrust.

This is particularly significant when it comes to working with young people who have been abused or otherwise exposed to traumatic experiences. This is because:

1. The abuse or trauma may have triggered a situation in which they have a very low level of trust towards adults.
2. Their level of self-esteem, and with it their level of self-respect, may have been eroded, and so giving and receiving respect could have become more difficult to achieve because of this.

3. As a result of bad experiences, the young person may display some testing behaviour which is literally testing – using perhaps extreme behaviour in an attempt to establish whether or not they are safe with the person concerned. This in turn can make giving and receiving respect more difficult.

In considering other aspects of communicating with young people, again the question of loss arises. Faber and Mazlish (2006) describe the losses associated with adolescence:

Loss of old, close relationship. (*Who is this hostile person living in my home?*)
Loss of confidence. (*Why is he acting this way? Is it something I've done ... or haven't done?*)
Loss of the satisfaction of being needed. (*'No, you don't have to come. My friends will go with me.'*)
Loss of the sense of ourselves as all-powerful protectors who could keep our children safe from harm. (*It's past midnight. Where is she? What is she doing? Why isn't she home yet?*) (p. xvi)

We can therefore learn a great deal about what makes young people 'tick' by tuning in to the significance of loss. This will especially be the case where there are other losses involved, and not just those that are typical of adolescence. This would include:

- Losses associated with abuse or trauma, as already discussed;
- In the case of young offenders, losses connected with possible deprivation of liberty;
- Loss of relationships due to family breakdown where it becomes necessary for a young person to be received into care or 'accommodated';
- Leaving school also brings losses, of course, even for young people who have not enjoyed school or flourished there.

ACTIVITY 7.3

How significant do you think loss experiences might be in children's and young people's lives, especially when they have experienced a high number of such losses? How might your understanding of such matters influence your practice?

To 'connect' with young people is not simply using the right words, the right tone of voice or the right body language (although these are all important) – it also involves having a good understanding of the world adolescents live in, which can be very different from the world that adults occupy. This involves having a good understanding of broad patterns and themes that apply to adolescence in general, but also being able to combine this with an understanding of the circumstances as they apply to this particular young person as well as empathically appreciating how all this looks from the point of view of that young person. Communicating with young people is therefore not simply a matter of developing a set of technical skills. Much also depends on having a good professional understanding on which to base our approach and thus our interactions.

PRACTICE FOCUS 7.5

Chen worked with young people for two years before going to university to gain a professional qualification. He had enjoyed his work for the most part, although he found it very challenging too and found that he was out of his depth at times, not really sure what to do. He was therefore delighted when, in the early stages of his course at the university, he found that there was so much to learn about young people. He was excited about how the combination of his hands-on experience and his new-found depth of knowledge could make him a much more effective worker. He realized that the course was going to be hard work and take a lot of commitment from him but it had not taken him long to recognize the value of the learning process he was embarking on. He was already looking forward to putting his new understanding into practice.

Building up our skills

There have been (at least) two recurring themes in this chapter. One is the importance of basing our practice in general and our communication in particular on a good understanding of human development, particularly as it applies to children and young people. That knowledge base needs to underpin our efforts at skill development. Without the necessary knowledge base, that skill development becomes much more difficult, if not impossible. The other theme has been the recognition that communicating with children and young people is a highly skilled understanding – it is not just 'common sense', nor will our everyday communication skills be sufficient to deal with some of the very challenging experiences members of the helping professions are likely to encounter in trying to support, protect and educate children and young people. In this final part of the chapter my focus is therefore on the skills we need and how to develop them. Realistically it cannot be an exhaustive or comprehensive account of such a large and complex topic, but it can at least lay the foundations for future learning.

Skill development is something that can happen spontaneously through experience without any formal training or study. For example, most parents learn their parenting skills in this way. So, it is possible to develop skills simply by doing the job. However, there is a strong and widely accepted argument that learning is much more effective if a more focused, intentional approach to learning is adopted – that is, by combining elements of spontaneous learning with a more deliberate, considered approach is what is likely to achieve optimal results. This is consistent with the idea of critically reflective practice. By reflecting on, and critically analysing, our work, we can draw out much more learning from it. In this way we can also incorporate learning from other sources – training courses, reading, discussion, supervision and so on. This enable us not only to draw upon the professional knowledge base available, but also to increase that knowledge over time, whereas relying on spontaneous, unfocused learning will not enable us to develop our knowledge base. On the contrary, such learning encourages us to stick with what we know and therefore to be quite limited in the range of things we can do and the creativity we could potentially bring to our work.

Voice of experience 7.3

❝I regularly have students on placement with me, and it is interesting to note how so many of them seem to arrive with the idea that they will learn simply from doing the job. They are surprised when I explain to them about the exercises we will be doing in supervision and about the guided reading I will expect them to do. But they all end up leaving at the end of the placement, glad that I have helped them to maximize their learning.**❞** *Rose, a practice teacher and mentor*

So, what are the skills we need to draw upon in communicating with children and young people?

The following suggestions should be seen as being necessary *in addition to* the other skills needed for effective communication in general, such as assertiveness, clarity, empathy and so on, and not as a replacement for them:

- Being able to recognize a child or young person's level of development; this is partly a matter of having the necessary knowledge base, but also requires a degree of skill in being able to draw upon that knowledge appropriately.
- Being adaptable; this means not only recognizing levels of development, but also being flexible enough to adapt our style accordingly.
- Not being drawn into 'sinking to their level'; when children or young people are being challenging or are testing you out, it is very easy to

slip into childlike or juvenile behaviour or language in response. This can potentially lead to a vicious circle in which each party's inappropriate behaviour encourages the other's. It is therefore essential to have the presence of mind not to allow ourselves to get drawn into this. We have to lead by example, however difficult that might be at times.

- Being able to use a wide range of communicative methods, including play and joining in activities so that we can use the opportunities for 'connecting' that these are likely to generate.
- Observing; we can learn so much from watching others (adults and children). Learning from observation is not simply a matter of copying – once again, what is needed is critically reflective practice (drawing out the learning from the experience).

Of course, we are communicating all the time, so we have excellent raw materials to draw upon in general. On those occasions we work with children and young people, we are again presented with rich learning resources from which we can develop both our knowledge and our skills.

But it isn't just about knowledge and skills; there are also values to consider. One value that is particularly important in communicating with children is being child centred – trying to see the world from their point of view, recognizing their vulnerabilities, but also recognizing their strengths and resilience – so that we are best placed to support and protect them and help them learn and develop. Much the same can be said of working with young people, but with the added complication of finding that delicate balance of not neglecting their remaining childlike needs, while also helping them to strive for adulthood and the relative independence it brings.

PRACTICE FOCUS 7.6

Roberta's work in adult mental health had taught her the importance of being person centred, as this was an important consideration in making sure that patients are treated as people and not simply as a diagnosis. So, when it came to working in a child-care context, she already had a head start when it came to adopting a child-centred approach. Because of the significance of children's differing levels of development, she knew she would have to adopt a more sophisticated approach, but it did not take her long to make the transition. She was quickly able to apply her knowledge and skills to her new context, with both of these underpinned by her values – particularly the value of being child centred in her approach. This would stand her in good stead in her work with children.

Conclusion

Some people see communicating with children and young people as a matter of 'common sense', just using the skills they have learned in their everyday lives. However, there are two problems with this. First, while such an approach may get you so far, it will have significant limitations – particularly in those more complex and demanding situations that arise (situations involving challenging behaviour and/or abuse, for example). Second, and perhaps more importantly, an uneducated, unenlightened approach to communication with children and young people could well be not only ineffective, but also counterproductive, actually doing more harm than good.

The need to develop the skills involved in communicating with children and young people is therefore a hugely important consideration. As we have seen, such skills need to be premised on a professional knowledge base. And, as we have also noted, both knowledge and skills need to be premised on values. This chapter will not be enough on its own to provide you with the knowledge, skills and values you need, but it is to be hoped that it will have at least laid a foundation on which you can build over time.

POINTS TO PONDER

- Why is it important to fit our level of communication to the child's or young person's level of development?
- What do you see as your main strengths in communicating with children and young people? How might you build on these?
- What do you see as your main areas for development? How might you be able to build these up over time?

CHAPTER 8

Working with groups

Introduction

Modern western societies tend to be based on a strong sense of individualism (Bauman, 2001). However, this focus on the individual can be misleading, as it can distract attention from the fact that so much of our lives takes place in groups. As we shall see, groups are not just the sum total of the individuals concerned. Groups take on a life of their own to a certain extent (see the discussion of 'group dynamics' below), and also complicate matters by interacting with other groups, sometimes in positive, helpful ways, and sometimes in negative, destructive ways. These are important issues for professional practice (including the practice of managers) in general, as groups influence various aspects of the situations we encounter, but they are particularly relevant when we focus on communication. Our focus in this chapter is therefore on the factors we need to consider when communicating in and with groups.

The chapter is divided into eight main sections. In the first I present an overview of how groups work and how and why they are very relevant to the helping professions. This is followed by a discussion of working with families (families are groups after all). Next comes a section on making presentations, something that many people find terrifying. This leads into a discussion of effective meetings, as meetings are a very important and common basis for communication, although complaints about their lack of effectiveness are sadly not uncommon. Undertaking groupwork as a therapeutic or problem-solving method comes next, followed by a discussion of promoting teamwork and the importance of leadership. Multidisciplinary collaboration is also a topic worthy of attention, as group factors can be very significant in relation to communication (and thus effectiveness) when it comes to multidisciplinary partnerships. Finally, I make some brief comments about the challenges involved in building up our skills in this aspect of the world of communication.

Understanding groups

This chapter explores various (but not necessarily all) ways in which our communicative efforts can involve interactions within or between groups. It can be helpful, therefore, to begin by having a picture of how groups work, as this knowledge will help us to make sure that our efforts to communicate are as effective as possible.

In an earlier work I commented that:

> Almost everybody is a member of one or more groups, whether they are formal, such as teams, clubs or societies, or informal, such as gatherings of friends and other associates. Such groups tend to serve as a powerful influence on us, both directly and indirectly. They can be a source of significant problems for us in terms of conflicts and tensions, but they can also be a significant source of solutions in terms of support, camaraderie and important resources to fall back on ... (Thompson, 2010, p. 92)

This helps us to appreciate that the group context of our communication is a significant set of factors to take into account. This can apply in one-to-one interactions which are influenced by the group context in which it is taking place as well as interactions that are across a group or even between groups.

In working with any group it can be important to know what the nature of the group is and what implications this has for our work. Different groups will have different characteristics and therefore different implications. Consider differences and similarities across the following situations: a therapy group in a psychiatric unit; a business meeting in a large commercial organization; a family meal; a multidisciplinary safeguarding meeting; a group of friends having a celebration. So, this needs to be our starting point – we need to ask ourselves: what sort of group context am I involved in? What difference might this make to how I need to communicate?

A key part of this is an awareness of the role and significance of group dynamics. This term refers to the significant interplays that characterize particular groups. Different groups will have different dynamics. The following factors are important 'ingredients' of group dynamics:

- *Conflicts*   Human interactions are characterized by conflicts, ranging from very mild and easily managed on the one hand to very severe and very challenging to deal with on the other. This applies just as much in groups if not more so. Conflicts can distort situations; they can push our interactions in one direction or make it harder to go in another. 'Tuning in' to any conflicts in the group concerned is therefore an important basis for making our communication as effective as possible.
- *Alliances*   These can be a way of dealing with conflicts and often arise from them. Alliances can sometimes be formed deliberately, with one or more people strategically developing a basis for cooperation in taking matters forward. At other times such alliances form spontaneously as a result of shared interests leading to a desire for

certain people to collaborate in terms of protecting or promoting those interests. It can be very helpful to be aware of those alliances so that (i) you can tailor your communications accordingly to suit the circumstances; and (ii) you can seek to ensure that you do not get 'stitched up' by an alliance of people who are happy to safeguard their own interests at your expense.

- *Phantoms*   This is a term used to refer to fears which, although they may have no objective grounding in reality, are none the less real in their consequences – in the sense that they are influencing the interactions in the group, the direction it is taking and so on (for example, consider a team who are under the impression that the forthcoming reorganization will result in the breaking up of the team; this belief will have a very real impact on them, even if ultimately it turns out not to have been true). Phantoms can significantly distort communication, so it can be very wise to be aware of them where possible.

- *Groupthink*   This refers to the tendency for groups – especially decision-making groups – to 'play it safe', with members not prepared to express concerns for fear of 'rocking the boat' and spoiling the collaborative working atmosphere in the group. This can be very dangerous, as it can lead to very ineffective decision making. Marsen (2006) lists the following ways in which groupthink can manifest itself:
    o The group has not fully considered alternatives.
    o The group has not clearly examined objectives.
    o The group has not taken into account the possible risks of their decision.
    o The group has not re-evaluated alternatives that it rejected at a previous stage of the process.
    o The group has not conducted a comprehensive information search and may therefore be ignorant of important issues.
    o The group has shown prejudice or bias in evaluating the information at hand.
    o The group has not worked out what to do in an emergency or if their decision proves ineffective. (p. 98)

  The overemphasis on conformity in groupthink means that communications based on conflict or opposing views will be largely or completely suppressed, possibly with dire consequences. Maximizing our communicative effectiveness in groups therefore needs to include the ability to recognize groupthink and to challenge it constructively where it does occur.

- *Cultural expectations*   Culture takes many forms: national and regional cultures; organizational cultures; professional cultures; and so on. Cultures are, in effect, sets of unwritten rules, taken-for-granted assumptions and habits. As such, they can have a major influence on the shape, tone, direction and effectiveness of communication. It can therefore be helpful to consider what effect the cultural context of the group is so that you can be aware of how cultural factors may be aiding or constraining the communicative efforts of those involved.

- *Gender dynamics*   It would be naive not to recognize that gender differences can play a significant part in shaping group dynamics. There is a high likelihood that, due to a complex set of psychological and sociological factors, all-male groups, all-female groups and mixed groups will operate in different ways. There is a significant literature base about gender dynamics that helps us to understand that these are significant factors that should not be ignored. See the discussion of gender and communication in Chapter 5.

- *Hidden agendas*   What goes on 'under the table' can be just as influential, if not more so, as what goes on 'over the table'. That is, people's private or 'hidden' agendas can be a major factor in either supporting or undermining the official agenda. This can often arise as a result of the development of alliances, as mentioned above. Being able to spot a hidden agenda can be a very useful way of preventing communication breakdowns and distortions.

A linking theme across these factors is the role of power. To a large extent group dynamics are power dynamics, and so we should not lose sight of the various ways in which power operates in social interactions (see Thompson, 2007).

PRACTICE FOCUS 8.1

Samir was asked to chair a working party on the implementation of the new legislation. He was keen to do a good job as he had never undertaken such a role before. A series of meetings was arranged to discuss and clarify what steps would need to be taken to comply with the new law. Samir expected it to be a constructive and relatively straightforward process. However, the reality turned out to be very different from his expectation. Different people seemed to be going off in different directions, alliances were forming, there seemed to be other issues at stake and not just the official aim of planning a response to the legislative changes. At first Samir was very confused by it all, and not a little disappointed. He also felt at a loss as to how to deal with it. Just before the next meeting he decided that he would need to watch very carefully what was going on and see if he could get to the bottom of it. However, without a knowledge of group dynamics, he was going to struggle to make sense of the complex processes that were going on.

Working with families

Just as groups in general have group dynamics, families can be seen to have family dynamics. That is, there will be significant recurring patterns and processes in families. They are not just a simple collection of related individuals. Family 'cultures' develop – established norms and expectations. In some ways these can be helpful and can be a positive benefit to the individuals concerned and to the family as a whole (for example, the ways in which members listen to each other and act supportively to one another). In other ways they can be harmful (for example, when conflicts are brushed under the carpet and not dealt with, leading to smouldering resentment and ill-feeling – and quite possibly triggering a vicious circle in which the resentment leads to further conflicts which are also not dealt with, thereby contributing to more resentment; and on it goes). What can also happen is that the family's characteristic ways of interacting have the effect of splitting the family. This is because some members will benefit while others will lose out. It is not simply a case of the family either benefiting or not (as a whole) from the way they tend to operate; rather, it is a matter of having winners and losers. For example, in terms of how household tasks are allocated in the family, there may well be (and often is) a distinct inequality in the division of labour.

ACTIVITY 8.1

What style of communication characterized the family you grew up in? What would you see as the characteristics of how communication took place within the family group? How might an understanding of such issues help you in your current work when it comes to communicating with groups?

For many years attempts to intervene in families were based on a simplistic systems model based on mechanistic thinking that failed to do justice to the *human* factors that are at work in family dynamics. More recently, however, families have been understood and worked with on the basis of the idea that they develop joint narratives, a shared story of what the family is all about, what is expected of individuals and so in. In effect, current understandings are predominantly based on the idea that families develop their own culture.

This has implications for our communications with families. This is partly because, without an understanding of the complexities of family dynamics, we may struggle to communicate effectively within a family context. For example, if we are not aware of unequal power relations within the family, we may wrongly assume that when a powerful person in the family speaks (the father, perhaps), he is speaking for the whole family because no one else offers an alternative perspective. The silence of the less powerful members of the family may be crucial, but someone unaware of how families operate may well be oblivious to this and therefore miss a key issue. It is also partly because, without an awareness of family dynamics, the professional may get drawn into those dynamics and become part of them. For example, if there is a power battle going on, an ill-informed worker trying to engage with that family may well unwittingly become a pawn in that battle.

Voice of experience 8.1

"The past three years of working with families has taught me just how complex they can be, just how many different strands there can be to what makes them tick. I can pick up on issues much faster now after all this time. My training stood me in good stead and my experience has built on that.**"**
James, a family therapist

Making presentations

Members of the helping professions, including managers, are likely to be called upon to make a presentation from time to time or even on a regular basis. This could be a presentation to a meeting or case conference or perhaps a contribution to a training course or other such staff development activity, or even a conference presentation. Whatever the setting the basic guidelines are the same:

- *Be not afraid!*   It is understandable that people who are not used to 'public speaking' will experience a degree of anxiety. However, if we are not careful, we can allow a counterproductive vicious circle of anxiety to develop: our anxiety impairs our ability to do the job smoothly and effectively; this in turn makes us more anxious, which then further impairs our ability to do what we set out to. In an earlier work (Thompson, 2006b), I have written about the importance of turning anxiety into fear – that is, of trying to work out exactly what it is that we are afraid of. We are then in a stronger position to prevent our fears from being realized. In particular, do not let your anxiety lead you into making the mistake of reading from a script – that does not go down well with an audience.
- *Be prepared*   While it can be a mistake to overprepare and turn your presentation into a stilted rehearsed speech, some degree of preparation is needed. As a minimum you will need to be clear about what points you want to get across and in what order. Cards with bullet points can be helpful but try not to write too much down, as the time it takes you to read your notes will slow you down – just a few key

words to remind you of what you wanted to say should be enough. Similarly, it is important to be prepared in terms of the appropriate dress code – feeling that you are not appropriately dressed for the occasion will not help keep your nervousness under control.

PRACTICE FOCUS 8.2

This was the third time Ian had made a presentation. The first time he did it he had not 'done his homework' – that is, he had not made any preparations. This was not through overconfidence. Rather, it was more a case of his anxiety causing him to keep putting it off until the day of the presentation arrived and he had only managed to put together some scrappy and not particularly coherent notes the night before. Not surprisingly, the presentation did not go well at all. He vowed that he would never go into a presentation so unprepared as he had found it quite a distressing and embarrassing experience.

The second time he made a presentation he went to the other extreme – that is, he *overprepared*. He made very detailed notes so that he felt much more secure as he went into the session. However, when his turn came to present, he had so much information in front of him in his notes that he found it difficult to focus on what he wanted to say. The presentation in effect turned into little more than Ian reading out his notes – an approach that was not well received by the group. Ian was aware of this as he was going through the presentation and so it made him feel worse, even more anxious and self-conscious.

So, this time, his third attempt, he was determined to get it right. He had sought advice from an experienced colleague who had made many successful presentations over the years. As a result of this advice, he had prepared some bullet points (in the order he wanted to present them) and used these as the basis of his presentation. This worked really well for him. It was just enough to give him a clear picture of what he wanted to say, but in a format that he could refer to quickly without losing himself in detailed notes.

- *Avoid the common pitfalls*   If you are using visual aids, make sure you do not stand in the way. Don't speak too slowly – or too quickly; don't mumble and don't shout (projecting your voice and shouting are two different things). Don't forget to introduce yourself (if necessary) and remember to say thank you at the end. Getting any of these wrong could spoil your presentation, undermine what you are trying to say and undermine your credibility too. So, they are nothing to get unduly anxious about but they do need your attention.

Effective meetings

The basic function of a meeting is to bring people together to facilitate communication. However, whether or not the meeting is effective in achieving its aims depends on a number of factors. Chief among these are the skill, commitment and performance of the meeting's chairperson. However, it would be a significant mistake to assume that this is the only factor. In reality, *every* participant has a part to play in making sure the meeting is effective, not just the person who is chairing it – the success or otherwise of a meeting is a *shared* responsibility.

Meetings are a complex matter and could easily form the basis of a book in its own right (see the 'Guide to further learning' at the end of the book). However, for present purposes I must restrict myself to outlining some key strategies for trying to ensure that our communication efforts achieve maximum effect in the context of the meetings we are involved in.

- *Preparation*   Are you clear about what you want out of the meeting? Do you know what you are expected to contribute (or what you can contribute)? Is the purpose of the meeting clear? Similarly, is the status of the meeting clear – that is, is it simply to share information, to make recommendations or to make decisions? Will you need to prepare a written report? Will you be expected to make a presentation? If this is a follow-up meeting, a regular meeting or part of a series of meetings, have you read the minutes of the previous meeting? If appropriate, have you followed up on any action points that relate to you?

- *Prioritizing*   It is primarily the chair's responsibility to ensure that the meeting runs smoothly, keeps to time and achieves its aims. However, there is no reason why other participants cannot assist him or her in terms of sticking to the agenda, making sure that relatively minor items do not take up too much time and leaving insufficient space for more important or pressing matters. I am not suggesting that you should 'take over' or act in such a way that the chair loses face or feels undermined, but the sensitive and skilful use of assertiveness skills (which are, after all, communication skills) can play an important part in making the meeting a success.

- *Participating*   There is no point in speaking up just for the sake of it, but going to the other extreme of not saying something that needs saying is potentially very problematic. This can happen because of nervousness, loss of concentration (in a long meeting it is inevitable that people will lose concentration from time to time) or because it is difficult to 'get a word in edgeways'. However, it has to be remembered that we have a professional responsibility to contribute appropriately to meetings even if that may make us feel uncomfortable from time to time. Doing the best for the people we serve as professionals is more important than remaining in our comfort zone all the time. Also, if we stay permanently in our comfort zone, we will not learn, grow or develop.

- *Planning*   There is a danger that, when we come out of a meeting, there are perhaps telephone messages waiting for us as well as emails that may need attention and other tasks to attend to, with the possible result that what has been discussed in the meeting quickly gets forgotten and recommendations and/or decisions made do not get carried through. It is therefore of great importance that, on leaving a meeting, we develop a plan of what we need to do as a result of that meeting before we get embroiled in other things.

PRACTICE FOCUS 8.3

Judith had been a member of the working party for three months now and had grown increasingly frustrated with how ineffective the meetings were. They took up a lot of time and achieved very little of positive value. This was partly because the chair of the working party was not very experienced or skilled in managing meetings and there were different factions within the group who were pulling in different directions, with the net result that no progress was being made. However, when Carla joined the working party things began to change. She was very skilful in helping the chair to focus. She asked all the right questions and made all the right comments to make sure that there was clarity about the aims of the group and what steps they needed to take to achieve them. This helped to bring to the surface the conflicting perspectives, and this then provided a platform for airing the differences and looking constructively at how to move forward. Carla was so skilled that she not only avoided offending or alienating the chair, she also gave him the opportunity to be more effective in doing his job. Judith was delighted with these changes and decided that, in the short term, she would do everything she could to support Carla in taking the group forward and, in the longer term, she would try and develop the advanced-level group communication skills she had seen Carla use to such good effect.

Undertaking groupwork

Social workers, psychologists, psychiatrists and psychiatric nurses, thera-pists of various kinds and community workers are among the many people who have found groupwork a helpful and empowering way of supporting people with their difficulties and making progress towards higher levels of well-being. Much of the value of groupwork comes from creating a safe, reliable forum in which communication can be facilitated so that the group members are able to develop supportive relationships with each other as well as the group leader.

An effective groupworker therefore needs to be able not only to communicate effectively, but also create the right atmosphere for group members to communicate with one another. Creating the right atmosphere or ethos is a key part of leadership, so it is in this sense that a groupworker is in effect a group *leader*. This does not mean that he or she makes all the decisions and spends his or her time giving orders. Groupwork is intended to be an empowering process, so the leadership role needs to be a facilitative one rather than a command and control one. The leader does need to be able to exercise authority in order to create a safe environment and a helpful focus and structure, but this should not extend into being the 'boss' of the group. Doel (2006), in an important text on the subject, comments helpfully:

> Part of the process of leadership is the exercise of control. Because of the pejorative connotations of words like 'controlling', groupworkers sometimes shy away from control, yet it is of fundamental value in groups. Ironically, fear of losing it is one of the main reasons why many do not practise groupwork. Group members will not attend a group they feel is out of control, since it will be perceived as unsafe, but exercising control in ways which is experienced as empowering demands skill. At all times you should think of yourself as exercising control *on behalf of the group*, until such time that the group can fairly exercise this control itself. (p. 101)

ACTIVITY 8.2

What skills would you associate with being a good group leader? How might you recognize that a group is not working well because of a lack of leadership? What might you be able to do about such a situation?

Groupwork skills can range from quite basic to very advanced, allowing scope for groupworkers to develop the quality, depth and scope of their skills. The following pointers can be helpful in developing our capabilities for effective communication in a groupwork context:

- *Preparation*   Beginning groupwork unprepared will make the job much harder. So, before getting a group off the ground you will need to give careful consideration to such important questions as:
    o What is the purpose of the group?

- o Who will be involved? Will membership be restricted to people who are invited to join (a closed group) or will it be possible for anyone who is interested to join in (an open group)?
- o How often will it meet? How long will the sessions be?
- o Will it be for a fixed period of time or will it be ongoing for as long as it is needed?
- o Will I be using any particular groupwork methods or activities?

- *Reading processes* Once the group is up and running it will be important to have the sensitivity and observation skills to be able to 'read' the interpersonal and group processes that are going on, to become attuned to the important dynamics that develop.

- *Guiding processes* Being able to read the processes also needs to be accompanied by the skills involved in guiding those processes. There is an important set of skills involved in being able to influence a group in a positive direction without taking over or being prescriptive. These are again advanced-level communication skills.

- *Handling silences* As Doel (2006) comments: 'Silences in groups are often difficult because they can provoke quick judgements about the cause of the silence' (p. 125). It is therefore important to get the balance right: not to panic or overreact when a silence occurs (reflective pauses can be very helpful), but being able to gently move the group on if a silence becomes too long and creates so much tension that it is becoming counterproductive.

- *Getting the practicalities right* This is partly about planning, as discussed above, but is also an ongoing issue. It involves addressing the following questions:
  - o Do you have a suitable venue that will be available on a regular basis at no cost or at a cost that your budget will run to? Are you able to book it well in advance?
  - o Is the venue disability friendly?
  - o Will refreshments be available?
  - o Can suitable transport and/or parking arrangements be made?
  - o Will you need any resources for particular activities?

Voice of experience 8.2

&&I was very lucky as I did a placement in a psychiatric unit where I had the chance to learn groupwork skills from an experienced colleague. She allowed me to work with her on a groupwork project helping people develop social skills. In the early sessions she took the lead and I played a supporting role, but then we switched so that I was leading, with her supporting me. It worked really well and I learned so much from it.&& *Khaled, a community development worker*

Promoting teamwork

A team, of course, is more than just a collection of individuals. A team develops its own dynamic (or set of dynamics) and with this its own culture (a set of habits, taken-for-granted assumptions and unwritten rules). This dynamic is largely spontaneous arising from the interactions among group members over time. However, a skilled leader can influence that dynamic in a positive direction by: (i) reinforcing those aspects of the culture that are helpful, constructive and of value; and (ii) undermining those aspects that are negative, destructive and problematic.

Within any team there will be considerable variety, and this can be both a benefit and a challenge. Diversity is now increasingly being recognized as an asset to society in general and to organizations in particular (Parekh, 2006; Thompson, 2011). Clutterbuck (2007) discusses how this applies to senior management teams, although the same arguments can also relate to other teams:

> Several studies have found that top management teams that have diverse backgrounds and capabilities make more innovative , higher-quality decisions than those that are relatively homogeneous [Bantel and Jackson, 1989; Murray, A. I., 1989]
>
> Being diverse isn't enough, however. Using diversity effectively in decision making demands that the team has processes that allow its members to have open and positively critical dialogue, to investigate issues with an open mind and to be willing to learn from the situation and from each other. They also need to be able to identify and understand others' perspectives and synthesize these into a decision that is better than that which might have emerged through the horse-trading and compromise that so often characterize management decision making. (pp. 55–6)

He goes on to argue that, while diversity can present difficulties at first, the benefits are likely to be felt further down the road. Indeed, being able to maximize the benefits of diversity is an important set of skills for leaders of teams. Part of this is the need for effective intercultural communication, a topic to which we shall return in Chapter 9.

A key part of promoting teamwork is having clear goals and a sense of direction inspired by them. This is because clarity about goals gives a sense of shared responsibility for achieving them, and this can have the effect of bringing people together. However, teams can sometimes become so busy and so immersed in their day-to-day duties that they lose sight of their overall goals. This can not only undermine teamwork, but also become counterproductive, in so far as busy but directionless activity can so easily become ineffective or even cause more problems than it solves.

Having clearly defined, shared goals is a necessary condition for optimal teamwork but it is not a sufficient condition. Also necessary is the ability to deal constructively with conflicts. It would be naive not to recognize that there will be conflict in every team. Most teams seem to manage their conflicts of perspective, approach priorities and so on without any major problems, although it is also the case that many teams have significant conflicts and are not very good at managing them. Unresolved conflicts can smoulder for a long time, with the risk that they can burst into flames at any point and do great harm. However, what can be even worse is that they fester over time, never developing to the point where they might erupt and then clear the air. The result is that the underlying conflicts lower morale (and thus motivation and effectiveness) and create a tense and unpleasant working environment. This can create a vicious circle in which the tension makes it less likely that the conflicts will be addressed and the ongoing conflicts ensure that the tension persists – the two sets of factors reinforce each other.

Communication is a crucial issue in relation to conflict. This is because poor communication can cause conflict or exacerbate existing conflicts, while effective communication can resolve or at least reduce conflicts. Ignoring conflict is therefore not part of being an effective communicator.

Earlier in the chapter I made the point that it is not only the chair of a meeting who can contribute to making the meeting an effective encounter. There is a direct parallel here, in so far as the team leader clearly has a primary responsibility for making the team work effectively as a collective entity, but of course every team member shares that responsibility to some extent.

PRACTICE FOCUS 8.4

Meg was delighted with her promotion, albeit a bit overawed by her new responsibilities. The friendliness of her new colleagues helped her settle and she soon felt much more relaxed. However, she soon developed new concerns, not about herself, but about how the team functioned. People seemed to be pulling in different directions, and there seemed to be no consensus on what the team was all about and what they were trying to achieve. Fortunately she was still on good terms with her previous manager who had offered to support her in her new post if she needed any guidance. Meg was glad that she took up the offer of this support as she gained some valuable advice about how it would be necessary to work with the team to establish some clear, shared goals and, in the process, to identify underlying conflicts and pave the way for addressing them constructively as a team. Meg again felt a bit overawed by what she needed to do, but with her previous manager's support, she felt confident that she would get the team where it needed to be in the end.

Communicating clearly within the team and on its behalf externally is clearly an important part of that.

Multidisciplinary collaboration

Working in partnership with colleagues from other agencies has always been important, but is now even higher on the agenda as a basis for high-quality care, support and assistance. Fundamental to effectiveness in this area is high-quality communication. For different professionals to work together as 'seamlessly' as possible, each has to have a good understanding of the others' roles and to 'connect' with them accordingly. This involves being a skilled communicator, someone who is sensitive to the context in which communication is taking place and 'tuned in' to where the other partners are coming from: their needs, their expectations, their priorities and so on.

Voice of experience 8.3

"I have had some very mixed experiences of multidisciplinary working. Sometimes it seems to click and everyone is supportive of one another and we work together to provide a really good service. But at other times, working with other professionals can be like walking through treacle – it's very messy and you don't seem to be getting anywhere.**"** *Chris, a children's centre worker*

Effective communication in a multidisciplinary context involves the following features, the four Cs:

- *Clarity and agreement about goals*   As with effective teamwork, clarity about goals is an important consideration. As Clutterbuck (2007) comments:

  > Communication within the team is helped by having clear goals and clearly defined roles, responsibilities and task structures. Clarity of goals and structures also reduces conflict and promotes the development of "shared mental models" [Madhaven and Grover, 1998] – common views of the work and the environment in which the team operates – that make communication between team members easier. (p. 61)

  This applies as much to multidisciplinary teams as it does to teams within the same organization. Similarly, it applies to both formally established multidisciplinary teams that work together on a full-time basis and *ad hoc* partnerships that come together only for specific projects or pieces of work. If the individuals involved in any form of multidisciplinary collaboration are not clear about the goals they (collectively) are aiming for, then there is a very real danger that the collaboration will be less effective than it could have been and may not be effective at all in some cases.

- *Clarity and agreement about how to achieve the goals*   Having agreement about the shared goals is only one part of what is needed. It also needs to be accompanied by agreement about what steps need to be taken to achieve the goals. Without this there could easily be a consensus about what needs to be achieved, but a failure to achieve it because different people are pulling in different directions.
- *Communication*   Partners in any multidisciplinary collaboration need to keep the channels of communication open throughout the process. This needs to involve communicating with each other respectfully and supportively, with any professional rivalries or jealousies kept to an absolute minimum. It also involves avoiding misunderstandings or ill feeling through the inappropriate use of jargon.
- *Conflict management skills*   There will inevitably be a degree of conflict in any shared endeavour and it would be naive to try and remove it altogether (as well as potentially counterproductive, as

PRACTICE FOCUS 8.5

Joe had been discharged from hospital at lunchtime the day after he was admitted as a result of drinking heavily and taking sleeping tablets the night before. On the evening of the day he was discharged he committed suicide with an overdose of paracetamol tablets. He had been depressed for the previous year or so and had received help from the local community mental health team until he told them he did not want any further input from them. Following this tragic event, his daughter, Lisa, made a formal complaint against the health authority. She argued that her father should not have been discharged, as his previous history of depression combined with concerns that his unsafe consumption of alcohol and sleeping tablets should have alerted the professionals to a possible suicide risk. Lisa told the health authority that, if she was not happy with the response to her complaint, she would consider litigation.

An independent investigator was asked to look into the matter and to write a report. The professionals involved were relieved to find that the investigator's report concluded that there had been no clear indication of suicidal intent on Joe's part (he had denied on the ward that his combination of alcohol and sleeping tablets had been an attempt to harm himself). However, the report was very critical of the lack of multidisciplinary communication. The investigator had been very disappointed in the lack of liaison across the professionals who had been involved in Joe's care.

conflict can be helpful and fruitful at times). We learn some degree of conflict management skill as part of our everyday lives – it is part of our upbringing. However, in a professional context we generally need a more advanced level of conflict management skill if we are to achieve optimal outcomes in our work. There is therefore much to be gained by building up our conflict management skills to as advanced a level as we can as part of the broader process of developing advanced-level communication skills.

Building up our skills

It has to be recognized that there is no shortage of opportunities for building up our skills in communicating in a group context. This is because so much of our interaction with others is set in the wider framework of one or more groups: families, teams, multidisciplinary networks and so on. However, it also has to be recognized that there are significant potential barriers to developing the skills required. Probably the most notable of these is anxiety. Feeling anxious about speaking up in front of others can be a major obstacle to developing the knowledge, skills and confidence to become a highly skilled group communicator. If this applies to you, then it is advisable that you seek support in trying to address the issues involved. Allowing anxiety to block progress means that you are paying a high price for such anxiety in terms of lost potential, and that price is one your clients/patients/service users also pay, as they lose out too.

ACTIVITY 8.3

What opportunities to work with groups are you likely to have in your chosen field of work? How could you develop or build on your confidence in this area?

A further potentially significant obstacle is a lack of self-awareness. If we are not able to 'tune in' to the processes going on around us, how they affect us and how we are playing a part in them, then we will struggle to achieve optimal communicative effectiveness. This lack of awareness may be linked with anxiety, as discussed above, or it may be due to a tendency to think in narrow, individualistic terms and therefore not recognize the significance of wider social factors in shaping what goes on. It may also be a personality factor. Many people have not learned as part of their upbringing to develop the insight needed to appreciate the subtle interactions between self and others, self and group. However, whatever the cause of the lack of self-awareness, it remains the case that its absence is a significant obstacle to developing our skills.

Having considered two major barriers to skill development in this area, it is important that we also explore positive ways forward. Chief among these is an emphasis on developing critically reflective practice. A reflective practitioner is someone who has a 'reflective conversation with the situation' (Schön, 1983) which means that they constantly make links backwards and forwards between the situation they are working with and their own knowledge, skills and values. They engage in their work in a carefully considered way rather than simply acting on the basis of habit, routine and guesswork. A critically reflective practitioner is someone who engages in reflective practice but does so *critically* – that is, they do not take things at face value (Thompson and Thompson, 2008). They adopt a questioning approach to both sides of the equation – the situation they are involved with *and* the knowledge, skills and values they are bringing to bear to make sense of it and to act upon it.

Adopting a critically reflective approach does not guarantee optimal effectiveness in group communication, but it does significantly increase the chances of doing so as it provides a sound foundation for doing the 'tuning in' that is needed to make the most of our communicative efforts.

PRACTICE FOCUS 8.6

June was not a particularly timid person, but nor was she the most confident in group situations. She was keen to do the best job possible and thought that she was until she attended a course on working with groups. The course made her realize that she tended to hold herself back in group situations. For example, she rarely said anything at meetings. She had not seen this as a problem until the course made her realize that she was not providing the best level of service she could if she was holding back in group situations. The course also helped her realize that if she continued to hold back she would be blocking her own learning as she would not be allowing herself to have the opportunities to learn, to develop the knowledge and skills necessary to make the most of group situations. There was a certain irony about this, as the trainer had very skilfully used the group setting of the training course to illustrate her point – namely that if participants did not join in the discussions on the course, they would not achieve optimal benefit from the training and, in turn, the people they served would not achieve optimal benefit from them, as opportunities for learning – and thus improvement of practice – had been missed. June realized that she would have to do more to make sure that she was making a fuller contribution to group situations, as the price for not doing so was quite a high one.

Conclusion

Everyone is an individual, of course, but most people spend a significant proportion of their time in group settings. Communication is not simply a matter of individuals connecting meaningfully with one another. It also involves individuals connecting meaningfully with groups of people and, indeed, groups communicating with each other. The group context of communication is therefore one that is worthy of close attention, and it is to be hoped that this brief chapter has provided at least a basic platform for further study and learning about these important issues.

One chapter cannot provide a comprehensive understanding, but it can flag up important issues. For example, Wit (2006) writes of conflicting forces in groups. There are pressures towards conformity that help the group retain a degree of stability, but there are also pressures towards innovation. The former, Wit argues, are associated with the majority, while the latter tend to stem from the minority. Sometimes the preponderance of conformity pressures will stifle innovation in the group and could put its very existence at risk in the longer terms if it is not able to adapt to changing circumstances. Where each of us stands as an individual communicator, as part of the forces towards conformity and stability or the forces towards innovation and development, will be highly significant, not only for each of us personally, but also for the group and the overall service we provide. This raises questions about how we see our role in groups, what confidence we have in being proactive and a positive influence or to what extent we are just part of the crowd being ushered along by the more skilful, confident and influential figures in the group and/or the very impersonal forces that arise through group dynamics. How effective we are in our work overall will therefore depend to a certain extent on how effective we are in communicating in a group context.

POINTS TO PONDER

- Why is the group context of communication so significant?
- What obstacles to effective communication in groups can you identify?
- How might you remove or get round these or minimize their impact?

CHAPTER 9

Communication difficulties

Introduction

Much of what I have written about in earlier chapters in relation to effective communication can be applied to a wide variety of situations if not across the board completely. In this chapter the focus changes to become a much narrower one, with an emphasis on those situations where there can be communication difficulties for various reasons. Such difficulties are not necessarily anybody's fault, but a degree of awareness about them can help us to be better placed to keep any problems to a minimum and thereby make a positive contribution to effective communication.

Once again it needs to be acknowledged that we are dealing with complex issues, and so there can be no simple formulaic ways of dealing with them. What is needed is an approach rooted in critically reflective practice – that is, one that is based on a critical engagement with the situation and informed by a professional knowledge base, professional skills and, of course, professional values.

It is important to be aware that there are numerous ways in which communication can be less than perfect for particular individuals and in particular circumstances. Examples would include a hearing impairment, a cognitive impairment (a learning difficulty or dementia, for example) or physical difficulties as a result of an illness or disability such as a stroke. A further example may be where the first language of the person you are speaking with is not the same as your own. The clear message of this book is that communication is without doubt a vitally important part of human existence. It is therefore important that some people are not excluded from this because we fail to recognize any difficulties that may be encountered in the practicalities of entering into interpersonal interactions. We should avoid the defeatist and inaccurate assumption that anyone who has a particular difficulty of communication is therefore not capable of full and worthwhile interaction with other people. While such complicating factors as a hearing impairment or a disability may make communication more difficult, this is certainly no justification for not making the effort to engage with people in social interaction. Indeed, to engage in such defeatism would amount to perpetrating yet another form of unfair discrimination. My point, then, is that we need to be sensitive to the range of communication difficulties that can arise and not use any anxieties about countering them to prevent us from entering into interpersonal encounters with a particular section of the community.

We also need to recognize that communication is not just about what is said. It is also a matter of how it is said, where and when it is said and the body language that accompanies it. In addition, we communicate through our behaviour – not only what we say (or write), but also both what we do (and how we do it) and what we do not do. This has implications for such social factors as inclusiveness. All these factors are important in minimizing the potential for communication to fail. Our approach to communication difficulties therefore needs to be broad based – *psychosocial* (incorporating both psychological and sociological factors), rather than simply individualistic.

The remainder of the chapter is divided into four main parts. In the first of these we explore the significance of intercultural communication and recognize that, while cultural diversity is a beneficial and enriching aspect of modern society, it would be naive not to acknowledge that a mismatch of cultural expectations can lead to significant communication difficulties. In the second part I provide an overview of the difficulties that can arise as a result of disability issues and relate these to a social model of disability. In the third part the subject matter is the difficulties that can arise from deafness or hearing impairment, and again a social model is adopted. In the final section I offer some suggestions about how we can develop our skills in responding to communication difficulties.

Before working our way through these four sections it is important to note that I have written this chapter from the perspective of someone who is not disabled and not deaf, partly because this is my own situation and partly because this will reflect the situation of the majority of readers. However, this should not mislead anyone into thinking that there are no deaf or disabled people working in the people professions or that those who do are in some way to be marginalized.

Cultural differences

Individuals exist in a cultural context – that is, we are constantly exposed to, and influenced by, a range of cultural factors, not least the following:

- *Taken-for-granted assumptions and meanings*   Our cultural context in large part shapes the 'horizon' from which we see the world, the frameworks of meaning we adopt to make sense of the world we encounter.
- *Unwritten rules*   As we grow up we learn what is acceptable and what is not ('taboo') within our culture. The price we pay for transgressing such rules can be very high (exclusion, ridicule and so on), and so these rules tend to be a very powerful influence on us.

- *Rituals and institutionalized patterns of behaviour*   Much of our behaviour is based on habit, and while our day-to-day habits are partly personal or individual characteristics, they are also largely reflections of the norms of behaviour associated with our culture.

ACTIVITY 9.1

Think about where you work (or study) now. What are the characteristics of the culture there? That is, what seem to be the taken-for-granted assumptions, unwritten rules, rituals and institutionalized patterns of behaviour? Compare notes with one or more colleagues to see what you can learn from this activity.

Holliday, Hyde and Kullman (2004) link culture and language through the concept of discourse (see Chapter 2):

'Discourses' with a capital 'D,' that is, different ways in which we humans integrate language with non-language 'stuff,' such as different ways of thinking, acting, interacting, valuing, feeling, believing, and using symbols, tools, and objects in the right places and at the right times so as to enact and recognize different identities and activities, give the material world certain meanings, distribute social goods in a certain way, make certain sorts of meaningful connections in our experience, and privilege certain symbol systems and ways of knowing over others. (p. 75)

PRACTICE FOCUS 9.1

Kate was involved in a community development project as part of her professional training. She had studied culture at university along with many other topics, but had not seen it as particularly significant. However, once she became immersed in the project it really came home to her how much of an issue culture was. She met people from a wide range of cultural backgrounds and this taught her how much of a difference a person's background made to the way they saw the world – and therefore the way they related to it. In addition to this, she became very aware of how big a part class made to culture. She was from a very middle-class background, but was now working mainly with people from a working-class background. She felt very uncomfortable at first, not sure how – or whether – she fitted in. However, people were very friendly towards her, so she soon started to settle and realized that cultural differences do not need to be a barrier. This gave her a lot more confidence in dealing with multicultural situations, although she realized too that she needed to learn a lot more.

In view of this, it should come as no surprise to learn that our communication will be strongly influenced by cultural factors. However, it is not simply a matter of each individual being influenced by their culture. The reality is much more complex than this. This is because of the prevalence of 'multiculturalism'.

The term 'multicultural' can be seen to apply in two senses. First, an individual can be multicultural, in the sense that they are and have been exposed to more than one set of cultural influences. Imagine, for example, a black person who is brought up for their first eight years as a Catholic in a working-class family in the south-west of England, adopted by a Protestant white, middle-class family (following the death of his single-parent mother) in Scotland who, in early adulthood, converts to Islam and moves to London. This may seem an extreme example, but complex multicultural contexts for individuals (and, indeed, families) are in fact very common. Second, societies will generally be multicultural, in the sense that there will be a variety of cultures living side by side – in some cases, peacefully, in others not so positively. Jandt (2007) captures this point well when he comments that: 'Intercultural communication refers not only to the communication between individuals of diverse cultural identities but also to the communication between diverse groups' (p. 13).

With each combination of cultural factors in a communication, there will be scope for the enrichment such diversity brings, but there will also be scope for misunderstanding and communication breakdown due to the potentially conflicting cultural perceptions, norms and frameworks of meaning.

Jandt (2007) refers to the work of Barna (1997) which discusses the various ways in which such difficulties tend to arise. Barna categorizes them under the following six headings:

1. *Anxiety* Where anxiety is at a high level it can act as a barrier to effective communication. Feeling uncomfortable in a situation where we do not know what is expected of us (where we are not sure of the unwritten rules and norms of the other person's culture) can very easily lead to a situation of high anxiety. That, in turn, can lead to a lower level of concentration plus a higher level of tension, a combination that can have a major detrimental effect on the effectiveness of communication. In the interests of improving intercultural communication we therefore need to consider how to avoid high levels of anxiety. This is particularly significant in dealing with situations where anxiety may be present anyway – for example, in relation to health concerns.

Voice of experience 9.1

❝An important part of my job is trying to make sure that tensions don't get too high. If they do, we end up with a vicious circle – communication gets more difficult, so tensions rise even more. It's partly about having good inter-personal skills, but also involves having a good knowledge of the people I'm working with and where they are coming from, culturally speaking.❞ *Angela, a community care worker*

2. *Assuming similarity*   This problem arises when people operate according to the norms and unwritten rules of their culture without realizing that different norms and rules may apply in a different cultural context. Consider the following example provided by Jandt:

> In 1997, a Danish woman left her 14-month-old baby girl in a stroller [buggy] outside a Manhattan restaurant while she was inside. Other diners at the restaurant became concerned and called New York City Police. The woman was charged with endangering a child and was jailed for two nights. Her child was placed in foster care. The woman and the Danish consulate explained that leaving children unattended outside cafes is common in Denmark. Pictures were wired to the police showing numerous strollers parked outside cafes while parents were eating inside. The Danish woman had assumed that Copenhagen is similar to New York, that what is commonly done in Copenhagen is also commonly done in New York. (2007 p. 73)

Assuming similarity can also cause significant ill-feeling – for example, when people feel offended by members of one culture failing to recognize important issues in another culture. One way in which this can occur is through a deliberate decision to assert one's own cultural norms at the expense of someone else's (see ethnocentrism below). However, it can also frequently arise unintentionally as a result of a lack of cultural sensitivity which in turn is likely to be based on a lack of knowledge or awareness. A wise move here, therefore, is to make sure that, in working with people whose culture is different from your own, you find out at least the basics of their culture. Often this can be done simply by asking the person(s) concerned.

3. *Ethnocentrism*   This is similar to assuming similarity, but goes a step further. Ethnocentrism quite reasonably begins with taking one's own culture as a starting point for making sense of the world (see Gadamer, 2004), but then takes the not-so-reasonable step of assuming that one's own culture is the one true way and that all other cultures are thereby 'wrong' or inferior. Clearly, such an attitude will present serious

barriers to effective intercultural communication, partly because of the distorted assumptions of the person relying on ethnocentrism and the reactions of the person(s) being treated as inferior. The power dynamics involved in this can be of very significant proportions, making a positive communicative interaction a much more difficult goal to achieve. From a practice point of view, the implications of this are (at least) twofold: first, we need to make sure that we are not allowing our own approach to other people to be based on ethnocentric assumptions; and (ii) we need to be able to develop our skills in 'elegant challenging' – that is, being able to challenge such assumptions skilfully and positively without alienating the person(s) concerned (Thompson, 2011).

4. *Stereotypes and prejudice*   A stereotype is an oversimplified and rigidly held view of a person or group of people. As such, they often serve as the basis of prejudice (that is, an unfair prejudgement). Unfortunately, intercultural communication is often impeded by a reliance on stereotypes on the part of one or more participants in the interaction. Effective communications relies on a number of factors, but two that are particularly significant are (i) accurate and reliable information; and (ii) each party being able to 'tune in' to the other's point of view. Both of these are compromised by stereotypes and prejudice. At best, the result can be a failure to 'connect' in a communicative sense, but at worst, the outcome can be an aggressive or even violent encounter brought about by the raised tensions and resentment involved, while misunderstanding and oppressive interactions are also possible negative consequences. In terms of the practice implications, these include making sure that we are aware of common stereotypes and prejudices, removing them from our own thinking and being prepared to address them when they become apparent in others, rather than colluding with them.

5. *Nonverbal misinterpretations*   Different cultures are likely to make use of nonverbal communication in different ways, and this then paves the way for misunderstandings based on how body language is interpreted. For example, in some cultures shaking one's head indicates 'no', whereas in others, it means 'yes'. Similarly, raising and showing the palm of one's hand can be a friendly greeting or an abusive gesture, depending on the cultural context involved. Once again, this means that we need to be aware of the cultural context in which we are working in order to make sure that we do not offend or alienate people (and thereby fail to communicate effectively with them) through a lack of knowledge, awareness or sensitivity.

PRACTICE FOCUS 9.2

Rachel was a very experienced bereavement worker and had found the careful, sensitive use of touch to be a very important way of 'connecting' with the people she was helping. She was very careful about not overdoing it and overstepping the mark. She recognized the importance of being entirely professional at all times. However, she was taken aback when she worked with a Palestinian woman who was clearly quite distressed when Rachel touched her arm in what was intended to be a soothing way. Rachel apologized straight away and had the poise to be able to continue the session in a helpful way. She apologized again at the end of the session. At first she thought it was simply an individual issue, that particular woman's preference. However, when she discussed the matter in supervision her supervisor suggested that it was probably a cultural matter rather than a purely individual one. At this point Rachel realized how naive she had been in not considering the cultural issues involved. Her supervisor helped her to recognize that it had been a serious mistake not to consider the use of touch in a cultural context.

6. *Language* This can prove to be a barrier in a number of ways. Different languages, different dialects of the same language, different styles of using language ('registers') – these are all ways in which different approaches to communication can lead to a mismatch and thus potentially to a breakdown in communication. Here we are touching on a complex set of issues that have different dimensions. For example, the choice of language use can be a political act – it can involve making a political statement (whether of defiance or of solidarity). There will also be cultural issues to consider, in so far as language is a major bearer (and reflection of) culture. And, of course, there will also be practicalities to take into consideration:

   o Will an interpreter be needed?
   o How readily available are interpreting facilities?
   o How skilled and experienced is the interpreter?

   This complex array of factors reinforces the importance of a concept discussed in earlier chapters, namely linguistic sensitivity – the need to be able to 'tune in' to the subtleties of language use.

Arguably these are not the only factors that stand in the way of successful intercultural communication. However, this overview of Barna's work should be sufficient to paint a picture of the complexities involved and therefore of the dangers of approaching intercultural communications without an adequate degree of knowledge, understanding and sensitivity. In a similar spirit, Holliday, Hyde and Kullman (2004) offer apt comment:

> Any study of culture will inevitably be complex and there are no easy off-the-peg definitions. It is, indeed, off-the-peg definitions that prevent a consideration of the complexities of culture, and prevent us approaching culture as a dynamic and interactive process. (p. 64)

Culture in general and intercultural communication in particular are prone to oversimplification. This brief snapshot should therefore help us to realize that, from a professional practice point of view, it is very unwise to adopt an uncritical approach to such issues and just rely on 'common sense', as what we regard as common sense is to a large extent a reflection of our own cultural norms and unquestioned assumptions. We run the risk of not only failing to communicate, but also of our communicative efforts being highly counterproductive if we are not suitably 'tuned in' to the significance of cultural differences.

Disability

Disability has traditionally been seen as a set of medical conditions affecting particular individuals who, as a result of such an impairment, are unable to do certain things. According to this traditional model there is no blame to be attached to a disabled person, but there is still none the less a sense that disabled people are somehow 'less than' other people. This can result in disabled people being pitied and regarded as objects of charity. This way of understanding disability has been strongly challenged by the emergence of what has come to be known as the social model of disability (see the 'Guide to further learning' for references relating to this approach).

ACTIVITY 9.2

Think about what the term 'disability' means to you. Do you think of it in broad social terms or narrow individual terms? What difference do you think it might make in terms of communication to think of disability in mainly social terms? If you are disabled yourself, consider talking to non-disabled colleagues about how they understand disability. If you are not disabled, consider asking a disabled colleague to discuss with you their perspective on disability. If it makes you feel uncomfortable to do that, think about why that may be. Consider where the discomfort is coming from and think about what that tells us about social attitudes towards disability.

The social model regards traditional approaches to disability as pathologizing and disempowering because they conceive of disability in individualistic (or 'atomistic') terms and fail to account for the role of wider social forces (both cultural and structural). The social model is based on the idea that it is society, through discriminatory assumptions, actions and inactions that *dis*ables people with an impairment. A basic example of this would be the recognition that it is the absence of a ramp (and the discriminatory assumptions that a ramp would not be needed) that excludes wheelchair users from certain buildings, not the use of a wheelchair *per se*. If we are to understand disability, then, we need to be able to think holistically about the broader context and not simply focus on the individual's capabilities.

PRACTICE FOCUS 9.3

Mark had worked in the same post for over three years when he decided that he needed a new challenge and moved to a multidisciplinary disability services team. In his previous post he had been part of a fairly harmonious work group, so he was surprised to find so much conflict in his new team. At first he struggled to make sense of why there was so much discord. However, it gradually became clear to him that the conflict seemed to be coming from different perspectives on disability. Some members of the team seemed to be working on the basis of a very traditional individualistic model of disability, while others had adopted a broader-based social model of disability. Mark was disappointed that the team manager had not realized this and had therefore not done anything about it. He wondered whether he would be overstepping the mark if he raised the issue at a team meeting. He was keen to move away from a disempowering individualistic model, but realized that he would have to be sensitive and tactful in how he dealt with the matter.

It is in this context that we need to understand communication difficulties associated with disability. We need to ask: whose difficulty? That is, we need to move away from the individualistic idea that most people have no difficulty in communicating, while some people do. The more complex reality is that society operates in ways that create communication difficulties when a group whose communication needs are not being addressed (for example, through knowledge of Makaton or other specialist language forms) interact with people whose communication needs are commonly met. Imagine, by way of analogy, a situation where some people who do not speak English are invited to an event where no interpreting or translation facilities are provided and all the discussions are in English. They are likely to find it nigh on impossible to contribute meaningfully to such discussions and would therefore be, in effect, excluded and marginalized. In such circumstances it would be very unfair and highly inappropriate to describe the situation as one in which the basic problem is their inability to speak English (rather than the organizers' inability to cater for their linguistic needs). This analogy captures well the position of disabled people who have different communication needs from the majority. Given the way disability and communication difficulties are generally presented and understood, it is easy – but none the less discriminatory and oppressive – to assume that any ensuing communication difficulties are a reflection of the 'inability' of the disabled person to communicate effectively.

Voice of experience 9.2

"It really annoys me when people who really should know better talk to disabled adults as if they were talking to children. It doesn't take much to tune in to somebody's communication needs if you make the effort – but that's the problem, some people aren't prepared to make the effort; they want everything their way.**"** *Diarmuid, a disability rights worker*

Having set the scene for exploring these issues in a way that does not pathologize or disempower, let us now focus on how such difficulties can arise and how we can best respond.

Disability-related communication problems can arise in four main ways:

1. *Learning difficulties* People with learning disabilities often communicate in different ways from others. For people who are not used to this and do not feel comfortable with it, there can be tensions that get in the way of effective communication. It is therefore important to ensure that we do not allow ourselves to create such difficulties. This is partly a matter of experience – that is, the more experience we have of communicating with people with learning disabilities, the more skilled we are likely to become – and partly a matter of attitude and values: are we sufficiently committed to equality and inclusiveness to make the necessary adjustments to enable effective communication to take place?

2. *Brain-related difficulties* Problems can arise as a result of a stroke, aphasia, dementia or related matters. Parr, Duchan and Pound (2003a) focus on the significance in particular of aphasia:

   aphasia is an impairment that affects language: the most powerful weapon in the armoury of the disabled people's movement. Aphasia compromises a person's ability to talk and write, and read and understand. Sharing and expressing ideas, and listening to others are critical functions in the process of mobilizing and politicizing a minority and bringing about change. When language is compromised by an impairment such as aphasia, negotiation, campaigning, education, debate and argument become difficult, if not impossible. For these reasons, people who struggle to communicate are often sidelined by a movement which should be representing them, championing their cause and sharing authority. (p. 7)

This passage illustrates that aphasia is not only *personally* limiting in terms of communication at the micro level, but also a matter of concern at a macro or sociopolitical level. This introduces a power dimension. Parr, Duchan and Pound (2003a) again offer apt comment:

People with aphasia require language and confidence to challenge and question those supporting them. When time and energy are limited, the temptation is to accept fast-track 'solutions' of suggested words and questions, to defer to those with professional or academic status and style of expression, and to underplay personal expression. (p. 8)

In line with this, Togher (2003) identifies the need to redress the power imbalance in interactions between professionals and people with aphasia. An important practice lesson from this, then, is that members of the helping professions need to be very sensitive in communicating with people with aphasia or other language-limiting conditions in order to ensure that we are not unintentionally misusing our power in such situations (Thompson, 2007).

3. *Difficulties relating to speech apparatus* This refers to impairments caused by conditions that impede the use of the speech apparatus – for example, breathlessness caused by severe emphysema. Here it is important to have patience, as an unwillingness to give people the time and space they need to communicate can create a vicious circle. Our impatience can raise tensions and create discomfort, which in turn add to the pressures which then make communication more difficult, leading to an even greater need for patience. In this context to be impatient is to give the message: 'My needs are more important than yours', which, of course, is not a firm basis for effective communication, especially in the helping professions.

4. *Disability discrimination* The development of the social model of disability (as discussed above) has alerted us to the prevalence and significance of disability discrimination. This is perhaps the most significant barrier to effective communication, particularly when it manifests itself as:

   o Assumptions that disabled people have nothing important to say, that it is therefore acceptable for professionals to speak on their behalf without being invited to do so; and o Feelings of pity that can be patronizing and pathologizing and thus potentially disempowering.

Effective communication with disabled people therefore needs to be based on principles of anti-disablist practice.

PRACTICE FOCUS 9.4

John had worked with disabled people for several years and had not been aware of any problems. However, he was both surprised and concerned when Layla, his line manager, told him that a complaint had been made against him. Jamie, a young man with spina bifida had registered a formal complaint, claiming that John had been patronizing towards him. He was informed that the complaint would be formally investigated and that he should have no contact with Jamie in the meantime. The time between being told this and actually meeting the investigator and getting more details of the complaint was therefore a very anxious one for him. However, he became even more anxious when he was told by the investigator that the basis of the complaint was that he had a tendency to speak on behalf of Jamie and other people with disabilities, rather than work towards empowering them to speak with their own voice. To begin with John rejected this claim, saying that he would never dream of patronizing people in this way. As the investigation proceeded, though, more and more people were supporting this view of John. He really struggled to understand this. Fortunately, Layla was very supportive in helping him to realize that he had perhaps been doing what he was accused of without being aware that he was doing so. Before long he had to acknowledge that there were clearly issues that he needed to address about how he communicated with disabled people.

A further factor to consider is the two-way relationship between communication and disability. Cross (2004) points out that: 'Communication problems can impair someone's ability to interact, manage their behaviour, learn and think' (p. 9). Consequently, a further vicious circle can be established in which disability (socially defined) can lead to communication problems, and then those communication problems can act as further social barriers to inclusion. Developing effective communication in working with disabled people is therefore more than simply following practical guidelines; it also involves having an awareness of wider sociopolitical concerns. In short, it needs to be based on critically reflective practice.

Deafness

Some readers may wonder why I have chosen to write about deafness in a separate section rather than include it under the heading of disability. This is because many people would not regard deafness as a disability. For example, Lane (2008) poses the question of whether deafness is a disability. He argues that there is no impairment involved – he sees deafness as a communication *difference* – an example of human variation – rather than a communication *deficit*. He makes the important point that: 'Unless Deaf people challenge the culturally determined meanings of *deaf* and *disability* … the day will continue to recede in which Deaf children and adults live the fullest lives and make the fullest contribution to our diverse society' (p. 290).

In a similar vein, Baynton (2008) argues that Deaf people should be recognized as a linguistic minority (note the capital 'D' as a political statement). Through the use of sign language Deaf people are able to communicate effectively with other sign language users, just as speakers of, say, Spanish can communicate with one another without having to translate what they are saying into another language.

Voice of experience 9.3

"Both my parents were Deaf and we had Deaf friends, but I attended mainstream schooling so I was in effect brought up in a bilingual environment. It has given me a distinct advantage in my work as I have a good understanding of what it means to be Deaf as well as some insights into how hearing people perceive deafness.**"** *Alli, a social worker working with hearing-impaired people*

The use of sign language is not a new phenomenon. Woll and Ladd (2003) give us some insight into the historical picture:

It is probable that deaf people who communicate by gesture or sign have existed as part of humanity from its inception; in the West, the first written evidence of their existence can be found at the rise of the Mediterranean societies in the fifth century BC. From that time onward, Greek philosophers like Herodotus, Socrates, Aristotle, and Plato, and their equivalents in Jewish and Roman society philosophized about the nature of Deaf people's existence and their place in society. (p. 154)

This should help us to realize that signing is not a secondary form of communication and needs to be understood in this broader social context. It is, in effect, a situation of bilingualism for many people. As such, it is a situation that needs to be understood in its full complexity if we are to do justice to the issues involved. An oversimplified approach could therefore be highly problematic.

ACTIVITY 9.3

Consider how people with a hearing impairment are regarded in society. What implications might this have for how we communicate together? Compare notes with other colleagues to see what you can learn about this important point.

Bauman (2008a) also reflects on the historical context and its significance:

In retrospect, we may now see that the historic misunderstanding of sign language is one of the enduring errors of human thought, leaving us with an incomplete understanding about the nature of human language – the implications of which have rippled throughout the centuries [Bauman, 2008b]. While effects of such a misalignment of thought can be traced throughout the history of Western thought, they have been felt most profoundly by deaf individuals whose intellectual abilities have been grossly misunderstood and their full humanity put into question. Indeed, the history of deaf individuals, like that of women, African Americans, Native Americans, gays and lesbians, and persons with disabilities, has been one of marginalization and misrepresentation. (p. 2)

This passage paints a picture of systematic discrimination, a phenomenon that is often referred to as 'audism'. It follows similar patterns to other established forms of discrimination (Thompson, 2006a). It is therefore not simply a matter of personal prejudice. This is an important observation, as it means that even individuals who have no prejudices against Deaf people may none the less be involved in unwitting discrimination because of institutionalized cultural assumptions about Deaf individuals or Deaf people as a group.

The notion of cultural assumptions is particularly significant because of the development of what has come to be known as 'Deaf culture'. This refers to the way in which Deaf people share not only a means of communication, but also a sense of community and belonging, a shared set of norms and assumptions – hence the use of the term 'culture'. This has implications for identity, as the extent to which a Deaf individual identifies with (or does not identify with) Deaf culture will have implications for their sense of self (just as the extent to which an individual identifies with any other culture to which they may belong is likely to have a significant bearing on their identity). This is an important point to note, as it would be a mistake to assume that a Deaf person necessarily identifies with Deaf culture (or indeed that they do not) – this is a matter to be established, not taken for granted either way. However, once this is established, the implications of this need to be taken into consideration in determining how best to interact.

Given the significance of Deaf culture, then, communication between users of oral language and Deaf people can be seen as a form of intercultural communication. In view of this, much of the discussion above about intercultural communication can be seen to apply here also.

PRACTICE FOCUS 9.5

Rana had always been intrigued by sign language and so she took the opportunity to learn how to sign by attending evening classes. Given her enthusiasm and her eagerness to learn, it was no surprise that she made rapid progress and did very well. Once she had become reasonably fluent she sought out opportunities to use her new skills in her work. The Deaf people she encountered clearly valued her ability to communicate with them in this way and she felt good that she had broadened her repertoire of communication skills. However, she soon began to realize that there was much more to interacting with Deaf people than being able to use sign language. She came to understand that, for the Deaf people she came into contact with at least, there was much more to being Deaf than communicating in a different way from most people. She felt a bit over-awed by this at first, but then came to see it as an important part of developing her professional understanding.

As Practice Focus 9.5 illustrates, learning sign language can be a helpful way of improving communication between Deaf and hearing people, but this also needs to be supplemented by an awareness of, and sensitivity to, the broader sociopolitical issues that characterize such intercultural communication.

Building up our skills

Sometimes people talk (or write) about knowledge and skills as if they were two entirely separate domains. However, the reality is that the two are closely interrelated much, if not all, of the time. Skill development depends on having at least a certain amount of relevant knowledge to draw upon, while knowledge is very limited if it is not broadened and deepened by its use in practice – that is, by the application of skills. I would argue that this is an important point in relation to the pursuit of effective communication in any professional work we undertake, but especially in those circumstances where the potential for communication difficulties is higher than would otherwise be the case – that is, in situations involving intercultural communication, some aspects of disability and interactions between Deaf and hearing people. While there certainly are skills that can be developed, there is also a great need for knowledge of the issues involved. Anyone ill-informed about such issues is likely to find dealing with such communication difficulties more of a challenge than they need to be, with the added consideration that the result of a lack of effectiveness may well be discrimination and marginalization. To avoid such unintended consequences we therefore need to make sure that our communicative efforts are suitably well informed. Building up our skills therefore needs to be premised on building up our knowledge (see the 'Guide to further learning' at the end of the book).

One of the skills (or set of skills) we clearly need is the ability to tune in to the communication situation we are dealing with and be sensitive to the potential difficulties that may arise so that we are better equipped to prevent them and to respond to them when they do occur. This level of awareness is, of course, a feature of critically reflective practice, so we again find ourselves revisiting this important theme. Routinized practices that lack reflective awareness of what is going on and the wider context in which it is taking place will leave the practitioner in a very weak position when it comes to rising to the challenges presented by communication difficulties.

One further factor to consider in terms of skill development is the need to find a balance between complacency and anxiety. At one end of the spectrum we need to avoid a complacent approach that does not prepare us for the difficulties we may encounter. If the potential for communication difficulties is not recognized in the first place, then there will be little or no opportunity to develop our skills and confidence in dealing with such matters. Complacency

---

PRACTICE FOCUS 9.6

Rick had recently graduated and was looking forward to this new phase in his career. He had done well on his degree in both the theory and the practice elements and he was to be working in a field where he had a lot of pre-course experience, so he was feeling very confident. However, it soon turned out that his confidence was spilling over into complacency, or so it seemed. He was quite taken aback when one of his more experienced colleagues took him on one side and told him that he needed to be more sensitive in how he communicated with people, that he needed to be more patient in relating to people in situations where – for various reasons – communication was more complicated than would otherwise be the case. His initial response was one of denial but when he was given various examples of how he could have done better, he realized that his colleague had a point. His next reaction was to become anxious about how he related to people – his confidence had been undermined. However, his colleague proved to be very supportive and helpful so he was soon able to start learning again, to put the anxiety behind him but without returning to his previous position of complacency.

can manifest itself in an approach that excludes people who do not fit neatly into the mainstream – for example, by taking no account of cultural differences, disability or deafness. At the other end of the spectrum we need to make sure that anxiety does not get in the way of effective communication. While some of the situations described in this chapter can be difficult and challenging, we should not lose sight of the fact that an anxious response to them can actually make the situation worse, in so far as they can lead to additional tensions. A balanced approach, then, neither complacent nor unduly anxious, is what is called for.

Conclusion

Of course, one short chapter cannot be comprehensive or exhaustive. There are many other aspects of communication difficulties that we have not been able to explore – for example, those arising from mental health problems, frailty in old age and other such factors that are not uncommon in the helping professions. However, it is to be hoped that the picture I have painted in this chapter is sufficient to provide a platform of understanding that can be built upon through further discussion, debate, study and reflection.

Communication difficulties can arise for various reasons and in various ways. Effective communication does not require us to be experts in communication difficulties, but it does require us to have at least a basic understanding of the issues involved so that we have a basis for critically reflective practice and for developing our knowledge, skills and confidence over time. We will then be much better equipped for the challenges involved so that we are better able to offer the best level of care, support and assistance to the people we serve. As Wiesmann comments, and it is worth repeating that comment here:

> Our ability to create and sustain our social world depends in large measure on how well we communicate. People's social skills are crucial to their well-being – individually and collectively. The importance of understanding skilled behaviour in all its complexities cannot be overstated. (cited in Hargie, 2006a, p. 1)

If we do not succeed in rising to the challenges discussed in this chapter because we oversimplify what is involved, then we run the risk that we will undermine the well-being of the very people we are seeking to help. Being able to communicate effectively in all situations and not just in the straightforward or mainstream ones is therefore an important ability to be able to develop over time.

POINTS TO PONDER

- What key factors do you need to bear in mind in dealing with people from a different culture from your own?
- How might discrimination against disabled people contribute to communication difficulties?
- What are the main implications of seeing deafness as a cultural matter rather than a disability issue?

CHAPTER 10

Putting it in writing

Introduction

While Chapter 3 explored some of the theoretical issues relating to the use of the written word, my aim in this chapter is to draw out some of the practice implications, based on both that theory base and my own experience in this area. This chapter will not make you into a highly skilled writer, but it should help you to improve your writing skills by helping to develop your understanding of what is involved in effective written communication.

The phrase 'putting it in writing' is one which immediately demonstrates the power of language, particularly in its written forms. Comments which are put in writing tend to acquire a formality and a power which can go far beyond the spoken word. I learned at a very early stage in my career that putting things in writing had a very pronounced tendency to give them an extra strength. For example, I realized that putting a request to a manager verbally had a certain amount of influence on the situation, but I found that committing such a request to writing gave it much greater voice. To a large extent, this power comes from our cultural expectations – that is, western cultures in particular ascribe considerable significance to the written word. We are therefore brought up to assume that something which is in written form has an extra degree of importance or weight. Indeed, this is a very strong cultural feature.

However, it is not simply a cultural matter, as there are also issues to do with the use of written materials as evidence – for example, in a court of law or some other form of formal inquiry or investigation. That is, while it is relatively easy to deny verbal comments made, it is far more difficult to deny something which can be produced in written evidence. Disputes about what was said and what was meant are much more easily resolved where there is a written version of events. Indeed, this is a major and significant characteristic of writing – its permanence. Committing something to writing can give it a relatively long shelf life, whereas a verbal comment can be made and disappear, never to have any influence again.

Given how important the written word is, it should be helpful for us to examine in this chapter a range of issues related to maximizing our effectiveness in written communication. In this respect, this chapter parallels Chapter

6 in which I looked at maximizing effectiveness in interpersonal interactions. Here, the focus is on maximizing effectiveness in what we could perhaps call written interactions – although one characteristic of writing which distinguishes it from the spoken word is that much of what is written is a one-way process, in the sense that much will be read without the reader responding to the author. For example, although I have had some people respond to what I have written in various books, articles and training resources, the vast majority of people who have read any of my published work have not interacted with me, nor would they reasonably be expected to.

A lot has been written about good practice in the use of the written word. There is no shortage of textbooks which claim to offer helpful guidance with what the authors see as the appropriate usage of the written language. However, the majority of these texts are prescriptive, in the sense that they tend to give instructions on what to do and what not to do. By contrast, what I am trying to do here is to engage in the broader process of facilitating learning about these issues, rather than simply to present 'cook book' prescriptions. The clear message from this book is that matters to do with communication are very complex indeed. It is therefore dangerous, and possibly counterproductive, to offer simple rules about language usage, whether verbally or in writing. My aim, then, is not to offer a set of rules, but rather to offer suggestions which should be used as the basis for developing a creative, reflective approach to the use of the written work. My suggestions should therefore not be seen as rules to be followed mechanically or unthinkingly. Of course, it could be argued that what I am presenting here is prescriptive, in the sense that I am seeking to put across what is my view of good practice and not so good practice. However, this is a far cry from the very common practice of authors offering what appear to be instructions on 'correct' usage.

The remainder of the chapter is divided into three main sections. First, under the heading of 'Effective writing', I shall examine a number of important questions we need to ask ourselves in order to make sure that we are using the written word to best effect. Following on from this, I present 12 pitfalls to avoid –12 areas where we can get ourselves into difficulties in writing if we are not aware of the dangers that lie ahead. Finally, I shall make some comments about the use of email as this has clearly already established itself as a major form of written communication and will no doubt continue to be widely used.

However, before beginning these discussions, there is one point I wish to emphasize. We need to remember that writing is a form of communication, and therefore the definition of communication as 'social interaction through messages' is one that we need to bear in mind. That is, whenever we are committing things to writing, we need to ask ourselves: What message are we seeking to put across? Confusing or misleading writing can be extremely problematic. It is therefore important, right from the beginning, that we are clear about what we are trying to say before we actually try to say it. From this, we can set up a very helpful 'checking loop'. That is, if we are clear about what message we are trying to put across before we start writing, we can then check what we have written to make sure that it does in fact convey the message intended. We should not underestimate how easy it is to put across the wrong message unwittingly. This chapter, then, is geared towards helping to ensure that what we write says what we want it to say – that it delivers the message we want it to deliver.

Effective writing

The topic of effective writing is a vast one, and so what I have to say here is necessarily selective. In particular, I am going to concentrate on five questions I feel you should be asking yourself before and/or during undertaking any writing tasks.

Why write?

This is an important question to begin with. Do you actually need to put what you want to say in writing? It is surprising how often communication takes place in a written form when either this is not necessary at all or there is a more appropriate form of communication. One of the challenges we face in this day and age is the problem of information overload. Indeed, it can be argued that the skills of information management are becoming increasingly important (Thompson, 2009b). We should therefore be careful not to add to this problem by writing things down when it is not necessary. On the other hand, there can be problems that arise when things are not recorded in writing when they should have been. Therefore, it is clearly an important skill to be able to decide what needs to be in writing and what does not. In some circumstances, there will be guidelines. For example, in many organizations there are policies and procedures which specify what information must be recorded and in what circumstances. However, in many cases, it is up to the individual to decide what is committed to writing and what is not. It is therefore important to be clear about what the criteria are for making such a decision. Without clarity about such criteria, you may find that some things which should have been committed to writing are not, while a lot of time and energy are wasted recording things that did not need to be in writing.

Clearly this can be problematic either way. The absence of written information can at times be a crucial factor in the collapse or failure of a particular project or endeavour. For example, I once encountered a student on placement who did an excellent job of recording all the relevant information from a person who made a telephone referral – except for one crucial thing: the address and telephone number of the caller. Her excellent work was spoiled by the fact that this simple oversight meant that she could not now follow up on that information and would have to wait for the caller to get in touch again, by which time it could have been too late to help.

At the other end of the spectrum, we can have problems if a lot of time and effort are wasted recording information unnecessarily. Indeed, the waste of time and effort can be twofold – first on the part of the person doing the record-ing, and second, on the part of other people who, at a later date, are called upon to wade through the mass of irrelevant material in order to identify impor-tant pieces of information. Sadly I have come across very many examples of files of information containing large quantities of irrelevant material and have had to devote a great deal of time to sifting through it in case there were any important nuggets of relevant information hidden in the dross of unprocessed description and tedious, unnecessary detail.

Another problem that can arise when people commit things to writing unnecessarily is that this can have an adverse effect on relationships. For example, I have come across a number of cases where relationships between managers and their staff were very poor indeed, with a lot of ill-feeling, if not hostility – with one of the main reasons for such poor working relationships being the overuse of memos or emails. It is understandable that people can become very resentful and feel undervalued when they are 'flooded' with such written communications, with little or no attempt on the part of the writing-obsessed manager to form personal relationships or to communicate at a more human level.

PRACTICE FOCUS 10.1

Pat understandably felt a little anxious in taking up his new post, wonder-ing whether it was a wise move. However, he was made to feel very welcome by his new colleagues, and so his anxiety was short lived. As time went on, he realized that making the move had been a very positive step for a number of reasons. In particular, he was delighted that his line manager, Janice, actually took the time and trouble to sit down and talk with staff members. This was a very pleasant change for him, as his previ-ous line manager rarely, if ever, communicated on a personal level. The nickname of 'Memo-man' he had acquired was one that was richly deserved, given that he would churn them out on a regular basis. This approach caused a lot of ill-feeling, a point which was brought to his atten-tion on more than one occasion, but without effecting any change in his behaviour. Pat felt very relieved to be in a work environment based on human contact, rather than bureaucratic defence mechanisms.

This is not to say that formal written communication should never be used, but rather that there is an important skill in being able to decide what needs to be committed to writing and what is best dealt with on a more informal basis through verbal communication. Not using this skill can so easily lead to the highly problematic situation of a manager who comes across as distant, uncaring and bureaucratic. This is a very serious issue, as a manager who is not perceived as supportive can easily become an additional source of pressure and stress for staff rather than a help in dealing with such work pressures (Thompson, 1999).

When to write?

There are two aspects to this. First, there is the question of: What time of day (or night) should you be writing? This is an important time management issue. As I have argued previously (Thompson, 2009b), some people are 'morning people' and some people are definitely not morning people. What I mean by this is that we all have our own rhythms and patterns of which are good times of day and which are not. Some people cope best early in the morning and perhaps tend to 'fizzle out' towards the end of the day, while others may take quite a while to get going early in the morning but continue functioning well long after some colleagues have given up the ghost. Effective writing needs clarity of mind and thus concentration. It is therefore helpful, wherever possible, for you to undertake any written duties you may have at a time when your concentration level is at its highest. For example, if you are someone who finds that you have an energy gap immediately after lunch, then that is clearly not the time to be writing a sensitive letter or a report that could have major consequences if its message is not communicated effectively. There is no standard or set time that is the best time for undertaking written work. It is up to each individual to work out their own best time.

Another important principle I would like to suggest in terms of when to write can be summarized as: 'the sooner the better'. This is because the longer we leave something before we write about it, the more difficult it may be to recall the detail of what we wish to write. For example, if your task is to write up the minutes of a meeting, then this is much more easily done soon after the meeting while events are fresh in your mind rather than leaving this task for some time and then having to struggle to remember what your notes refer to. The same goes for 'running records' – the sooner after the discussion to which they refer, they are written up, the less effort is involved in doing so, and the more accurate those records are likely to be. Undertaking such tasks earlier rather than later can also help to alleviate any anxiety about writing and can raise levels of confidence. It would be naive not to recognize that many people feel anxious about writing and are not very confident in undertaking such tasks. Therefore, the longer we leave it in terms of undertaking writing tasks, the greater the anxiety can get and the lower our level of confidence.

ACTIVITY 10.1

Consider your own 'body clock'. When is the best time for you to do your best writing, to be at your best when it comes to concentrating? Consider also what implications this might have for how you organize your time at work.

What to write?

When people have a written task to complete, a common question that is asked is: What should I include and what should I leave out? Of course, the short answer to this question is: 'It depends'. It can depend on many things but, in general, there are two main ones to consider. The first one relates to the purpose of what you are writing. It is important to ask yourself: Why am I writing this? What am I hoping to achieve in doing so? This will not necessarily give you a direct answer to what to include and what to leave out, but it will give you a great deal of guidance on what is relevant to what you are writing:

> what form a report (or other written communication) should take will depend to a large extent on the desired end product. In other words, the purpose of a particular piece of written work will be a major influence on the shape that work takes. It is therefore important to consider carefully the purpose of any particular piece of written work before writing begins. This should help to make the written output compatible with its intended purpose. Without this, a great deal of time and effort may be wasted and the results may be disappointing. (Thompson, 2009b, p. 127)

For example, if you are writing a report for another person or organization, you would need to ask yourself:

- Why do they want this report from me?
- What information are they likely to need from me?
- What would they find helpful?

It is by asking questions such as this that we can begin to establish what is relevant to the writing task in hand.

Voice of experience 10.1

❝I used to struggle with record keeping until I attended a training course that emphasized the importance of being clear about what I was writing, why I was writing it and who I was writing it for. It was one of the most helpful training courses I have ever been on.**❞** *Lysette, a mental health development worker*

Often there are set formats for particular pieces of written work. Such formats can give us helpful clues about what sort of information we are expected to include. It is unfortunately the case that I have often come across examples of writing where people have ignored the format set and, as a result of this, have either omitted significant information or have included extraneous information which is of no use to the person receiving the piece of writing, thereby wasting the time of both parties. We should therefore be careful not to allow anxieties about writing to allow us to rush into the task without first examining whether or not there is a set format that the written work needs to follow.

One important factor that I have noted from my experience of working in adult education over a period of years is the high number of people who leave compulsory education with a distinct lack of confidence about the use of the written word, in their own attempts both to communicate in writing and to make use of written sources as study materials. For very many people, therefore, there is a very real challenge in seeking to overcome any barriers that may stand in the way of developing confidence in the use of written language. However, there is no shortage of people who have successfully got past such barriers and managed to develop an impressive set of writing skills. The barriers can seem daunting at first, but it is clear that they can be overcome.

How to write?

This is a very big question! Indeed, it would be possible to write a whole book in response to that question alone. One long-standing approach to this that has stood the test of time is what Lanham (1983) refers to as the CBS approach: clarity, brevity and sincerity. While this can be a helpful format to work to in some respects, we once again encounter the problem of a simplistic, prescriptive approach. Consider, for example, the emphasis on brevity which is something that is shared by many other writers (for example, Morris, 1998; Hopkins, 1998a). However, it is not simply the case that 'the briefer the better'. This is not least because, very often, a less brief way of stating something is actually easier for the reader to digest and make sense of. If you are not convinced by this, try looking at a philosophy book and seeing just how many ideas are often squeezed into one page. People who are used to reading philosophy texts will generally tell you that they take a lot longer to read because of this established style of expressing complex ideas very succinctly indeed. Rather than focus on brevity, I would argue that we should focus on providing written work that is easily digested, which means aiming to be neither too over elaborate nor too succinct, but rather an appropriate balance between the two extremes.

While I would certainly not advocate waffling, I would also not want to go to the opposite end of the spectrum of assuming that expressing something briefly is automatically better than expressing it more fully. It is very often the case that repetition and emphasis are needed in order to get the point across. Indeed, there is much to be said for the idea that, if we have something important to say, it is worth saying it twice to make sure that we have got the message across. That is, while unnecessarily repeating something can be both irritating and a waste of time for both parties, sometimes what we have to say is important enough to bear repetition.

The section below headed 'pitfalls to avoid' should be useful in helping you to avoid some of the common mistakes and problems in writing. However, the two most important points in terms of making sure that your written work is appropriate are clarity and effectiveness. That is, you should be making sure that you are expressing yourself as clearly as possible, doing your best to avoid confusion and ambiguity, and also as effectively as possible – which can be summarized as follows:

- It is consistent with its intended purpose – that is, it fulfils its aims and has not drifted off the point.
- It will be helpful to the intended reader in the specific circumstances.
- It contains all the relevant points (to avoid significant omissions) and only the relevant points (to avoid information overload and distracting people from the point of your communication).
- It is pitched at the appropriate level in terms of formality, style of language and so on.
- It is in an appropriate format.

PRACTICE FOCUS 10.2

Aisha had never felt very confident in putting things in writing, largely as a result of negative experiences in her school days which had seriously affected her confidence. She therefore attended the *Effective Writing Skills* course with mixed feelings. On the one hand she was hoping she would get some practical help so that she could improve her skills and boost her confidence. On the other hand, she was anxious about the possibility that the course might confirm what she had feared for a long time now – that she was just not bright enough to reach the level of literacy skills her job required of her. Fortunately, the course was a very successful one and Aisha found it very reassuring, as she was able to learn quite a few 'tricks of the trade' that she felt would stand her in good stead when she returned to work. She also found it very helpful to become aware that there were many other people on the course who were less than confident in using the written word and this made her much happier in realizing that she was not alone in having anxieties about developing her writing skills.

How do I avoid discrimination?

I argued in Chapter 6 that it is important to avoid a simplistic political correctness approach and, in its place, to develop what I refer to as linguistic sensitivity. That is, it is important that we become sensitive to those forms of language that can in some way reinforce discrimination. The points that I made in that chapter can also be applied here. You may therefore wish to revisit that section of Chapter 6 and consider the comments made there in relation to the use of the written word. However, there are two main differences – one positive and one negative. The first is that, in a written piece of work, we have the positive benefit of having an opportunity in most circumstances to review what we have written and to reflect on it before we present it to other people. We therefore have a great opportunity to develop linguistic sensitivity. The second, and not so positive one, is that what we write may stay on record for many, many years, warts and all. That is, what we write may come back to haunt us a good deal later. We should therefore be very careful about what we commit to posterity by committing it to writing.

Pitfalls to avoid

I have now been involved for a very long time in a world of work in which the written word plays a vitally important part. As a practitioner, a manager and an educator, and in the other related roles that I have fulfilled over the years, I have had to be very sensitive to issues relating to language in general and the written word in particular. Through that experience, I have become aware of a number of problems that can easily arise. Here I present 12 of those problems or pitfalls to enable you to be aware of them so that you can take whatever steps you feel are necessary to avoid the problems described. Of course, I am by no means suggesting that the 12 pitfalls presented here are by any means the only ones. Rather, they are the ones that I am most familiar with from my own experiences of working with a wide variety of people who rely on the use of the written word.

1. Failure to plan

As we have noted, putting something in writing can be an onerous task, as what we write may be available for many years to come. Clearly, this is a heavy responsibility and one that can be quite daunting. However, the positive side of this is that, unlike speech and conversation, we do not have to 'think on our feet'. We can plan what we write by thinking carefully about what message or messages we are trying to put across before we put pen to paper (or finger to keyboard). An important point to recognize here is that unclear thinking will produce unclear writing. That is, if we are not clear about what we are trying to convey before we start writing, we should not be surprised when what we write emerges as unclear. At times, people may feel the pressure to 'just get on with it' but this is a temptation to resist if we can. This does not mean that you have to plan every last detail before you begin writing, but it does mean that the clearer you are about what you are trying to say, the easier it will be to say it. An important time and workload management principle (Thompson, 2009a) is that it is wise to invest time in order to save time. This very much applies to planning what we commit to writing. For example, a mistake made by saving a few moments' worth of time by not planning could lead to whole days being spent on trying to rectify the problem or make up for the harm done.

PRACTICE FOCUS 10.3

When Darren submitted his first assignment he was not sure what the tutor would make of it, as he had no previous experience of higher education and was not entirely sure what was expected of him. He felt confident, though, that he had at least done enough to pass. He was therefore both disappointed and upset when he discovered that he had failed the assignment. The tutor's comments stated that the work presented was too jumbled and incoherent to achieve a pass grade. At first, Darren felt a little bit insulted to have his work described as 'incoherent' and therefore went to see the tutor concerned to raise his objections to this comment. The tutor explained that she had not been able to follow the thread of Darren's argument and had been unable to work out what he was trying to say. Although he still felt a little aggrieved about having his work described as incoherent, he did have to admit that there was no thread of argument to follow and he too had not been sure what he was trying to say in the assignment. He learned the hard way that his written work would have to be much more focused, and that he would have to be much clearer about what he wanted to say before he started to say it.

One helpful way of looking at this is that effective writing is generally characterized by the writer gently leading the reader through the message(s) he or she is trying to put across. Careful planning can help to make sure that this is achieved.

2. Not listening

Much written work is a response to other written work – for example, a letter in response to someone else's letter, or a report written as a result of receiving other documents. As noted in Chapter 6, in relation to speech and conversation, not listening to someone is a recipe for poor communication. And, of course, the same can be seen to apply in terms of written communication. For example, if you receive a letter which asks a number of questions, but your response does not respond to all of those questions, then it should not come as a surprise if the writer of the original letter is dissatisfied with how you have responded. Similarly, my experience over the years as a tutor is that the most common reason for a student to fail an essay is that he or she does not address the question set when preparing the assignment. It is not uncommon for students to write the essay which responds to the question they would have liked to have been set, rather than the one that was actually set. It is therefore important that we are focused in ensuring that what we write responds appropriately to whatever triggered off the need for undertaking the writing task.

3. Lack of structure

The structure of a piece of written work is an important aid to digestion – that is, something that is carefully and appropriately structured is much easier to read and understand than something which lacks structure. Consider, for example, the difference between a piece of writing which has a clear structure and one which rambles from point to point, with no apparent thread linking them together. Which would you find easier to read?

This returns us to the earlier point about planning. We need to plan not only what we want to write, but also the order in which we should write it. A very common structure which can be very helpful in most circumstances is to divide the piece of written work into three parts: the first is the introduction in which you set the scene by giving the reader a picture of the purpose of what you are writing and its contents; the second part should be the main body in which you put forward the points you need to convey. These should be presented in a logical order. It is up to you to decide what is the best order to present your ideas, but generally a little thought and advance planning will enable you to decide. The third part should be the conclusion in which you draw your piece of work to a close, summarizing the main points and explicitly identifying any conclusions you wish to draw.

While this is a well-established format and widely used across letters, reports, essays and other forms of written work, we should be careful not to overgeneralize its use. Some forms of written work will require a more complex or sophisticated structure. For example, some reports will need to separate out general conclusions from specific recommendations. Also, as noticed earlier, we should bear in mind that some pieces of written work have a specified or predetermined format. It is therefore important that we give some thought to structure before launching into what we are trying to get across.

> **ACTIVITY 10.2**
>
> Find a number of different examples of written work (reports and so on).
> Look at each one to see whether it follows the three-part structure high-
> lighted above. Then think about which reports work best, those with a clear
> structure or those without.

4. Airs and graces

Morris (1998) makes the point that 'too many people write correspondence
with the aim of sounding important, or of putting up a defence – not to communicate' (p. 1). Similarly, Hopkins (1998a) alerts us to the dangers of writing
which is geared towards impressing rather than informing. Unfortunately, I
have come across many examples of writing where the author has tried to
sound academic or elegant and has failed on both counts. Many people would
therefore argue that it is important that we should keep our writing simple and
to the point. However, once again, I would be wary of oversimplifying the
matter. Rich, elegant and sophisticated language can be very influential and
can be a very powerful tool in many work settings (as well as being a significant source of satisfaction and thus motivation in its own right). Therefore,
rather than seeking to discourage people from using such rich prose, I would
want to pose a question: Are you sufficiently skilled and experienced to be
able to write in an elegant and sophisticated way? If so, then I would suggest
that there is much to be gained by making the most of this ability. However,
it is also important to recognize our limitations. Therefore, if you feel that you
are not sufficiently skilled or experienced to produce this level of writing, then
I think it is important not to attempt to do so, as crude attempts to write at a
high level can be very counterproductive – at best, they can sound pretentious
and at worst can be embarrassingly wrong. If you are not sure where the limits
of your writing ability fall, you may wish to enlist the help of a friend, relative
or colleague to give you feedback. However, if you do so, you would be well
advised to choose the person carefully, as some tactless feedback may succeed
only in undermining your confidence.

A related point is the use of jargon. Hopkins (1998a) describes jargon as
'the curse of the modern age' (p. 72). However, he then goes on to add that it
can be a useful shorthand. While broadly agreeing with the spirit of what
Hopkins is trying to convey, I would take a slightly different slant on this
issue. To my mind, jargon is an extremely useful form of specialist language
that can be much more precise than everyday terminology. If people working
in specialist fields had to communicate with one another in everyday speech,
then their communications would have to be much lengthier and more time
consuming, and they would also lose a lot in the translation in terms of the
subtlety and sophistication that is commonly associated with many forms of

PRACTICE FOCUS 10.4

Bernard was able to write assessment reports that very vividly brought to life the people he had been working with. He had a very rich talent when it came to describing people and the interactions that had gone on as part of the assessment process. Everyone commented on how well he was able to use language to paint a very helpful picture that captured the complexities and subtleties of some very sensitive issues. Over the years some colleagues had tried to imitate his style and produce comparable work. However, one by one, they had realized that they did not possess his rare talent and were better off sticking to less ambitious forms of written communication. They had therefore returned to more conventional forms of report writing, but remained grateful that Bernard had not had the quality of his writing knocked out of him by a simplistic approach which left no room for more advanced language skills.

technical language. Jargon in itself, then, is not a bad thing. In fact, when used appropriately, it is an extremely good thing. Where problems arise, however, is not from the use of jargon itself, but from the *inappropriate* use of jargon. For example, I can use sociological jargon in conversing with a sociologist friend, or psychological jargon in communicating with a psychologist colleague and, in both cases, have a very fruitful and satisfying communication. However, if I were to use sociological or psychological jargon in a conversation with somebody who does not have a background in either of these disciplines, then it is likely that he or she would find the experience very frustrating, and it is very unlikely that my communicative intentions would have been fulfilled in those circumstances.

In my experience, problems with jargon can arise in one of two main ways. First, people can sometimes forget that a particular term is part of their professional jargon and confuse it with everyday terminology. This is understandable if people are constantly using technical terms and become very accustomed to them. However understandable it may be, it is none the less not acceptable, as it can be a serious barrier to communication. This is an example of failing to ensure that one's communication fits the situation. Second, and this is where we return to the theme of airs and graces, many people deliberately use jargon in what I would regard as an inappropriate way in a misguided attempt to impress people. Some people seem to feel that they will gain more respect by using technical language in non-technical situations, perhaps without realizing that they risk being seen as arrogant or pretentious. This type of inappropriate use of language is also, of course, an inappropriate use of power, as the net effect of it can be significant disempowerment for the people who are on the receiving end of such poor practice.

Voice of experience 10.2

"One of the things I end up doing a lot of in my job is translating officialese into English. Professionals who write in ways that their clients can't understand can be a real problem. I think they lose the plot sometimes. I don't think they realize how writing like that creates distance instead of bringing people closer together.**"** *Holly, an advocacy worker*

5. Not making the purpose clear

Practice Focus 3.4 describes a situation in which foster carers received a letter from a school informing them of a review meeting in respect of a child they were looking after at the time. What was not clear to the recipients of this letter was whether it was simply for information purposes or was actually an invitation for them to attend that meeting. This is a good example of what not to do in a written communication. It should be perfectly clear to the person receiving your written work as to why you have written it. Considerable confusion and misunderstanding can arise if you make false assumptions about the intended reader's expectations of the purpose of what has been written.

It is often helpful to make the purpose clear by explicitly spelling out why the written work concerned has been produced – for example, by stating something like: 'This report has been prepared in order to … '. This can not only help people digest what you have to say and help to avoid misunderstandings, it can also help people decide whether they want to read it or not. Of course, it can be very irritating when someone has to read something to find out whether it is something they want or need to read!

6. Poor presentation

Hopkins (1998b) makes the point that, if the way your work is presented gives the impression that you do not care about it, then you run the risk that the reader will not care about it either. Similarly, it can be argued that the way you present your work can be read as an indicator of the respect that you hold for your reader, with carefully presented work representing a high level of respect and sloppy work representing little or no respect for the reader.

It is also important to be aware that poor presentation can, in itself, lead to poor communication. While some people become quite obsessive about, for example, the use of punctuation, it is none the less the case that such matters as punctuation, spelling, word order and so on can make a difference to the meaning of what you write. In terms of punctuation, consider for example the difference between 'Sam said Kim is stupid' and 'Sam, said Kim, is stupid' (for a discussion of punctuation, see Seely, 1998). Similarly, in terms of spelling, 'cite', 'site' and 'sight' all sound the same but, of course, have very different meanings. Sometimes, even where a word is misspelled, we can understand the meaning from the context, but this is not always the case. And finally, missing words out or putting them in the wrong order can have a drastic effect in changing the meaning of what you are trying to convey. For example, I once came across a situation in which a letter stated: 'We help your value' when it should presumably have read: 'We value your help'. I presume no harm was done by that error, but there are many other cases where a presentation error can be very costly indeed.

Poor presentation can present problems not only of meaning being distorted, but also of a very negative impression being given. A low level in terms of presentation quality can give a very distinct impression of amateurishness, lack of care, lack of credibility and even a lack of commitment. There is therefore a lot to be lost by producing written work to a poor level of presentation. Some people may argue that it should not matter, as long as the message content of the communication is as it should be. However, I would suggest that this is a naive view that fails to recognize the complexities of communication. This is because poor-quality written work sends out 'metamessages'. That is, it conveys not only the information that was intended, but also these other messages about how much care was taken, how professional the organization is and so on.

7. Being vague

In everyday conversation, we can often afford to be quite imprecise without causing any significant difficulties. However, in formal correspondence, reports and so on, a lack of precision can be quite a problem. As mentioned above, sometimes the vagueness in writing stems from the vagueness in thinking that has preceded it, whereas, in many other cases, it is a failure to express oneself

---

PRACTICE FOCUS 10.5

Niamh was not sure what was happening about the proposed appointment of the new staff who were needed as a result of the new project funding that had been received. She therefore sent an email message to the Head of Human Resources to seek clarification about what process would be followed and to what timescale. She was very disappointed with the response she received as it did not answer her questions and seemed to talk around the issues rather than actually address them. She therefore sent another email, apologizing if her earlier message had not been clear and restating the questions as clearly as she could. When she received another message that was equally vague and unfocused, she resolved to deal with the Deputy Head of Human Resources in future and accept that the Head was someone who struggled to provide a simple answer to some simple questions. She later discovered that this situation was not an isolated incident, and that others too had encountered difficulties as a result of this person's very vague style of communication.

clearly and precisely which causes the problem. It is therefore important to ask yourself at times: Am I expressing this clearly or am I allowing vagueness to creep in?

Consider, for example, the discussion in Chapter 2 of the multiple meanings of the word 'go'. Its ability to mean so many different things in so many different contexts can lead to confusion and misunderstanding if we use language too loosely in writing. What may be apparent in a conversation as a result of paralanguage, body language and the overall social setting of the communication may be far less apparent in a written piece of work. That is, we can get away with being imprecise far more readily in speech than we can in writing.

8. Using the wrong word

There are many pairs of words which sound similar but which have very different meanings. For example, 'uninterested' means lacking in interest – that is, bored – whereas 'disinterested' means objective or impartial. To say that the referee was disinterested is not to say that he or she was bored! Another common confusion relates to 'affect' and 'effect'. To affect means to have an effect upon someone or something. To effect means 'to bring about' (for example, to effect a change). Often the context will indicate to the reader that the wrong word has been chosen, and so the writer's intended meaning will still get through. However, this is not always the case, and problems can arise from these confusions. For example, if I sign a contract to undertake a certain amount of work for an organization over a two-year period and to be paid for this work on a six-monthly basis, then I should ensure that the person drafting the contract has not confused biannual (every six months) with biennial (every two years). Of course, it is generally much simpler and much safer to avoid such terms and to be more precise in, for example, stating 'six-monthly'.

People can often confuse singular and plural forms of certain words, although this is not likely to lead to major problems, as it is usually clear from the context whether singular or plural is intended. Common examples would include:

Singular	Plural
criterion	criteria
phenomenon	phenomena
consortium	consortia

9. Incoherence

It is amazing how often I come across something that simply does not make sense. Perhaps there is a word missing that renders the passage meaningless, but more often I think it is simply that the writer has not paid enough attention to what they are writing and how it will come across to the reader. Here are two real examples that I have previously come across:

1. The decision was made after the couple's marriage was reviewed and police involvement had intervened while there is no recourse in the pressure, the situation has reapplied, but without being recorded.
2. The children had been visited at school, with the consequences were not transmitted to the agencies, after parental consent was not registered.

After a lot of effort invested in looking closely at the context in which the comments were written, I was eventually able to get some vague idea of what (2) meant, but (1) remains a complete mystery to me, and no doubt to anyone else who reads it.

In view of the danger of incoherence, it is important that we (i) think carefully about what we write while we are writing it; and (ii) check it over once we have written it.

10. Neglecting confidentiality

It perhaps seems obvious to state that confidential information should not be provided in non-confidential documents. However, in my experience it is sadly the case that this is often overlooked. For example, as an external examiner at various universities, I have seen many reports relating to student placements which have included confidential information, even though the guidelines provided to students made it clear in explicit terms that this should not happen. Sometimes the problem arises simply because the writer does not mark a confidential document as 'confidential'. What can also happen is that, in work environments where people are handling confidential information as a matter of course on a daily basis, the need to handle such information sensitively can be forgotten. That is, people can become complacent if they are regularly handling confidential information. While such problems may be understandable, they none the less remain unacceptable, as a breach of confidentiality can have very significant detrimental consequences for the person to whom the information relates, the person who provided the information and for the person who breached the confidentiality (if it becomes a matter of disciplinary action, for example).

In committing information to writing we should therefore always be clear about what is confidential and what is not. We need to make sure that we are not revealing information to people who have no right to receive it. The boundary between confidential and non-confidential information is therefore an important one to police very carefully. In running training courses on these issues I have found it useful to ask participants to consider how they would feel if sensitive information about themselves were carelessly handled and, as a result, made available to people who should not have that information. This can be a good source of motivation to ensure that we do not become complacent about such matters.

11. Inviting litigation

The point was made earlier that putting something in writing means that it is relatively permanent and can be used as evidence in future. Care therefore has to be taken that what is written down is not harmful to anyone. Such problems can arise in a number of ways, but there are three in particular that are worthy of comment. First, there is the problem of confusing fact and opinion. In many cases, it is better to avoid giving opinions altogether but, where an opinion is called for, it should be made clear that it is an opinion and not necessarily a statement of fact (see Practice Focus 10.6). Second, we have the problem of inaccuracy. If you confuse Mr Jones of Waverley Street (who embezzled £50,000 from his employers) with Mr Jones of Waverley Court (who did no such thing), then the consequences of such a mistake could be disastrous. Third, there is the problem of making defamatory comments. We have to make sure that what is written down is not something that could be interpreted as libel or defamation of character – even if you believe what you write to be true. It is therefore important to make sure, as far as is reasonably possible, that what you are committing to writing is accurate and appropriate, and that opinions are clearly identified as such.

PRACTICE FOCUS 10.6

In her report of the work she had done with the Spencer family, June described Mr Spencer as a violent man. June had found him to be very intimidating, largely because of his large physical presence, his booming voice and his aggressive tone of voice and body language. She had found it a very difficult piece of work and was glad that it was now at an end, so that she could concentrate on working with families that she found less threatening. However, when her line manager read her report she was taken aback by the use of the word 'violent'. Following discussion of the report, June came to realize that 'violent' was not the right word. While she clearly feared that Mr Spencer would become violent, she had no evidence at all to show that he had ever actually been violent. On her line manager's advice she therefore amended her report, deleting reference to him as violent (an unsupported opinion) and referring to the actual facts of how he had presented to her.

In all three cases (failing to separate fact from opinion, inaccuracy and defamatory remarks) the unfortunate result may in some cases be litigation.

That is, if you record something that is unfair or inaccurate and the person or organization to which it refers feels they have suffered harm as a result of your actions, you and/or your employers may find yourselves in a position of having to justify your actions in a court of law. I would certainly not advocate adopting a defensive approach in which your primary motivation is to keep yourself out of trouble, as I believe such a narrow approach tends to cause more problems than it solves, in so far as it can contribute to our losing sight of what we are doing and why we are doing it. However, we can be alert to possible problems without becoming unduly defensive and concentrating too much on 'covering our backs'.

12. Closed worlds

This refers to forms of writing that may well make sense to the person doing the writing, but do not 'connect' with the world of the person(s) being communicated with. One example of this is reflected in Voice of experience 10.2 which reflects how practitioners working in a bureaucratic setting can get drawn so far into officialdom that they forget that much of what they write will at best confuse many people and, at worst, alienate them.

Another relates to multidisciplinary working which can be undermined by members of one profession not taking on board the perspectives, needs or priorities of members of other professions. For example, a health professional may use medical terminology that others cannot understand (I have read many reports where I have had to look things up because I was not aware of what that particular term meant), while someone involved in the legal system may make assumptions that are not shared with those reading the communication

PITFALLS TO AVOID	
1	Failure to plan
2	Not listening
3	Lack of structure
4	Airs and graces
5	Not making the purpose clear
6	Poor presentation
7	Being vague
8	Using the wrong word
9	Incoherence
10	Neglecting confidentiality
11	Inviting litigation
12	Closed worlds

Figure 10.1 Pitfalls to avoid

– assumptions based on knowledge of the legal world that people outside of that world are unlikely to have.

One very important implication of this is that, before communicating with people in writing, we need to make sure that we are not making assumptions that make perfect sense within our own professional context, but which may have little meaning outside of it.

As I indicated earlier, these 12 pitfalls are not necessarily the only ones. However, what I have presented should be sufficient to get across the point that there are numerous ways in which we can experience problems with attempting to communicate effectively in writing. Clearly, care does need to be taken to ensure that, as far as possible, we do not make the mistakes that have been outlined here. Of course, forewarned is forearmed, and so it is to be hoped that by being aware of these common pitfalls, you will be less likely to fall into them. These are mistakes that have been made many times before and so we now have the chance to learn from other people's mistakes without having to make them for ourselves.

Using email

The use of electronic mail has grown in the past ten years from a very special-ized usage on the part of a relatively small part of the population to a main-stream usage by a growing number of individuals and organizations. It is now not unusual for some people to have more or less all of their communication with particular individuals or organizations by email. Given its speed (more or less instant communication across the world) and relatively low cost, it is not surprising that it has become so well established. It is more instant and more flexible than formal written communication, such as letters and memos, and also has the advantage over telephone communication that the person you want to communicate with does not have to be present when you are trying to get hold of them (it is 'asynchronous', to use the technical term).

However, despite its clear benefits, email is not without its problems. The following are just some of the difficulties that can arise:

- *Netiquette* Etiquette about the use of the Internet and email has grown up over the years in the form of a number of 'rules' about appropriate usage. Sometimes a lot of bad feeling can be generated when people do not 'stick to the rules'. For example, it is considered bad form to write entirely in capitals as this is regarded as the equivalent of shouting.
- *Misunderstanding* Given its speed, flexibility and relative informality, it is not surprising that people generally give less attention to the emails they send than any formal letters they would send out. And

similarly, people can often read emails less carefully than they would read a formal letter. This can create considerable scope for misunderstanding and being at cross-purposes with one another.

- *Information overload*   Given the benefits of email, it is not surprising that it is used very heavily. However, this can easily lead to overusage, with some people being flooded with messages – perhaps to the point where they become overwhelmed and experience stress as a result.

It can also often be the case that people use email inappropriately, perhaps because they have come to rely on it so heavily as such an easy means of communication. Whelan (2000) makes an important point when he argues that:

E-mail is not always the best way of communicating. Some things are best dealt with in other ways.

To some people e-mail is an ideal way in which they can:

- *take part in office politics*
   'I'll copy this to the CEO so that he can see who's really driving this deal forward.'
- *pass the buck*
   'I've forwarded the message to Purchasing so it's no longer my problem.'
- *cover their backs*
   'I've copied the message to Accounts so that I can't be blamed if the bill doesn't get paid.'

These characteristics are not common to all companies. Nevertheless they do occur and e-mail can be a contributing factor. (p. 9)

Email is therefore something that needs to be used carefully and sensitively. It is a powerful tool, and like any tool, can do a lot of good if it is used properly but a lot of harm if it is not.

ACTIVITY 10.3

Talk to colleagues about their experiences of using email and, in particular, what problems they may have experienced over time. Make some notes from these discussions and then think about what lessons can be learned about email as a contribution to effective communication.

In using email as a means of written communication it is important that you should ask yourself the following questions:

- *Is email the appropriate means of communication?*   For example, if you are responding to a complaint, a formal letter may be more appropriate. Another example would be someone sending an email marked 'urgent' to somebody who is on a week's leave and thus not in a position to respond.

- *Am I communicating with the right person(s)?* Sometimes people send out the same message to a large number of people 'for their information'. However, this can lead to problems if some of the recipients then find themselves with messages that they do not want cluttering up their inbox. Even deleting unwanted messages can be very time consuming by the time you have worked out that you do not want them and actually gone through the process of deleting them.
- *Am I saying enough?* Often email messages are problematic because either they do not have enough information in them or they have too much. It is important to think carefully before giving somebody a message which either leaves them wondering what you are talking about or contributes to the increasingly common problem of information overload.
- *Am I using the right tone?* Email is a relatively informal means of communication, but that does not mean all social rules of formality go out of the window.
- *Am I being sufficiently discreet?* Email is not as private as many people think. We therefore have to be very careful about communicating sensitive or confidential information by email.

These questions will not guarantee that you do not have any difficulties, but they should help to limit the chances of problems arising.

Voice of experience 10.3

“Thankfully I have not upset anyone in an email yet, but I have seen it happen so many times. We tend to use the damned thing so much these days – and get so many messages to deal with – that it is easy to just bang out a reply without thinking carefully about what you are saying – or how you are saying it. We really do need to be more careful in our use of it.**”** *Steph, a hospital social worker*

Conclusion

A major aim of Chapter 3 was to establish just how important writing is as a form of communication and this chapter has no doubt reinforced that message. Of course, few if any people will get everything right all of the time when it comes to writing. Mistakes are there for us all to make, and so it would be highly unrealistic to expect a 100 per cent record in dealing with such matters. However, it is to be hoped that, by giving you a raised level of awareness of some of the complex issues relating to writing, this chapter will enable you to be in a stronger position to use this important form of communication to best effect. Effective writing is a powerful tool, and so the efforts needed to develop the knowledge and skills you need and to continue to build upon them as far as possible should be well repaid in the medium to long term, if not in the short term.

If you are fortunate enough to be someone who is already a skilful and effective writer, then I hope that this chapter has at least reinforced your confidence and perhaps also given you some pointers for further development. However, if you are not confident in your ability to use writing to best effect, then it is to be hoped that you will find this chapter a positive foundation on which to build. Of course, it will not give you everything you need, but it should at least help you to move in the right direction. It should give you food for thought as well as some indicators of steps you can take to try and boost your skills and confidence.

Effective writing can be not only a useful part of your repertoire of skills in dealing with people and their problems, but also a significant source of pride, job satisfaction, high morale and motivation. I therefore very much hope that you will be able to build on whatever foundations you currently have in order to be able to maximize your effectiveness in the use of the written word.

Having now explored some of the key issues involved in effective written communication, we now arrive at the final chapter of the book. The topic for this is managing communication. Some readers who are not employed as managers may be tempted at this point to think that they have now finished the book, that the final chapter does not apply to them. However, this would be a serious mistake. Managing communication effectively is a challenge for everyone, and not just for managers. The final chapter has some important things to say to everyone who is involved in trying to promote effective communication, and so it is to this that we now turn.

POINTS TO PONDER

- How significant is it that written records could be available for others to see years after they were first written?
- What harm could poor written communication do (for example, a letter sent to a client or patient in 'officialese' rather than in a style of language geared towards effective partnership working)?
- Why is it important not to be vague in our written communications?

CHAPTER 11

Managing communication

Introduction

Our starting point for this chapter is the fact that effective communication is not simply a matter of personal skills and individual efforts. Rather, it also depends on such important matters as organizational systems, cultures and structures. It was noted in Chapter 5 that the context of communication is a significant factor in shaping its outcomes. The organizational context is no exception to this. A major implication of this is that, for communication to be used to best effect, it needs to be actively managed and not just left to chance. The focus of this final chapter can therefore be summed up in one question: How do we manage communication?

It is important to be clear at the beginning that, by management, I do not simply mean administration. In my view, an important element of management is leadership. Administration is concerned purely with day-to-day operational matters, but the leadership dimension of management brings in a strategic focus. In terms of communication, what this means is that we need to go beyond simply using skills to avoid or circumnavigate barriers to communication and develop a more holistic approach. Being strategic involves adopting a more holistic approach, looking at the overall picture, including barriers to communication, and seeing what can be done to remove them. It is a proactive approach which rises above day-to-day concerns to look at wider issues which stand in the way of progress. This is an important part of developing successful organizations. We have already seen how important communication is, and so we can also see that an organization which is defeatist or ineffective in relation to barriers to communication will fare far worse than a proactive organization which adopts a strategy of seeking to remove such barriers.

However, as I noted at the end of Chapter 10, we should not allow this talk of management and leadership to mislead us into assuming that this chapter is for managers only. I would argue that all staff, whether managers, practitioners, educators or support staff, have a part to play in making sure that communication is well managed. While managers will generally have more responsibility for such matters than others within the organization, this is not to say that they are the only ones to carry such responsibility.

The remainder of the chapter is divided into four main sections. In the first one, I look at what I refer to as 'the big picture'. This is my attempt to help to develop a more holistic understanding of communication within and between organizations. The second section looks at communication systems and considers some of the important issues here for making sure that these are working as effectively as possible. The third section examines the role of organizational culture in shaping communication, and the fourth section explores issues of structure and power as they affect the management of communication.

The big picture

An important concept to draw upon here is that of 'helicopter vision'. This refers to the ability not only to rise above a situation to get 'the big picture', but also to descend back into the day-to-day reality and deal with it on the basis of the understanding gained from achieving an overview (see Thompson, 2006b, for a discussion of this). There is no point having a holistic overview if we are not able to make the insights gained from it pay dividends in terms of actual practices. This is an important issue, as there is no shortage of examples of situations that have gone tragically wrong as a result of either a failure to obtain an overview or a failure to learn and apply the lessons that such a holistic overview can give us.

Developing such an overview involves looking at organizational systems for the storage, retrieval and transmission of information; factors relating to the organization's culture and how shared meanings affect communication; and the power lines along which the organization is structured. I shall consider each of these three main elements within this chapter. However, before I do so, there are some other important points about the big picture that need to be made.

The first point to emphasize is that communication problems can be both the cause and effect of difficulties within an organization. Few, if any, organizations are entirely free of communication difficulties. However, we need to be careful not to oversimplify the situation by assuming that, where an organization is having major difficulties – including communication difficulties – the communication problems are the source of the other difficulties. A more realistic understanding of such situations is that the two sets of problems (those that are directly associated with communication and those which are not) enter into what is known as a dialectical relationship. That is, rather than one simply 'causing' the other, they enter into a relationship of mutual cause and effect. They influence each other. A badly run organization is unlikely to manage its communication well. However, it is also the case that an organization which does not manage its communication effectively is likely to find it very difficult to be an efficient and effective organization in other respects. The two sets of issues are interconnected.

> **PRACTICE FOCUS 11.1**
>
> When Ryan was promoted to the position of team manager, the team were quick to tell him that they had concerns about communication both within the team and between the team and other sectors of the organization. Ryan therefore decided that one of his first tasks in his new job would be to analyse and evaluate communication systems. This he did with gusto, and soon found a number of relatively simple ways in which he could improve communication. However, once he had made these changes he realized that there were still significant problems that needed to be addressed. By looking carefully at the situation, he became aware that, in some ways, the communication problems, although significant in their own right, had actually been masking more deeply embedded problems – for example, in terms of the skills mix within the team. He had to be careful to make sure that he got the balance right – to give the importance of communication its due recognition but without failing to recognize the role of other factors that could significantly interact with communication.

Another important issue to address is the need for an *inclusive* approach to managing communication. Of course, it is clear that organizations depend on people, and where people are unnecessarily excluded, then it is not difficult to predict that there will be detrimental consequences arising from this in terms of communication. For example, what can happen in such circumstances is not simply that communication fails to happen, but rather that the wrong type of communication occurs. If an individual or a group of people within an organization feel disaffected because they feel excluded from the channels of communication, then it is unlikely that they will simply remain silent but, rather, they will engage in communication of a more destructive nature – for example, rumour, innuendo, gossip (possibly of a malicious nature) or other general expressions of dissatisfaction and alienation. Such talk can be very destructive in terms not only of the morale and the overall well-being of the workforce, but also the possible scenarios that can arise as a result of such talk – complaints, grievances, valued staff leaving and so on. The need to ensure that everyone is included in the appropriate networks of communication is therefore a very important task because of the positives it brings and the (often very serious) negatives it avoids.

A lack of inclusion can arise for a number of reasons, not least the following:

- *Special communication needs* Where someone's first language is not English or where he or she has a hearing impairment or other disability which could impair communication, it may be necessary to take additional steps to ensure that such individuals are not disadvantaged in terms of how the organization's communication systems work (see the discussions in Chapter 9).

- *Use of inappropriate language*   As noted in earlier chapters, some forms of language can have the effect of excluding certain groups. For example, gender-biased language in a male-dominated workforce may leave many women feeling that they are not involved in what is going on.
- *Bullying and harassment*   In recent years we have come to realize that such destructive practices as bullying and harassment are far more widespread than we had previously been aware (Thompson, 2000b). It does not take much imagination to work out that such practices are likely to have a seriously detrimental effect on communication processes at work in that particular organization.

Voice of experience 11.1

❝I have been lucky, I suppose, in that I have worked in organizations where communication was very badly managed and everything was very haphazard and also in well-run organizations where communication problems are very few and far between. Having that breadth of experience has helped me to appreciate what makes for effective communication and what gets in the way of it. That has been helpful for the training that I deliver about communication skills.**❞** *Geraldine, a training and development manager*

We should also ensure we do not forget that communication operates at different levels and therefore has to be managed at different levels, not least the following three:

1. *Within the organization* Successful internal communications are, of course, essential to the success of an organization in achieving its goals. If an organization cannot 'get its act together' internally, then clearly it is going to struggle when it comes to communicating in the wider arena. Poor communication at this level will also contribute to the organization concerned having a less than favourable reputation or image in the eyes of outsiders if its internal communicative deficits become apparent (and they frequently do).
2. *Between the organization and its stakeholders (clients, customers, patients and so on)* Of course, the success of a commercial organization depends very much on how it treats its customers. Failing to communicate appropriately with customers is likely to turn them into ex-customers. Similarly, within the public sector where the emphasis is on public service, a lack of effective communication between the organization and those people it is seeking to serve is likely to seriously

undermine the organization's ability to achieve its goals and is also likely to lead to a high level of dissatisfaction – for example, in terms of the number of complaints received.

3. *Between organizations* It is increasingly the case within the present political climate that organizations are working together to achieve shared or overlapping goals. If such organizations which are seeking to work together fail to communicate in satisfactory ways, then the outcome may be not only to fail to achieve their goals, but also to encounter far worse consequences, such as the collapse of a particular project or enterprise in its entirety. There can be many reasons why interorganizational communication problems arise, due in large part to the highly complex dynamics that occur when organizations seek to work together (Harrison et al., 2003).

PRACTICE FOCUS 11.2

The partnership had been set up across six agencies and, while the majority of people involved welcomed the opportunity to work together, they were also aware of how difficult it would be to do so, given the different cultures, value systems and priorities of the organizations involved. To begin with, everything went very well, and the staff involved were pleasantly surprised. Things continued to go well for some months and people were feeling confident about how things were developing and how they were well on the way to achieving their initial aims. However, what they had not bargained for was the impact of the summer holiday season. Two meetings had to be abandoned because there were too few people present for them to be quorate as a result of several people being on leave. Once the summer was over the impetus had been lost and the partnership never really got going after that. It was as if the extended gap between meetings had spoiled the rhythm that the group had built up from their very positive start, and there was no one person or agency that took the responsibility to pull things together again. There was an important lesson to be learned here about anticipating difficulties and planning for such eventualities.

It should be clear, then, that managing communication involves attempting to meet the challenges of effective communication at all three of these levels. For example, there is little point in an organization having extremely good internal communicative systems when communication becomes very poor as soon as that organization interacts with its clients or customers or other stakeholders.

ACTIVITY 11.1

Think about the organization you currently work (or study) in. How is communication managed in it in relation to the three levels outlined above? Can you think of any ways in which it could perhaps be improved? See if you can find out what other people think about this.

A further important issue or set of issues in this regard is what I shall refer to as the information balance. I use this term to refer to the importance of ensuring that we are neither flooded by having far too much information to deal with, but nor are we at a disadvantage because we have too little information for our communication needs. The problem of information overload is one of major proportions in today's society. This is due partly to developments in information technology and partly to increased access to the technology as a result of the lower costs of acquiring and using such technology. This problem is a major one because, not only does it lead to unnecessary pressures and stress for staff who are in danger of being swept away by the flood of information, but also too much information can lead to significant pieces of information being missed. For example, a key message may not be taken on board if it is only one out of a very large number indeed of messages received by that particular person on that particular day. What is needed, therefore, is an information management strategy which seeks to protect employees from the problems of information overload, while also being clear about what information is essential. We have to move away from the old idea that the more information we have, the safer we are. The notion of 'the more the better' does not work in this technological age where there is just so much information so readily available to us from a wide variety of channels. We have to be more realistic and selective. For example, I once worked as a consultant with an organization where a trade union representative requested copies of the minutes of all the relevant management committee meetings. However, within a matter of three weeks, he had had to cancel that request, as he was horrified by the huge amount of paper that came his way in response. He realized that it would be a more or less full-time job simply to keep up to date with the torrent of management information that was coming his way through these minutes.

The information balance therefore involves establishing systems and mechanisms which seek to ensure that people are not weighed down with too much information, but nor do problems arise as a result of crucial information being missed or lost. This is clearly a major challenge for all concerned. It involves ensuring that the organization has not only established appropriate and adequate channels of communication, but also has in place mechanisms for deciding what is to be communicated and what is not.

PRACTICE FOCUS 11.3

Craig was keen to help his staff to become involved in policy development. He therefore made use of opportunities for basic grade staff to make a contribution. It was with this in mind that he asked Katie to undertake some research on a matter that was to be discussed at a forthcoming management meeting and to write a report for him. He asked her to have the report ready for him by the day before the meeting. Katie was pleased to have this opportunity and so she promised faithfully to get the report to Craig on time. However, Craig had not specified how detailed a report he wanted and Katie, in her enthusiasm, had produced a very long and detailed report – far more than Craig could comfortably read in the time available to him in between receiving the report and attending the meeting. He therefore had to make do with skim reading the report and hoping that he did not miss anything crucial – and he felt very uncomfortable about that. However, he realized it was his own fault, as he had failed to brief Katie properly, and so he undertook to set aside some time to talk to her about report writing, the use of executive summaries and so on.

One final point I wish to emphasize in relation to the big picture is that of self-management or personal effectiveness. If we are to make the most of communication, then we must not only manage the systems of communication, but also manage ourselves in terms of ensuring that our personal effectiveness is at an optimal level as far as possible. Systems of communication will only work if the people using them are sufficiently well organized to ensure that the necessary processes actually take place. Consider how many examples of communication breakdown are not due to a lack of communication skills on the part of a particular individual but, rather, owe much more to that individual's inability to manage his or her time effectively. For example, many problems arise because someone fails to make an important communication because they did not get round to it or they were distracted from doing so, rather than because they did not have the skills to do so. There is little point in being highly skilled communicators if we are so badly organized and so out of control in terms of our workload that we fail to take the opportunity to use those skills when they are needed. (For a discussion of self-management skills, see Part I of Thompson, 2009b.)

Communication systems

Information technology (or IT for short) is commonly assumed to refer to the use of computer equipment for the storage, retrieval and processing of information. However, the term is actually broader than that. Pens, pencils and paper are also forms of information technology. It is my view that we need to think broadly about information and communication technology and not simply to focus on the use of computers. Indeed, there are many organizations that have begun by looking at the computer systems and then tried to fit these into their organization. However, it takes relatively little thought and analysis to work out the folly of this approach. Clearly, what is likely to be far more suitable is to undertake a systematic analysis of the information and communication needs of the organization and then design a system or set of systems around those needs.

It is likely that computers will feature significantly in implementing any such plan developed from an analysis of needs, but we should, none the less, avoid making the mistake of beginning and ending our thinking with computers. For example, forms play a major role in most organizations' attempts to manage their communication and information needs. Although many forms are now available in a computerized format, we are still a long way from the day when paper forms no longer have a significant role in organizations. It would therefore be a mistake to ignore the design and use of forms in seeking to develop and implement an information and communication strategy. Indeed, it is well known that forms can cause significant problems. Unless they are carefully designed and matched to their specific purpose, forms can cause a great deal of confusion and lead to a great deal of time being wasted.

In this regard, I find it useful to borrow (and take liberties with) a phrase from architecture, namely 'form follows function'. What I mean by this is that it is important to ensure that forms actually do what we want them to do – that they fulfil their function. Important questions to be addressed are:

- *Are we clear what the purpose of the form is?* If people are not clear about the intended purpose of a form, we should not be surprised if they do not fill it in properly, or do not feel motivated enough to fill it in at all. In this day and age we have become so used to filling in forms that we can easily start to do so without giving a moment's thought as to what purpose the form is intended to fulfil.
- *Are the forms we are using fulfilling their purpose?* I am no longer surprised by how often I encounter badly designed forms that are not well suited to their purpose. We should not make the mistake of assuming that, because a form has been in use for a long time, it is therefore a form that works well in achieving its objectives. It is often the case that the use of forms is not reviewed, and so inappropriate forms can remain in use for a long time.
- *If they are not, how can we change them to ensure that they do?* Do you have the authority to change the forms you use? If not, how can you bring your concerns to the attention of those who do have the

authority to do so? It is a sad reflection perhaps of our bureaucratic society that it can often seem as though forms are written in stone rather than paper, and therefore cannot possibly be changed. I have had many incredulous looks when suggesting to staff in particular organizations that they should consider changing one or more of their forms. However, I have also had many experiences of organizations changing the design of a form because, as a result of my involvement as a trainer or consultant, staff have been motivated to pursue this as a line of action rather than just assume that change is not possible.

- *If they are, can they be improved further?* While some forms may well fulfil their basic function quite effectively, this does not mean that there is no scope for improvement. A review of form usage can often lead to forms being improved quite significantly. Again we have to be wary of bureaucratic inertia leading to the assumption that forms cannot possibly be changed.

- *Do the forms request unnecessary information, thereby wasting time and risking creating ill-feeling?* This refers back to the point made earlier that we need to move away from the traditional idea of gathering as much information as we reasonably can. Some people take great comfort from gathering as much information as they can, regardless of what they actually need. When such people design forms, the result can be one which asks for far more information than is necessary. Also, circumstances and needs can change. Information that was needed when the form was first designed may no longer be necessary in the circumstances that currently apply.

- *Do the forms omit significant information that would be helpful to us?* The people who design forms are not necessarily the people who will be using them. They may therefore not realize how significant a particular piece of information may be, and consequently could omit any mention of it from the form. This returns us to the notion of the 'balance of information' – neither too little nor too much.

This is an example of what I referred to earlier as leadership. An administrator is someone who would ensure that existing forms are used appropriately within existing parameters. A leader, by contrast, is someone who would look at whether the forms are fulfilling their strategic purpose and, if not, make the necessary arrangements to resolve the situation wherever possible. An administrator makes sure the system is working, whereas a leader takes a broader view than this by seeking to maximize system effectiveness (and seeks to change the system where this is needed) rather than simply keep the wheels turning.

PRACTICE FOCUS 11.4

Laura got to the point where she was very fed up with the complaints about various forms and their perceived inadequacies. She was also aware that some forms were used very inconsistently across the staff group. She therefore decided the time had come to review all the forms and look carefully at what they were intended for, whether they actually did what they were intended to, and what changes needed to be made to improve the situation. She divided the forms up into two categories – those that were internal to her field of management responsibility and could therefore be changed without reference to others, and those that were from the wider organization and would need permission from the powers that be for changes to be made. She decided to prioritize the former so that, if all went well, she could widely publicize the benefits gained from changing their own forms and use this to try and influence those above her in the organization with a view to encouraging a wider review of form usage.

Czerniawska (1997) argues that information systems drive change within organizations. She goes on to argue that research has shown that such systems are the most important internal driver for change. They are therefore significant influences on organizational dynamics and, as such, are important elements of organizational life that need to be taken seriously by all concerned, rather than being left to the technical experts who may well be extremely well versed in their own technical sphere, but who may not have the necessary understanding of the organization's information and communication needs. As I have already argued, information and communication systems are much, much more than just technical systems.

ACTIVITY 11.2

Consider what level of understanding you have of the communication systems of the organization you currently work (or study) in. How good is this understanding? How can you improve it further? Also, consider why it is important for you to have such an understanding.

Czerniawska also warns of the dangers of computer systems not meeting the needs they were designed for:

We can hear the impact that computer-speak continues to have all around us. How many times have we heard someone exclaim: 'But it doesn't do what I asked for! You haven't listened to what I told you.' Of course, there are many reasons why IS [information systems] fails to meet its expectations – needs change, technology arrives late, systems have bugs, projects go over budget. But it is still my belief that the language we use to talk about IS still has a significant impact on its results. (p. 72)

Although computers have amazing processing abilities, we should remember that they are not intelligent. That is, they will do only what they have been designed and programmed to do (although it often does not seem to be that way and, on many an occasion, I have had to remind myself that my computer cannot possibly have a personal grudge against me). Czerniawska also argues that many of the problems people continue to encounter in attempting to design and implement computer systems owe a great deal to the language we use in discussing such matters. She argues that we have allowed technical computer language to dominate in attempts to manage communication and information. This is something I would agree with, and I would further argue that computers and their systems are a means, not an end. Our focus should be on communication and information systems and how computers, amongst other things, can fit in with those systems (rather than the other way round). It is very unfortunate that the allure of modern technology has had the effect in many places of making the acquisition of state of the art equipment a more important goal than having hardware and software that actually achieve what they were purchased to do.

Another problem arising from the dominance of 'IT speak' is that such language has contributed to what can be called 'technophobia'. Of course, computers in themselves are nothing to be afraid of, but it has unfortunately become the case that many people do have a fear of them (particularly, it would seem, of 'pressing the wrong button' and wreaking havoc). However, building on Czerniawska's arguments, I would suggest that much of the fear arises from the fact that so many suppliers of computer equipment do not provide operating instructions in plain English. Their reliance on 'techno babble' tends to have the effect of undermining confidence and increasing the mystique of computer use. If we are to get the most out of the computer-based elements of communication and information systems, then it is important that we find ways to counter technophobia. Managers can play a part by trying to ensure, as far as possible, that appropriate guidance in understandable English is available to the staff who will be using the hardware (for example, in making this part of the contractual arrangements when they enter into a commercial agreement with a supplier of computer equipment). Users of computer equipment can also play a part by raising objections when they are faced with computer speak that they do not understand, rather than simply accepting it as a fact of life these days.

Voice of experience 11.2

❝We really struggled with our new computer system at first, as no one could really understand it, and the instructions we were given were not exactly helpful either. We were lucky, though, that our training department was able to find a really good trainer who explained it all to us in simple language. There aren't many like him around, unfortunately.**❞** *Kareem, a manager in a voluntary organization*

The use of computers is, at root, all about the management of communication and information systems, and so it is both ironic and perhaps unacceptable that the use of computers can be hampered by the dominance of forms of language which obscure more than they clarify and hinder more than they help. This is another example of the relationship between language and power. Such is the power of technological discourses in today's organizational world that it is relatively easy for largely unintelligible computer speak to be accepted by many people without challenge.

Increasingly the term 'IT' is being replaced by ICT (information and communication technology). This indicates the importance of not only storing and retrieving information, but also of transmitting it. One particular aspect of this which is causing some consternation in many quarters these days is the use of email. It is very common these days for people to feel that they are flooded with email messages, with many people receiving as many as 200 per day. Clearly, this is an unacceptable state of affairs and, while the individual can help in some regards, there is also work that needs to be done here at a communication management level. Many organizations are now developing much stricter policies on the use of email to ensure that frivolous or unnecessary usage is not allowed to clog up the system. Email can be an excellent and extremely useful form of communication when used (and managed) appropriately. However, I am also aware that if managers are not careful, it can be a major source of stress. Hoping that people will be sensible and not contribute to the problem of 'email flooding' is clearly not enough. A more proactive management approach to these issues is needed if they are not to continue to be the source of major concern.

What is needed, then, is a clear, workable and helpful policy in relation to the use of email. The factors to be addressed in such a policy should include:

- Guidelines on the circumstances in which email should and should not be used (including whether or not limited private use is permitted and, if so, in what circumstances and with what limitations).
- Information about what sanctions will be applied in the event of email being misused.
- Clear parameters in relation to confidentiality.

- Advice on how to avoid email flooding and the stress associated with it.
- Details of how the policy will be implemented, monitored and reviewed.

As email becomes more and more established as a very useful form of communication, it will become all the more important to have a clear and effective strategy for making the best use of it and avoiding the problems it can bring. For a more detailed discussion of email policies, see Whelan (2000, Chapter 6).

PRACTICE FOCUS 11.5

When email facilities were made available to all the staff as a result of the installation of a new computer system, it was understandable that, at first, staff would make full and enthusiastic use of the system, including sending each other jokes, recipes and other such non-essential matters. Jeff, the ICT manager, felt that this was not a problem as people experimented and familiarized themselves with the facilities and their capabilities. However, after three months, he could see no sign of this extensive use of the system abating. He therefore felt the need to raise the issue with the senior management team, with a proposal that they develop a strategy for the appropriate use of electronic communication. He was concerned that they would pay little heed as they had previously made it clear that they had little interest in ICT matters. However, he was prepared to give it a try in order to try and get the message across that, while he was able to deal with the technical and operational aspects of the system, senior managers still needed to take account of such matters at a strategic level in order to make sure that communication and information needs were successfully integrated into the overall organizational strategy, rather than treated as 'add-ons'.

Organizational culture

The term 'culture', as we have noted, refers to shared ways of seeing, thinking and doing. In other words, it consists of a set of discourses, established patterns of language and action which are very powerful in shaping our sense of reality and therefore our actions and interactions. The term 'culture' can also be applied within organizations. That is, we can see that organizations develop shared ways of seeing, thinking and doing – sets of unwritten rules and unquestioned assumptions which are very powerful in influencing behaviour and attitudes within the organization concerned. For example, some organizations have a culture of openness where there are few secrets and people express their views openly without fear of being penalized in some way for doing so, while other organizations have much more secretive cultures where it is 'not the done thing' to speak openly on issues. People who go against the culture of their organization can often find that it is a very uncomfortable experience and they can easily be seen as 'not fitting in'.

This is very important in terms of how communication is managed within an organizational setting. This is because, as we saw in Chapter 5, communication is largely shaped by the context in which it occurs. This applies no less to the organizational context and we can see that organizational culture can act as a form of cultural filter, shaping and constraining the way communications take place (or do not take place). There are likely to be cultural habits or unwritten rules about what is communicated (and what is not) and how such communication takes place. For example, some organizations have a very strong oral culture where relatively little is written down or where what is written down has little or no influence on what actually happens. Many organizations have policies which are in effect only paper policies, in the sense that they do not drive actual day-to-day practice. Other organizations by contrast will have a very strong written culture where the written word has immense power. Both these scenarios can lead to problems. In the former case, there may be an unacceptable level of inconsistency because there is no formal policy to unify approaches to a particular issue. In the latter case, there can be difficulties which arise because of, for example, an excessive use of memos and other forms of written communication which lead to information overload and, perhaps, important messages being missed in the flood of paper.

Some organizations develop what can be called a culture of blame. This is unfortunately often the case in relation to issues relating to equality and diversity. This is mainly because for many years attempts to promote equality and value diversity were handled extremely crudely and dogmatically (see Thompson, 2009c, and 2011, for a discussion of these issues). In many places, people are reluctant to discuss issues relating to discrimination and related matters for fear of 'saying the wrong thing' and thereby being labelled racist, sexist and so on. This therefore hampers debate and discussion about these important issues, and this, in turn, hampers learning. Consequently, many organizations have failed to progress in terms of putting a stop to unfair discrimination and realizing (in both senses of the word) the benefits of diversity.

Some organizations also have a culture of defensiveness in which the focus is not so much on achieving the organization's goals, but rather on 'covering your back'. This is clearly a dangerous position to be in. It is well established – for example, in child protection services – that focusing on not getting into trouble, rather than focusing on the safety and welfare of the child, is ironically much more likely to get staff into trouble. It is so easy, in focusing on covering your back, to lose sight of what you are trying to achieve, and there-fore to find yourself in even worse difficulties. This can also be seen to apply to a number of organizations in terms of how they deal with matters of stress. Many focus defensively on how not to get sued by disaffected staff, rather than on how to ensure, through appropriate staff care measures, that staff are not disaffected and stressed in the first place.

Clearly in the case of both a culture of blame and a culture of defensive-ness, communicative effectiveness is likely to be severely reduced. Another way in which communication can suffer, or even break down altogether, is through the failure of interorganizational collaboration which, in turn, is likely to owe much to different cultures within those organizations. For example, returning to the case of child protection services, there are many examples on record of situations that have gone seriously wrong as a result of the break-down in communication between, for example, social services and health services.

ACTIVITY 11.3

Think about how organizational culture affects the working relationships across different organizations. From your experience, how effective would you regard this aspect of the management of communication? What could possibly be done to develop cultures that improve partnership working across organizations?

One clear implication of my comments here is that if we wish to improve communication and how it is managed, then we need to address issues of orga-nizational culture and, where necessary, set about making changes to the culture concerned. This is again where leadership comes into its own. An administrator is someone who works within the existing culture regardless of whether it is a 'healthy' or positive culture or not. A leader, by contrast, is someone who recognizes that his or her brief includes efforts to bring about organizational culture change where required. In my view, what is often needed in order to improve an organizational culture in order to enhance the manage-ment of communication, is a movement towards a culture based on valuing and supporting the people involved. A culture based on the idea that people are dispensable and have little intrinsic worth is likely to be a culture which struggles to promote effective communication and interpersonal engagement. By contrast, a culture based on principles of staff care and dignity at work is likely to improve morale and levels of organizational commitment, thereby laying a very firm foundation for effective organizational and interorganiza-tional communication.

Structure and power

Organizations are influenced not only by their culture, but also by their structure – that is, the network of power relationships which map out the hierarchy. This has the effect of establishing power lines, and such power lines will be very significant in terms of communication. This is because information tends to flow more easily from the more powerful to the less powerful. Consider a practical example. It is much easier for the Chief Executive of an organization to get his or her point of view across to the workforce than it is for an individual member of that workforce to represent his or her views to the Chief Executive. What needs to be recognized is that sometimes this can lead to problems in terms of communication. It can mean that people who have both significant and meaningful contributions to make may not have their voice heard. More enlightened organizations will therefore put in place systems which allow communication to flow in all directions, not just from the top down. While power can facilitate communication in one direction, in so doing it can have the effect of blocking it in the opposite direction.

Montgomery (2008) makes a significant point when he poses the question:

> Is it possible, one might ask, that men sometimes miss the point of what is said to them, because in order to find it they would have to understand the utterance from the position of a subordinate in a relation of power? (p. 171)

Here Montgomery is raising an important issue, in so far as he is suggesting that, while power relations may well play a significant part in keeping the wheels of an organization turning (including its wheels of communication), such relations can at times be an obstacle to effective communication, and may therefore be a significant problem for the organization concerned.

It is also worth noting that it is often through the abuse or misuse of power in organizations that such problems as discrimination, bullying and harassment and stress occur. If all staff are to make a positive contribution to an organization, regardless of their gender, skin colour and so on, then it is important that the distribution of power within the organization is not such that less powerful members become marginalized. I would argue that effective organizations rely on the appropriate use of power. However, it can clearly be seen that the inappropriate use of power has the opposite effect – undermining the effectiveness of the organization and making it a very negative place to work.

Of course, making sure that power within an organization is used appropriately is something that is more easily said than done. However, while wishing to avoid naive idealism about this subject, I would also want to make sure that we do not go for the opposite extreme and become cynical and defeatist. All staff, particularly those in leadership roles, can play at least a small part in seeking to influence the ways in which power is used within the organization

---

PRACTICE FOCUS 11.6

Frank was an experienced personnel officer who had worked in a number of different industries. However, until he moved to his present post, his experience had been entirely in male-dominated industries such as engineering and construction. He now found himself working in an area of work that was still predominantly male but where there were none the less significant numbers of women employees also.

What he did not realize until it was forcefully pointed out by a female union steward was that his behaviour towards women was often unacceptable. He would use inappropriate language (referring to adult women as 'girls', calling them 'love' and so on); he also made assumptions about women's role in the organization (making coffee and generally supporting the men in doing the 'important' work) and sometimes indulged in inappropriate touching (putting his arm around young women, for example). At first he tried to dismiss the complaints against him, but changed his view when he was warned that he would face a harassment claim if he did not start treating the female staff with dignity and respect. (Source: Thompson, 2000b)

---

and, of course, it is interesting and important to note that being able to influence one's organization will depend very much on one's skills in communication and the effective use of language.

Communicative sensitivity

In Chapter 1, I commented on the significance of 'communicative sensitivity' – the ability not only to communicate effectively, but also to recognize when communication is needed, with whom and so on. This is a concept which is worth revisiting in relation to managing communication. This is because organizational factors can play an important role in creating (or preventing) an environment in which:

1. There are clear procedures and protocols in place which help staff and managers know what needs to be communicated, to whom, in what circumstances and so on.
2. There are safeguards in place (for example, supervision) to make sure that appropriate communication has taken place.
3. There is a culture which promotes openness and thus communication.
4. Employees are not so overloaded (with work or information) that they lose sight of their communicative responsibilities.
5. Employees are adequately supported (for example, through training) in being aware of when communication needs to take place.

If an organization hinders rather than helps when it comes to promoting communicative sensitivity, it runs the risk of developing major problems in relation to communication, even where there are high levels of knowledge and skill, sophisticated systems and no shortage of commitment. The communication challenge that organizations face is not only that of seeking to eradicate poor-quality communication, but also of avoiding the problem of communication not taking place at all when it should have. Communicative sensitivity is therefore something that organizations should seek to promote wherever possible.

Voice of experience 11.3

❝We came close to having a disaster on our hands. The family moved to another area and notified the housing association, but neither the family nor the housing association told us. After three visits when no one seemed to be at home, we eventually found out what had happened. The housing association people knew the children were on the child protection register, yet they didn't think to tell us about the move. We contacted Children's Services in their new area and they picked up the case; thankfully, nothing untoward had happened in the meantime, but it so easily could have.**❞** *Fran, a child protection worker*

Conclusion

Organizations can be complex and bewildering places in a variety of ways. Given their complexity, it is not surprising that communication is often far from perfect. This chapter will certainly not 'cure all the ills' of organizational communication, nor has it made any claim to do so. However, I hope that what it has done is to provide considerable food for thought around these important issues and has stimulated thought, reflection, debate and analysis. Given the complexity of the issues, it is important that people attempting to improve the ways in which communication is managed in their organization have at least a basic understanding of the issues. If this chapter has contributed to developing that greater level of understanding, then it will have served its purpose.

It is to be hoped that, in future, organizations and the people working within them will be in a better position to recognize, and work constructively with, the complex dynamics of organizational life in general and those associated with communication and language in particular. Improving these aspects of organizational life is vitally important, because organizations (and the ways in which they are managed) have far-reaching effects on so many people's lives, for good or ill. A badly managed organization can have very serious detrimental effects on not only those who work within it, but also other 'stakeholders'

– that is anyone with some form of investment in that organization and its effectiveness, such as clients, customers, shareholders, elected representatives, board members, trustees, suppliers and contractors.

> **POINTS TO PONDER**
>
> - What do you understand by the term 'organizational culture'? How does a culture affect how communication is managed?
> - Why is the management of communication important for everyone and not just for managers?
> - How significant is power in shaping how communication is managed in an organization?

Conclusion

In the space available I cannot possibly draw out all the implications of the 11 chapters that make up the book or explicitly identify all the conclusions that could be drawn from the points I have made, the arguments I have presented and the views that I have represented (my own and those of the authors from whose work I have drawn). What I shall present here, then, by way of conclusion, is a summary of some of the key points and 'messages' I have tried to convey, together with some thoughts about future directions of study and learning in tackling this enormous (and enormously important) field of study and practice. I shall divide my comments into five sections, namely: the importance of communication; communication and the individual; communication and society; communication and equality; and integrating theory and practice.

The importance of communication

The central role of communication in so many aspects of social life is something that cannot be doubted. When we look more narrowly at the context of working with people, their problems and their challenges across a range of settings (as discussed in the Introduction), we can see that the role of communication is even more important than in many other aspects of social life. When people are ill, distressed, vulnerable, grieving, under threat or in difficulties of some other kind, connection with other people can become even more important, if not crucial. And, of course, it is through communication that such connection is achieved.

When people have problems and are in need of help or care of some kind, emotional issues are often to the fore, and understandably so. Our ability to communicate in ways which recognize, and respond sensitively to, the emotional dimension of our interactions with others is therefore a very important component of our skills repertoire if we are to be effective in supporting people in rising to the challenges they face. Communication, then, is not simply a matter of sending and receiving messages, but also involves sensitivity to emotional factors and the complex and subtle dynamics that operate between people as part and parcel of our communicative encounters. Moss (2008) captures this point nicely when he comments that:

communication is a far more complex phenomenon than a set of discrete skills. It is something to do with the whole person, the context in which we work, and ultimately the societal values that serve as a backdrop for the work we undertake. (p. 3)

Of course, we should not forget that communication is also important in its written forms. What becomes a written record can be very influential in shaping future developments. For example, reports written for specific purposes can play a major role in decision making. A well-written, high-quality report can provide important information, careful analysis and a balanced view of the situation, all of which can be vital in ensuring a fair and appropriate outcome of a decision-making process. By contrast, a poor-quality report can stand in the way of effective decision making, distorting the situation, misleading people, creating ill-feeling and contributing to problems and unfairness rather than tackling them.

Clearly, so much of 'people work' not only involves communication, but actually relies on it – in fact, we could go so far as to say that our work is 'constituted' by language. Communication indeed informs a large proportion of the work undertaken in so many different settings. High-quality work without high-quality communication is not really the order of the day. Any serious commitment to achieving high standards of practice must certainly include a commitment to high standards of communication as a foundation.

POINTS TO PONDER

- In what ways does communication play a part in your work (or the type of work you are training for)?
- What problems (may) arise as a result of breakdowns in communication in your line of work?
- What positive contribution to your work could be made by an improvement in your communication skills?

Communication and the individual

One very important aspect of the relationship between communication and the individual is that of identity. It has been argued that identity is best thought of not so much as a fixed essence (as in so much of personality theory), but rather as a fluid process strongly influenced by social factors and our interaction with other people and the social world more broadly. Processes of communication can therefore be seen as fundamental parts of the development and maintenance of identity. That is, our sense of who we are owes a great deal to the messages we receive about ourselves from others. And, of course, the messages we receive from others about ourselves in turn owe a great deal to the messages we give others about ourselves. There is a dialectical interplay based on communication, and it is largely through this that we are able to sustain our sense of who we are.

In terms of working in the people professions, identity can be seen as a very important factor, in so far as a person's identity is often threatened at times of crisis, loss, distress or other such vulnerability. A person's behaviour may reflect the fact that their identity is threatened, and so it is important that we ensure that our communicative endeavours do not make this problem worse but rather, where possible, actually improve the situation. For example, if someone is feeling threatened and undermined in their sense of who they are (perhaps because they have experienced one or more major losses), then an insensitive or ill-chosen remark may lead that person to react in an aggressive or even violent way (consider the discussions in Chapters 1 and 6 of the important role of 'face' in social interactions). The relationship between communication and identity is therefore a very important one, and one that we neglect at our peril. If we wish to make sure that our communication is *effective* communication, we need to take account of identity issues as they affect our interactions (see Joseph, 2004).

POINTS TO PONDER

- In what ways does communication affect your own identity, your own sense of who you are and how you fit into the social world?
- What problems do you envisage encountering if you pay less than adequate attention to identity factors?
- In what ways could you ensure that you take such matters into account in communicating with other people?

Communication and society

It is not only individual identity that is linked to communication and language. We can also see that society hinges on communication, in the sense that social structures, formations, patterns and institutions are created and daily recreated in and through social interactions. When we communicate together, we are interacting with one another and, in so doing, we are reproducing the social and cultural patterns on which society depends for its existence – no social interaction, no society.

In this way we can see that communication 'feeds into' the social order, but we also have to recognize that this is a two-way or dialectical relationship, in so far as the social order also 'feeds into' our patterns of communication and language use. For example, when I speak or write I do so as a unique individual.

However, I am not just a unique individual, I am also 'socially located'. That is, I am bound to reflect to a certain extent at least:

- *my class background* – both my class of origin or 'working-class roots' and my more middle-class standing currently as a professional trainer, consultant and author;
- *my gender* – both the pressures to conform to conventional images of masculinity that were part of my upbringing and my own attempts to move away from them towards less problematic forms of masculinity;
- *my race and ethnicity* – being white and thus part of the dominant group, but also being Welsh and therefore subject to no shortage of ethnocentric discrimination over the years;
- *my age and generation* – my experience being shaped by not only the stage in life that I have now reached, but also the generation (or 'age cohort') of which I form a part;
- *my (dis)ability* – while my work experience and my political interests make me very aware of disability issues, the fact that I am not disabled means that I cannot write or speak from such a perspective;
- *my sexual identity* – the degree of approval/disapproval that is commonly associated with a person's sexual orientation in a society which is characterized by discrimination against some forms of sexual identity.

What these comments should indicate is that communication factors are linked with not only a person's unique identity and sense of self, but also the social factors and structures which influence who we are, how we interact with one another or how we 'connect' (or fail to).

POINTS TO PONDER

- Which aspects of your own social background affect how you communicate?
- Can you identify situations where communication with a person from a background different from your own may be hampered?
- How could you try to make sure that social differences do not become a barrier to communication?

Communication and equality

The point has already been made that communication is closely intertwined with social patterns, structures and institutions. Given the fact that discrimination can be seen as integral to much of the social order (Thompson, 2011), we should not be surprised to find that there are close links between communication and language on the one hand and discrimination, disadvantage and oppression on the other. This is not to argue the case for so-called political correctness, as I have argued both in this book and elsewhere that such a dogmatic, oversimplified approach to these complex issues is certainly not to be welcomed or embraced.

In place of the simplistic rigidity of political correctness I have proposed what I like to refer to as *linguistic sensitivity* – appreciating the power of language in general and the power of language to discriminate against and oppress in particular. It is unfortunate indeed that the predominance in recent years of a reductionist 'PC' approach has distracted attention from the very real issues of how language and communication can be very problematic when it comes to guarding against unfair discrimination. Such an approach has also devalued genuine attempts to develop more appropriate and less problematic forms of language and communication and has sadly had the effect of undermining such efforts. This has often left proponents of linguistic sensitivity open to ridicule due to the excesses of some people who have attempted to tackle discriminatory forms of language and communication but have done so with only a very limited understanding of:

- the complex and intricate workings of discrimination and oppression;
- how language and communication work; and
- how people learn.

A low level of understanding of these issues has led to some disastrous attempts to promote equality and diversity in relation to communication and language, resulting in: considerable ill-feeling and resentment, if not actual distress; a wariness of, and resistance to, further debate, discussion or training about such matters (contributing to a culture of defensiveness); in some cases a backlash against equality initiatives (because they have become associated with 'extremism'); and a level of anxiety about 'saying the wrong thing' that discourages people from communicating openly and participating in debate, discussion, learning and development. We therefore have to adopt a much more sensitive, constructive, carefully thought-through approach to addressing the relationship between communication and discrimination.

POINTS TO PONDER

- Can you identify ways in which some forms of language use can reinforce discrimination (for example, by reinforcing discriminatory stereotypes)?
- How can you contribute to an atmosphere where people feel it is sufficiently safe and supportive to discuss sensitive issues about discrimination and communication?
- What support are you able to draw upon in tackling these difficult and complex issues?

Integrating theory and practice

In planning this book I was very careful to ensure that it would be concerned with both theory (the underpinning knowledge base, broadly defined) and practice (the actual use of such knowledge in situations of working with people, their problems and their challenges in a variety of contexts and settings). I have argued elsewhere (Thompson, 2000a, 2010) that the relationship between theory and practice is not a simple or straightforward one and that we should be wary of exhortations to 'apply theory to practice' as if it were a one-way relationship.

What is needed is what I like to refer to as 'reflective practice' (drawn from the work of Schön, 1983; 1987; 1992). This refers to the ability to draw upon the wealth of professional knowledge available to us and to tailor it to the specific situations we encounter in practice and to adjust and expand our professional knowledge base in line with that experience (Thompson and Thompson, 2008). That is, we should avoid the destructive and unhelpful extremes of (i) expecting the professional knowledge base to provide answers in a simple or straightforward way; and (ii) rejecting all theory and research as being of little or no value to practice (the 'I prefer to stick to practice' mentality).

This book has been designed as an aid to critically reflective practice, in so far as it has:

- Presented much of the basic knowledge base you will need to draw upon if you are to have a good grasp of the complexities of communication.
- Set down signposts to further study, learning and development through the provision of references and suggestions for further reading.
- Given a flavour of the relevance of the concepts being discussed by providing 'practice focus' illustrations, other in-text examples of practice and 'voice of experience' quotes.
- Provided chapters which specifically address a wide range of practice issues, but without simply providing a set of prescriptions for practice.
- Encouraged a critically reflective approach by critiquing some aspects of the established wisdom of the existing professional knowledge base.
- Provided a conclusion which includes 'points to ponder' – questions to encourage and facilitate further thought and debate about the issues.
- Tried to practise what its author 'preaches'.

I can now but hope that it has served its purpose well in this regard and will encourage you to continue to study these fascinating and vitally important aspects of human existence and the very many challenges for you of working with people, their problems and *their* challenges.

POINTS TO PONDER

- How can you now build on the foundations of knowledge this book has given you about communication?
- How can you use your knowledge base to develop your skills on an ongoing basis?
- What are the various ways in which you can try to ensure that your communication is as *effective* as possible?

Guide to further learning

Voice and representation

The point was made in the Introduction that, as an author, I am not able to provide the voice of the people we serve. It is, however, important that, in a spirit of empowerment and inclusion, we listen to their voices and support them in having a voice. The following offer a good start: Schneider (2010) on listening to people with schizophrenia; Gelfand et al. (2005) on stories from people facing end-of-life issues; Goldman (2002) on the experiences of carers; Victor et al. (2009) on loneliness in old age; Bytheway et al. on older people's experiences of discrimination. Please note that these are just some of the wide range of texts that are available.

General texts on communication

Cobley (2001b), Fiske (1990), Marsen (2006), McQuail (2000), Rosengren (2000) and Stanton (2004) are all useful introductory texts which present an overview of communication theory. Hargie (2006b) is also very informative. Moss (2008) is an ideal reference resource and, although the title refers specifically to health and social care, there is much of value in this book for readers from across the people professions.

General texts on language

The works of Jean Aitchison (2000; 2004; 2007) are an excellent starting point, as are the works of David Crystal (1987; 1995). Finch (2005) is also helpful. Abley (2003) is an interesting study of minority languages across the world. Huang (2007) is an interesting, albeit not very accessible, text on the use of language or, to use the technical term, pragmatics.

Language and society

Downes (1998), Holmes (2008), Montgomery (2008) and Trudgill (2000) are all good introductory guides to the social context of language. Millar (2005) provides a fascinating account of the relationships between language, nation and power. Joseph (2004) provides a very interesting discussion of the relationship between language and identity. Goldsmith (2008) explores how messages of social support are communicated in situations involving care provision.

Culture and cultural studies

Barker and Galasinski (2001), Kendall and Wickham (2001), Schirato and Yell (2000), Wetherell et al. (2001a) offer interesting accounts of culture and cultural theory, much of which is very relevant to communication and language. Two other important texts in this area are During (2007) and Barker (2007). Please note, however, that it is not unusual for books in this area to use a less than accessible style of language.

Communicating with children

Faber and Mazlish (2001) is a helpful practical guide to communicating with children, while Faber and Mazlish (2006) provides a similar text in relation to communicating with teenagers. Stapert and Verliefde (2008) offers an interesting approach to the area of communicating with children. Cross (2004) focuses on communication problems in childhood.

Communicating with groups

Working with families is covered in many of the child care texts – for example, Hart and Blincow (2007). This topic also featiures n the family therapy literature – for example, Dallos and Draper (2010). For guidance on making presentations see Esposito (2008).A key text in relation to groupwork is Doel (2006), while Preston-Shoot (2007) is also a valuable source. Promoting teamwork is helpfully explored in Clutterbuck (2007).

Communication difficulties

Cross-cultural communication is well covered in Holliday et al. (2004), Jandt (2007) and Scollon and Scollon (2001). Disability-related communication problems are covered in Anderson and Shamas (2010), Hartas (2005) and Joffe et al. (2008). For interesting discussions of deafness and hearing impairment, see Bauman (2008c) and Marschark and Spencer (2003).

Written communication

Derrida (1978) offers a very interesting perspective on written language but, ironically, his style of writing is a largely impenetrable one. By contrast, the work of Hopkins (1998a; 1998b) is far more accessible as practical guide as to effective writing. King (2009a) and King (2009b) are useful introductory texts. Morris (1998) and Seely (1998) offer prescriptive guidelines on 'correct' writing. Thompson (2009b) contains a chapter on written communication. Whelan (2000) is a very useful text on the use of email.

Speech, paralanguage and interpersonal encounters

Thompson (2009b) has chapters on verbal and nonverbal communication and a further chapter on interviewing skills. Hargie (2006) is a very thorough and helpful text, as is Stanton (2004). There are a number of 'popular' books on interpersonal communication which vary considerably in quality, and a very large literature relating to counselling skills.

Context and meaning

Discourse analysis and related topics are well covered in Barker and Galasinski (2001), Kendall and Wickham (2001) and Schirato and Yell (2000). Rabinow (1984) provides a useful introduction to the work of Foucault. Social constructionism is a complex subject, but both Burr (2003) and Gergen (2009) present helpful and interesting introductions.

Managing communication

Policies relating to email are helpfully discussed in Whelan (2000). Deetz (1995) and Miller (1995) are two texts which offer a lot of useful and interesting food for thought in relation to managing communication. Stohl (1995) is also a helpful text. Ling and Donner (2009) offers some interesting insights into mobile communications.

References

Abley, M. (2003) *Spoken Here: Travels Among Threatened Languages*, London, William Heinemann.

Aitchison, J. (1997) *The Language Web: The Power and Problem of Words*, Cambridge, Cambridge University Press.

Aitchison, J. (1999) *Linguistics: An Introduction*, 2nd edn, London, Hodder & Stoughton

Aitchison, J. (2000) *Language Change: Progress or Decay?*, 3rd edn, Cambridge, Cambridge University Press.

Aitchison, J. (2001) 'Language Change', in Cobley (2001b).

Aitchison, J. (2004) *Teach Yourself Linguistics*, 6th edn, London, Teach Yourself Books.

Aitchison, J. (2007) *The Articulate Mammal: An Introduction to Psycholinguistics*, 5th edn, London, Routledge.

Anderson, N. B. and Shames, G. H. (2010) *Human Communication Disorders: An Introduction*, 8th edn, London, Allyn & Bacon.

Antia, S. D. and Kreimeyer, K. H. (2003) 'Peer Interaction of Deaf and Hard-of-Hearing Children', in Marschark and Spencer (2003).

Austin, J. L. (1955) *How to Do Things with Words*, Oxford, Clarendon Press.

Baker, L. and Cantwell, D. P. (1987) 'A Prospective Psychiatric Follow-Up of Children with Speech and Language Disorders', *Journal of the American Academy of Child and Adolescent Psychiatry*, 26, pp. 546–53.

Bakhtin, M. M. (1986) *Speech Genres and Other Late Essays*, Austin, University of Texas Press.

Bales, R. F. (1976) *Interaction Process Analysis: A Method for the Study of Small Groups*, Chicago, University of Chicago Press.

Bantel, K. A. and Jackson, S. E. (1989) 'Top Management and Innovations in Banking: Does Composition of the Top Team Make a Difference?', *Strategic Management Journal*, 10, pp. 107–12.

Barker, C. (2007) *Cultural Studies: Theory and Practice*, 3rd edn, London, Sage.

Barker, C. and Galasinski, D. (2001) *Cultural Studies and Discourse Analysis: A Dialogue on Language and Identity*, London, Sage.

Barna, L. M. (1997) 'Stumbling Blocks in Intercultural Communication', in Samovar and Porter (1997).

Bates, J. (1995) 'An Evaluation of the Use of Information Technology in Child Care Services', *Social Work Education*, 14(1).

Bates, J. and Thompson, N. (2002) 'Men, Masculinity and Social Work', in Gruber and Stefanov (2002).

Bateson, G. (1972) *Steps to an Ecology of Mind*, New York, Ballantine.

Bauer, L. and Trudgill, P. (eds) (1998) *Language Myths*, Harmondsworth, Penguin.

Bauman, H.-D. L. (2008a) 'Introduction: Listening to Deaf Studies', in Bauman (2008c)

Bauman, H.-D. L. (2008b) 'On the Disconstruction of (Sign) Language in the Wesyern Tradition: A Deaf Reading of Plato's Cratylus', in Bauman (2008c).

Bauman, H.-D. L. (ed.) (2008c) *Open Your Eyes: Deaf Studies Talking*, Minneapolis, MN, University of Minnesota Press.

Bauman, Z. (2001) *The Individualized Society*, Cambridge, Polity.

Baynton, D. C. (2008) 'Beyond Culture: Deaf Studies and the Deaf Body', in Bauman (2008c).

Beauvoir, S. de (1984) *Adieux: A Farewell to Sartre*, trans. Patrick O'Brian, Harmondsworth, Penguin.

Bell, V. (1993) *Interrogating Incest: Feminism, Foucault and the Law*, London, Routledge.

Bendelow, G. and Williams, S. J. (eds) (1998) *Emotions in Social Life: Critical Themes and Contemporary Issues*, London, Routledge.

Berger, B. M. (1991) 'Structure and Choice in the Sociology of Culture', *Theory and Society*, 20.

Berger, P. and Luckmann, T. (1967) *The Social Construction of Reality*, Harmondsworth, Penguin.

Bernstein, B. (1971) *Class, Codes and Control*, Vol. 1: *Theoretical Studies Towards a Sociology of Language*, Philadelphia, University of Pennsylvania Press.

Bernstein, B. (1973) *Class, Codes and Control*, Vol. 2: *Applied Studies Towards a Sociology of Language*, Philadelphia, University of Pennsylvania Press.

Billig, M. (2001) 'Discursive, Rhetorical and Ideological Messages', in Wetherell et al. (2001a).

Bourdieu, P. (1991) *Language and Symbolic Power*, Cambridge, Polity.

Bryson, B. (1990) *Mother Tongue*, Harmondsworth, Penguin.

Bryson, V. (1999) *Feminist Debates: Issues of Theory and Political Practice*, Basingstoke, Macmillan – now Palgrave Macmillan.

Burr, V. (2003) *Social Constructionism*, 2nd edn, London, Routledge.

Bytheway, B., Ward, R. Holland, C. and Peace, S. (2007) *Too Old: Older People's Accounts of Discrimination, Exclusion and Rejection*, London, Help the Aged.

Camarata, S., Hughes, C. and Ruhl, K. (1988) 'Mild/Moderate Behaviourally Disordered Students: A Population at Risk for Language Disorders', *Language, Speech and Hearing Services in Schools*, 19, pp. 191–200.

Cameron, D. (1998a) 'Introduction', in Cameron (1998c).

Cameron, D. (1998b) 'Lost in Translation: Non-Sexist Language', in Cameron (1998c).

Cameron, D. (ed.) (1998c) *The Feminist Critique of Language: A Reader*, London, Routledge.

Cheshire, J. (1978) 'Present Tense Verbs in Reading', in Trudgill (1978).

Cheshire, J. (1982) *Variation in an English Dialect*, Cambridge, Cambridge University Press.

Clutterbuck, D. (2007) *Coaching the Team at Work*, London, Nicholas Brealey International.

Cobley, P. (2001a) 'Introduction', in Cobley (2001b).

Cobley, P. (ed.) (2001b) *The Routledge Companion to Semiotics and Lingustics*, London, Routledge.

Cook, V. J. and Newsom, M. (1996) *Chomsky's Universal Grammar: An Introduction*, 2nd edn, Oxford, Blackwell.

Cooley, C. H. (1902) *Human Nature and the Social Order*, New York, Scribner.

Coupland, N. and Jaworski, A. (2001) 'Discourse', in Cobley (2001b).

Coupland, N. et al. (1991) 'Intergenerational Discourse: Contextual Versions of Ageing and Elderliness', *Ageing and Society*, 11, pp. 189–208.

Cross, M. (2004) *Children with Emotional and Behavioural Difficulties and Communication Problems*, London, Jessica Kingsley Publishers.

Crystal, D. (1987) *The Cambridge Encyclopaedia of Language*, Cambridge, Cambridge University Press.

Crystal, D. (1995) *The Cambridge Encyclopaedia of the English Language*, Cambridge, Cambridge University Press.

Crystal, D. (1997) *English as a Global Language*, Cambridge, Cambridge University Press.

Czerniawska, F. (1997) *Corporate Speak: The Use of Language in Business*, London, Macmillan – now Palgrave Macmillan.

Dallos, R. and Draper, R. (2010) *An Introduction to Family Therapy*, 3rd edn, Maidenhead, Open University Press.

Davies, B. and Harré, R. (2001) 'Positioning: The Discursive Production of Selves', in Wetherell et al. (2001a).

Deetz, S. (1995) *Transforming Communication – Transforming Business: Building Responsive and Responsible Workplaces*, Cresskill, NJ, Hampton Press.

Derrida, J. (1976) *Of Grammatology*, Baltimore, MD, Johns Hopkins University Press.

Derrida, J. (1978) *Writing and Difference*, London, Routledge & Kegan Paul.

Doel, M. (2006) *Using Groupwork*, London, Routledge.

Downes, W. (1998) *Language and Society*, 2nd edn, Cambridge, Cambridge University Press.

Doyle, M. (1995) *The A–Z of Non-Sexist Language*, London, The Women's Press.

Doyle, M. (1998) 'Introduction to the A–Z of Non-sexist Language', in Cameron (1998c).

Drakeford, M. and Morris, S. (1998) 'Social Work with Linguistic Minorities', in Williams et al. (1998).

During, S. (ed.) (2007) *The Cultural Studies Reader*, 3rd edn, London, Routledge.

Elmes, S. (2005) *Talking for Britain: A Journey Through the Nation's Dialects*, London, Penguin.

Erickson, F. and Schultz, J. (1982) *The Counselor as Gatekeeper, Social Interaction in Interviews*, New York, Academic Press.

Esling, J. H. (1998) 'Everyone Has an Accent Except Me', in Bauer and Trudgill (1998).

Esposito, J. (2008) *In the Spotlight: Overcoming Your Fear of Public Speaking and Performing*, Mankato, MN, Capstone.

Faber, A. and Mazlish, E. (2001) *How to Talk So Kids Will Listen and Listen So Kids Will Talk*, London, Piccadilly.

Faber, A. and Mazlish, E. (2006) *How to Talk So Teens Will Listen and Listen So Teens Will Talk*, London, Piccadilly.

Finch, G. (2005) *Key Concepts in Language and Linguistics*, 2nd edn, Basingstoke, Palgrave Macmillan.

Fischer, A. H. (ed.) (2000) *Gender and Emotion: Social Psychological Perspectives*, Cambridge, Cambridge University Press.

Fishman, J. A. (1977) 'Language and Ethnicity', in Giles (1977).

Fiske, J. (1990) *Introduction to Communication Studies*, 2nd edn, London, Routledge.

Fiske, J. (1994) 'General Editor's Preface', in O'Sullivan et al. (1994).

Foucault, M. (1977) *Discipline and Punish: The Birth of the Prison*, London, Allen Lane.

Foucault, M. (1979) *The History of Sexuality*. Vol. 1: *An Introduction*, London, Allen Lane.

Foucault, M. (2007) 'Space, Power and Knowledge', in During (2007).

Fowler, B. (ed.) (2000) *Reading Bourdieu on Society and Culture*, Oxford, Blackwell.

Fraser, C. and Burchell, B., with Hay, D. and Duveen, G. (eds) (2001) *Introducing Social Psychology*, Cambridge, Polity.

Gadamer, H.-G. (2004) *Truth and Method*, London, Continuum.

Gelfand, D. E., Raspa, R., Briller, S. H. and Schim, S. M. (2005) *End-of-Life Stories: Crossing Disciplinary Boundaries*, New York, Springer.

Gergen, K. J. (1999) *An Invitation to Social Construction*, London, Sage.

Gergen, K. J. (2009) *An Invitation to Social Construction*, 2nd edn, London, Sage.

Giles, H. (ed.) (1977) *Language, Ethnicity and Intergroup Relations*, London, Academic Press.

Gilligan, C. (1982) *In a Different Voice*, Cambridge, MA, Harvard University Press.

Gilligan, S. and Price, R. (eds) (1993) *Theraputic Conversations*, New York, Norton.

Ginott, H. G. (1969) *Between Parent and Teenager*, London, Macmillan.

Glastonbury, B. (1992) 'The Integrity of Intelligence', *New Technology in the Human Services*, 6(2).

Goffman, E. (1990) *The Presentation of Self in Everyday Life*, Harmondsworth, Penguin.

Goldman, C. (2002) *The Gifts of Caregiving: Stories of Hardship, Hope and Healing*, Minneapolis, MN, Fairview Press.

Goldsmith, D. J. (2004) *Communicating Social Support*, Cambridge, Cambridge University Press.

Goleman, D. (1996) *Emotional Intelligence: Why it Can Matter More than IQ*, London, Bloomsbury.

Good, D. (2001) 'Language and Communication', in Fraser and Burchell (2001).

Goodman, S. and Graddol, D. (eds) (1996) *Redesigning English: New Texts, New Identities*, London, Routledge.

Graber, D. (2003) *The Power of Communication: Managing Information in Public Organizations*, Washington DC, CQ Press.

Graddol, D. (1996) 'The Semiotics of a Wine Label', in Goodman and Graddol (1996).

Green, J. and Burleson, B. (eds) (2003) *Handbook of Copmmunication and Interaction Skills*, Mahwah, NJ, Lawrence Erlbaum.

Gruber, C. and Stefanov, H. (eds) (2002) *Gender and Social Work: Promoting Equality*, Lyme Regis, Russell House Publishing.

Guirdham, M. (1999) *Communicating Across Cultures*, London, Macmillan – now Palgrave Macmillan.

Gumperz, J. (1982) *Language and Social Identity*, Cambridge, Cambridge University Press.

Hargie, O. (2006a) 'Editorial Introduction', in Hargie (2006b).

Hargie, O. (ed.) (2006b) *The Handbook of Communication Skills*, 3rd edn, London, Routledge.

Harlow, R. (1998) 'Some Languages Are Just Not Good Enough', in Bauer and Trudgill (1998).

Harrison, R., Mann, G., Murphy, M., Taylor, A. and Thompson, N. (2003) *Partnership Made Painless*, Lyme Regis, Russell House Publishing.

Hart, A. and Blincow, D., with Thomas, H. (2007) *Resilient Therapy: Working with Children and Families*, London, Routledge.

Hartas, D. (2005) *Language and Communication Difficulties*, London, Continuum.

Heritage, J. (2001) 'Goffman, Garfinkel and Conversation Analysis', in Wetherell et al. (2001b).

Holliday, A., Hyde, M. and Kullman, J. (eds) (2004) *Intercultural Communication: An Advanced Resource Book*, London, Routledge.

Hollinger, R. (1994) *Postmodernism and the Social Sciences: A Thematic Approach*, London, Sage.

Holmes, J. (2008) *An Introduction to Sociolinguistics*, 3rd edn, London, Longman.

Honey, P. (1990) *Face to Face Skills*, Aldershot, Gower.

Hopkins, G. (1998a) *Plain English for Social Services: A Guide to Better Communication*, Lyme Regis, Russell House Publishing.

Hopkins, G. (1998b) *The Write Stuff: A Guide to Effective Writing in Social Care and Related Services*, Lyme Regis, Russell House Publishing.

Huang, Y. (2007) *Pragmatics*, Oxford, Oxford University Press.

Hugman, R. and Smith, D. (eds) (1995) *Ethical Issues in Social Work*, London, Routledge.

Jandt, F. E. (2007) *An Introduction to Intercultural Communication: Identities in a Global Community*, London, Sage.

Jenks, C. (1993) *Culture*, London, Routledge.

Joffe, V., Cruice, M. and Chiat, S. (eds) (2008) *Language Disorders in Children and Adults: New Issues in Research and Practice*, Oxford, Blackwell.

John, B. K (2007) *Entry from Backside Only: Hazaar Fundas of Indian-English*, New Delhi, Penguin.

John, M. (1988) *Kids' Lib: The Politics of Childhood*, Unit 2 of the Open University Course, D211 Social Problems and Social Welfare, Milton Keynes, The Open University.

Johnston, J., Roseby, V. and Kuehnle, K. (2009) *In the Name of the Child: A Developmental Approach to Understanding and Helping Children of Conflicted and Violent Dovorce*, 2nd edn, New York, Springer.

Joseph, J. E. (2004) *Language and Identity: National, Ethnic, Religious*, Basingstoke, Palgrave Macmillan.

Kendall, G. and Wickham, G. (2001) *Understanding Culture: Cultural Studies, Order, Ordering*, London, Sage.

King, G. (2009a) *Improve Your Writing Skills*, London, Collins.

King, G. (2009b) *The Complete Writing Guide*, London, Collins.

Kitzinger, C. and Frith, H. (2001) 'Just Say No? The Use of Conversation Analysis in Developing a Feminist Perspective on Sexual Refusal', in Wetherell et al. (2001).

Knight, S. (1995) *NLP at Work: The Difference that Makes a Difference at Work*, London, Nicholas, Brealey.

Kress, G. (2001) 'From Saussure to Critical Sociolinguistics: The Turn Towards a Social View of Language', in Wetherell et al. (2001a).

Labov, W. (1972) *Language in the Inner City: Studies in the Black English Vernacular*, Philadelphia, University of Pennsylvania Press.

Lane, H. (2008) 'Do Deaf People Have a Disability?', in Bauman (2008c).

Lanham, R. A. (1983) *Literacy and the Survival of Humanism*, New Haven, CT, Yale University Press.

Ling, R. and Donner, J. (2009) *Mobile Communication*, Cambridge, Polity.

Lovell, T. (2000) 'Thinking Feminism With and Against Bourdieu', in Fowler (2000).

Madhaven, R. and Grover, R. (1998) 'From Embedded Knowledge to Embodied Knowledge: New Product Development as Knowledge Management', *Journal of Marketing*, 62(4), pp. 1–12.

Maltz, D. and Borker, R. (1982) 'A Cultural Approach to Male–Female Misunderstanding', in Gumperz (1982).

Man, J. (2002) *The Gutenberg Revolution: The Story of a Genius and an Invention that Changed the World*, London, Review.

Marschark, M. and Spencer, P. E. (eds) (2003) *Deaf Studies, Language and Education*, Oxford, Oxford University Press.

Marsen, S. (2006) *Communication Studies*, Basingstoke, Palgrave Macmillan.

Maybin, J. (2001) 'Language, Struggle and Voice: The Bakhtin/Volosinov Writings', in Wetherell et al. (2001a).

McKay, M., Davis, M. and Fanning, P. (1995) *Messages: The Communication Skills Handbook*, 2nd edn, Oakland, CA, New Harbinger Publications.

McLuhan, M. (1964) *Understanding Media*, London, Routledge & Kegan Paul.

McQuail, D. (2000) *McQuail's Mass Communication*, 4th edn, London, Sage.

Millar, R. M. (2005) *Language, Nation and Power*, Basingstoke, Palgrave Macmillan.

Miller, K. (1995) *Organizational Communication: Approaches and Processes*, London, Wadsworth.

Milroy, L. (1998) 'Bad Grammar is Slovenly', in Bauer and Trudgill (1998).

Montgomery, M. (2008) *An Introduction to Language and Society*, 3rd edn, London, Routledge.

Morley, D. and Chen, K.-H. (eds) (1996) *Stuart Hall: Critical Dialogues in Cultural Studies*, London, Routledge.

Morris, R. (1998) *The Right Way to Write*, London, Piatkus.

Moss, B. (2008) *Communication Skills for Health and Social Care*, London, Sage.

Murray, A. I. (1989) 'Top Management Group Heterogeneity and Firm Performance', *Strategic Management Journal*, 10, pp. 125–41.

Myers, S. (2008) *Solution-Focused Approaches*, Lyme Regis, Russell House Publishing.

Nelson, D. (1997) *Off the Map: The Curious Histories of Place Names*, New York, Kodansha.

Noel, L. (1994) *Intolerance: A General Survey*, London, McGill – Queen's University Press.

O'Hanlon, B. and Weiner-Davis, M. (1989) *In Search of Solutions*, New York, Norton.

O'Sullivan, T., Hartley, J., Saunders, D., Montgomery, M. and Fiske, J. (1994) *Key Concepts in Communication and Cultural Studies*, 2nd edn, London, Routledge.

Panza, C. and Gale, G. (2008) *Existentialism for Dummies*, Hoboken, NJ, Wiley.

Parekh, B. (2006) *Rethinking Multiculturalism: Cultural Diversity and Political Theory*, Basingstoke, Palgrave Macmillan.

Parr, S., Duchan, J. and Pound, C. (2003a) 'Setting the Scene', in Parr et al. (2003b).

Parr, S., Duchan, J. and Pound, C. (eds) (2003b) *Aphasia Inside Out: Reflections on Communication Disability*, Maidenhead, Open University Press.

Parton, N. and O'Byrne, P. (2000) *Constructive Social Work: Towards A New Practice*, Basingstoke, Macmillan – now Palgrave Macmillan.

Payne, M. (2006) *Narrative Therapy*, 2nd edn, London, Sage.

Penketh, L. (2000) *Tackling Institutional Racism: Anti-Racist Policies and Social Work Education and Training*, Bristol, Policy Press.

Pinker, S. (1994) *The Language Instinct*, Harmondsworth, Penguin.

Postman, N. (1983) *The Disappearance of Childhood*, London, W. H. Allen.

Poupeau, F. (2000) 'Reasons for Domination, Bourdieu versus Habermas', in Fowler (2000).

Preston-Shoot, M. (2007) *Effective Groupwork*, 2nd edn, Basingstoke, Palgrave Macmillan.

Price, S. (1997) *Communication Studies*, London, Longman.

Rabinow, P. (ed.) (1984) *The Foucault Reader: An Introduction to Foucault's Thought*, Harmondsworth, Penguin.

Rogers, E. M. (1995) *Diffusion of Innovations*, 4th edn, New York, Free Press.

Rosengren, K. E. (2000) *Communication: An Introduction*, London, Sage.

Rubinstein, D. (2001) *Culture, Structure and Agency: Towards a Truly Multidimensional Society*, London, Sage.

Rymaszewska, J. and Philpot, T. (2006) *Reaching the Vulnerable Child: Therapy with Traumatized Children*, London, Jessica Kingsley.

Samovar, L. A. and Porter, R. E. (eds) (1997) *Intercultural Communication: A Reader*, Belmont, CA, Wadsworth.

Sartre, J.-P. (1948) *Existentialism is a Humanism*, London, Eyre Methuen.

Sartre, J.-P. (1958) *Being and Nothingness*, London, Methuen.

Sarup, M. (1996) *Identity, Culture and the Postmodern World*, Edinburgh, Edinburgh University Press.

Schirato, T. and Yell, S. (2000) *Communication and Culture: An Introduction*, London, Sage.

Shazer, S. de (1988) *Clues: Investigating Solutions in Brief Therapy*, New York, Norton.

Schneider, B. (2010) *Hearing (Our) Voices: Participatory Research in Mental Health, Toronto*, University of Toronto Press.

Schön, D. A. (1983) *The Reflective Practitioner*, New York, Basic Books.

Schön, D. A. (1987) *Educating the Reflective Practitioner*, San Francisco, Jossey Bass.

Schön, D. A. (1992) 'The Crisis of Professional Knowledge and the Pursuit of an Epistemology of Practice', *Journal of Interprofessional Care*, 6(1).

Scollon, R. and Scollon, S. W. (2001) *Intercultural Communication: A Discourse Approach*, 2nd edn, Oxford, Blackwell.

Searle, J. (1969) *Speech Acts*, Cambridge, Cambridge University Press.

Seely, J. (1998) *The Oxford Guide to Writing and Speaking: The Key to Effective Communication*, Oxford, Oxford University Press.

Seidler, V. J. (1998) 'Masculinity, Violence and Emotional Life', in Bendelow and Williams (1998).

Shannon, C. and Weaver, W. (1949) *The Mathematical Theory of Communication*, Urbana, University of Illinois Press.

Shotter, J. (1993) *Cultural Politics of Everyday Life: Social Constructionism, Rhetoric and Knowing of the Third Kind*, Buckingham, Open University Press.

Soydan, H. and Williams, C. (1998) 'Exploring Concepts', in Williams et al. (1998).

Stanton, N. (2004) *Mastering Communication*, 4th edn, Basingstoke, Palgrave Macmillan.

Stapert, M. and Verliefde, E. (2008) *Focusing with Children: The Art of Communicating with Children at School and at Home*, Ross-on-Wye, PCCS Books.

Stohl, C. (1995) *Organizational Communication: Connectedness in Action*, London, Sage.

Tannen, D. (1990) *You Just Don't Understand: Women and Men in Conversation*, London, Virago.

Tannen, D. (2001) 'The Relativity of Linguistic Strategies: Rethinking Power and Solidarity in Gender and Dominance', in Wetherell et al. (2001a).

Thompson, N. (1992) *Existentialism and Social Work*, Aldershot, Avebury.

Thompson, N. (1999) *Stress Matters*, Birmingham, Pepar.

Thompson, N. (2000a) *Theory and Practice in Human Services*, 2nd edn, Buckingham, Open University Press.

Thompson, N. (2000b) *Tackling Bullying and Harassment in the Workplace*, Birmingham, Pepar.

Thompson, N. (2006a) *Anti-Discriminatory Practice*, 3rd edn, Basingstoke, Palgrave Macmillan.

Thompson, N. (2006b) *People Problems*, Basingstoke, Palgrave Macmillan.

Thompson, N. (2007) *Power and Empowerment*, Lyme Regis, Russell House Publishing.

Thompson, N. (2009a) *Practising Social Work: Meeting the Professional Challenge*, Basingstoke, Palgrave Macmillan.

Thompson, N. (2009b) *People Skills*, 3rd edn, Basingstoke, Palgrave Macmillan.

Thompson, N. (2009c) *Promoting Equality, Valuing Diversity: A Learning and Development Manual*, Lyme Regis, Russell House Publishing.

Thompson, N. (2010) *Theorizing Social Work Practice*, Basingstoke, Palgrave Macmillan.

Thompson, N. (2011) *Promoting Equality: Working with Difference and Diversity*, 3rd edn, Basingstoke, Palgrave Macmillan.

Thompson, N., Murphy, M. and Stradling, S. (1996) *Meeting the Stress Challenge*, Lyme Regis, Russell House Publishing.

Thompson, S. (2005) *Age Discrimination*, Lyme Regis, Russell House Publishing.

Thompson, S. and Thompson, N. (2008) *The Critically Reflective Practitioner*, Basingstoke, Palgrave Macmillan.

Thomson, P. (1996) *The Secrets of Communication*, London, Simon & Schuster.

Togher, L. (2003) 'Do I Have Green Hair? "Conversations" in Aphasia Therapy', in Parr et al. (2003b).

Trenholm, S. (1999) *Thinking through Communication*, Boston, Allyn & Bacon.

Trudgill, P. (ed.) (1978) *Sociolinguistic Patterns in British English*, London, Edward Arnold.

Trudgill, P. (2000) *Sociolinguistics: An Introduction to Language and Society*, 4th edn, Harmondsworth, Penguin.

Truss, L. (2003) *Eats, Shoots and Leaves*, London, Profile Books.

Turner, B. S. (2000a) 'An Outline of a General Sociology of the Body', in Turner (2000b).

Turner, B. S. (ed.) (2000b) *The Blackwell Companion to Social Theory*, Oxford, Blackwell.

Uchida, A. (1998) 'When "Difference" is "Dominance": A Critique of the Anti-Power-Based Approach to Sex Differences', in Cameron (1998c).

Victor, C., Scambler, S. and Bond, J. (2009) *The Social World of Older People: Understanding Loneliness and Social Isolation in Later Life*, Maidenhead, McGraw-Hill.

Waismann, F. (1997) *The Principles of Linguistic Philosophy*, 2nd edn, ed. R. Harré, Basingstoke, Macmillan – now Palgrave Macmillan.

Weiner-Davis, M. (1993) 'Pro-constructed Realities', in Gilligan and Price (1993).

Weld, N. (2009) *Making Sure Children Get HELD: Ideas and Resources to Help Workers Place Help, Empathy, Love and Dignity at the Heart of Child Protection and Support*, Lyme Regis, Russell House Publishing.

Wetherell, M. (2001) 'Themes in Discourse Research: The Case of Diana', in Wetherell et al. (2001b).

Wetherell, M., Taylor, S. and Yates, S. J. (eds) (2001a) *Discourse Theory and Practice: A Reader*, London, Sage.

Wetherell, M., Taylor, S. and Yates, S. J. (eds) (2001b) *Discourse as Data: A Guide for Analysis*, London, Sage.

Whelan, J. (2000) *E-mail at Work*, Harlow, ft.com.

Williams, C., Soydan, H. and Johnson, M. R. D. (eds) (1998) *Social Work and Minorities: European Perspectives*, London, Routledge.

Williams, S. (2001) *Emotion and Social Theory: Corporeal Reflections on the (Ir)rational*, London, Sage.

Wiesmann, J. (2003) 'Foreword', in Green and Burleson (2003).

Wise, S. (1995) 'Feminist Ethics in Practice', in Hugman and Smith (1995).

Wit, A. (2006) 'Interacting in Groups', in Hargie (2006b).

Wittgenstein, L. (1953) *Philosophical Investigations*, Oxford, Blackwell.

Woll, B. and Ladd, P. (2003) 'Deaf Communities', in Marschark and Spencer (2003).

Woodward, K. (ed.) (1997) *Identity and Difference*, London, Sage.

Index